INTO THE KAZAKH STEPPE

Also by Beatrice Teissier

Russian Frontiers

Eighteenth-century British Travellers in the Caspian, Caucasus and Central Asia

Signal Books, Oxford 2011

INTO THE KAZAKH STEPPE

John Castle's Mission to Khan Abulkhayir

Edited by Beatrice Teissier

Signal

Signal Books
Oxford

This edition first published in 2014 by
Signal Books Limited
36 Minster Road
Oxford
OX4 1LY
www.signalbooks.co.uk

A catalogue record for this book is available from the British Library.

ISBN 978-1-909930-08-7

Production: Tora Kelly
Cover Design: Tora Kelly
Images © The British Library Board, 9455.bb.36, Plates 1-13.
Cover Image © The British Library Board, 9455.bb.36, Plate 1.
The young Sultan Erali, flanked protectively on the left by Monsur, an
akhun (a high ranking cleric) from 'Buchar' holding a Koran, and a fully
armed, prominent Kazakh *batyr* (warrior of repute) on the right.
Printed in India

CONTENTS

ACKNOWLEDGEMENTS

I am particularly grateful to the British-Kazakh Society for facilitating a research trip to Almaty and to Alexander Morrison for reading and commenting on this work. The help and support given to this project by Galya Appleby, Yulduz Baizakova and Irina Erofeeva are also greatly appreciated. Professor Meruert Abusseitova kindly facilitated my research in Almaty, and Beknazarov Rakhim Agibaevich, Akhmet Toktabai and Nuzmandova Ditzhan were good enough to discuss the project with me. Gratitude is also due to and the staff at the TsGARKaz and the National Library in Almaty, who were exceptionally helpful and professional. I would like to thank the staff at the Slavonic Library, notably Elena Vassilieva and Jessica Semeniuk, and Lidio Ferrando at the Oriental Institute, Oxford for their friendly assistance. And crucially, warm thanks to Sarah Tolley, the translator of this difficult text. All mistakes are mine.

i.m.
Till

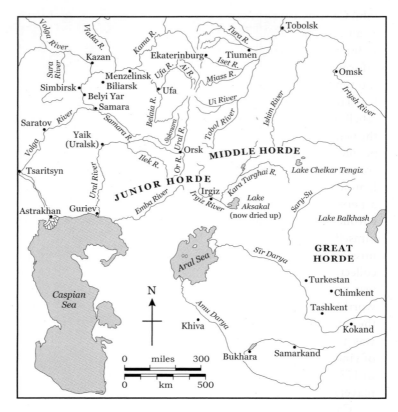

Map 1 Regional Map and Distribution of the Kazakh Hordes

INTRODUCTION

John Castle's 'extremely necessary and happily completed' journey as an envoy to Khan Abulkhayir of the Kazakh Junior *Zhuz* in 1736, reluctantly sanctioned by the Russian authorities, was informed throughout by the complex and turbulent context of the times. The onslaught of the Orenburg expedition (the first Russian attempt to colonize the Kazakh steppe), a major Bashkir rebellion, the Russo-Turkish war, volatile Kazakhs calculating the benefits of Russia's 'protection', Russian troops and disaffected people on the move were all reported on (and corroborated from contemporary sources) by Castle. Extreme physical discomfort, famine and obstruction also played their part. The mission was a personal odyssey, in which Castle, having been enrolled (or enrolled himself) in the Orenburg expedition, tried to prove himself to the Russian authorities not only by his diplomatic mission to Abulkhayir but by various other actions, including the collection of geological samples intended for the Crown. But he was not an expert: some of these samples appear to have been worthless, others were confiscated and appear never to reached the court as intended (pp.106-7). This, together with other slights, was a major source of grievance to him, and resulted in a letter of vindication and complaint written to Empress Anna Ivanovna in 1737.[1] For their part, the Russians thought him increasingly a maverick, to be dispensed with if of no use.[2]

Castle dedicates his journal to the Crown and while the journal occasionally turns into a self-aggrandizing diatribe over his treatment by certain Russian officials, Castle never hints at the despotism discourse that often characterized other western travellers' accounts of Russia.[3] But it is precisely the fact that the journal is written from the point of view of a foreigner in the service

---

1 RGADA f. 248, kn. 1164, ll.73-75 (copy in the TsGARKaz: Central Archives of the Republic of Kazakhstan, Almaty).
2 Matvieskii 1958, pp.139-40, nn.51-2 (TsGIAL now RGIA f.1329, kn.89, ll.410, 421ob.).
3 Teissier 2012, pp.254-57.

of the Russian state that distinguishes it from other (published) contemporary sources of the time and makes it valuable to the historian. Another highly valuable aspect of Castle's journey was his close contact with Khan Abulkhayir and other Kazakhs: the journal is full of anecdotal observations on religion, law and other Kazakh customs. This ethnography was then supplemented by Castle in a special section at the editing stage (see Text below). The prints (Plates 1-13), including a portrait of Abulkhayir himself, are unique among published records of Kazakhs at the time, and are not only highly informative but more naturalistic than the mannered poses given to the 'peoples' of the empire in some later Academicians' publications.[4]

The journey itself can only be broadly reconstituted. Some place names, which may have been local, do not occur in contemporary records and/or have changed with time. The journey consists of two parts (i) from Orenburg/Orsk south-east to meet Khan Abulkhayir, then back up almost to Orenburg/Orsk turning west between the Ural/Yaik and the Ilek rivers, then crossing the Ural, up to Sakmarsk (getting lost on the way) and back to Orenburg/Orsk and (ii) voyage along the Ural to Simbirsk, via Yaik (Uralsk) town and Samara, going back and forth between Simbirsk and Samara. Simbirsk and Samara were then the command headquarters against the Bashkir rebellion.

Castle was one of a number of foreigners associated with the newly formed Orenburg expedition.[5] This was a military expedition, sanctioned by an Imperial decree of 1734 (Rychkov, *Istoriia*, p.10) and impelled by the reports and recommendations of A.I. Tevkelev (a Tatar noble who was the principal intermediary between the Russians and the Kazakhs in the mid eighteenth century) and I.K. Kirilov (*IKRI* 3). Its aims were to establish the fort and trading centre of Orenburg and secure and colonize the southern Bashkir frontier by building a line of defensive forts; to quell the Bashkirs; to control the Empire's new Kazakh 'subjects';

---

4 Notably in Georgi, 1776-77 e.g. Pls. 38-40; but also Falk 1786, e.g. Pls. 37-39. See also Teissier 2011, p.269.
5 The role and numbers of foreigners in this expedition has not been comprehensively addressed (see n.162 p.104 for Captain Elton).

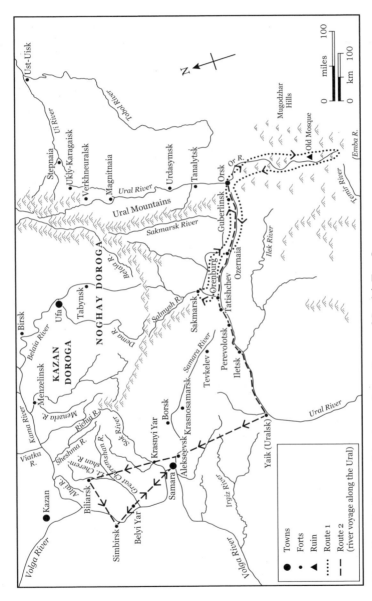

Map 2 Frontier Forts and the Approximate Routes of Castle's Two Journeys

to gain access to Central Asian trade by building a port on the Aral sea and to investigate the natural resources of the region. Thus, besides army units, the expedition included scientists, engineers, naval officers, surgeons, clerks, builders, a priest, merchants and others (Rychkov, *Istoriia*, pp.10-16; Donnelly 1968, pp.64-71).

The expedition's goals were soon thwarted by the Bashkirs, who initiated a full-scale rebellion (Rychkov, *Istoriia* pp.16 ff.; Donnelly 1968, p.72 ff. and see n.3, pp. 19, 23-26 ff.). This rebellion (1735-37) (the second of the early eighteenth century)[6] was predictable given Russia's renewed efforts through the Orenburg expedition to further advance into the Urals and surround the Bashkirs with fortification lines. Russian expansion in the area had been active since the seventeenth century onwards: the Bashkirs' continued grievances included seizure of land, rising levies, appropriation of resources and the influx of Russian, Tatar, Chuvash and Cheremis migrants (Demidova 2002, e.g. nos.69, 74, 98; Donnelly 1968, pp.45-48, 75-95). As shown in Castle's diary not all Bashkirs took part in the rebellion: some had been co-opted by Russian advancement and other rewards (cf. Aldar, pp.20, 64, n.109). Known as 'friendly' or 'loyal' Bashkirs, they fought on the Russian side. The revolt was nevertheless a major one, and took place in three main areas around the Urals: the Kazan, Nogay and Siberian *dorogas* or districts, and was brutally repressed. Documents covering this rebellion show the careful Russian monitoring of the situation and the brutality of this war: the burning of Bashkir villages, their deliberate starvation, the deportation, execution and torture of captives and the removal of children (Demidova 2002, e.g. nos. 74, 92, 98, 107, 171). Bashkir rebels were themselves destroying Tatar, Cheremis and Russian villages, ambushing and attacking troops (Demidova 2002, passim).

The story of Abulkhayir's oath(s) of allegiance to the Russian Crown, which marked the point of no return for the Kazakhs, will only be summarized here as it is well known and documented.[7]

---

6 The first c. 1705-1711.
7 e.g. Rychkov eds. 2010, 1896; Levshin ed. 1840; Bodger 1980; Khodarkosvsky 2004; Erofeeva 1999, 2005, 2011.

Abulkhayir (c. 1680-1748) became Khan of the Junior (*Kishi Zhuz*) Kazakh Horde in c.1719, despite having been born into a minor family of Sultans.[8] The khanship was won through the support of strong allies, such as *batyr* Janibek Koshkaruli (d.1751) of the Middle Horde (*Orta Zhuz*) and the influential Bashkir *tarkhan* Aldar Isiangeldin (see the Diary for both). His reputation was earned through his victories over the Jungar Oirats in the Kazakh-Oirat wars of 1723-30. This nevertheless resulted in the loss of Tashkent, Turkestan, Sayram and surrounding villages. This drove Senior numbers of the Kazakhs of the Junior and Middle Hordes westwards across the Sïr-Darya into Mawara' al-nahr, devastating the nomadic and sedentary life of the region.[9] The approach to Russia was driven by the precarious position of the Junior Horde (the westernmost of the three Kazakh hordes)[10] *vis à vis* its close neighbours (the nominally Russian subject Bashkirs and Kalmyks) and Abulkhayir's ambition to further his own advancement within the Junior *Zhuz* (see below). The horde's rights to movement and pastures were also being severely curtailed by encroaching Kalmyks, Cossacks and settlers. This was deliberate Russian policy as forts were built around and into the steppe as part of the Bashkir and Orenburg projects. The Jungars at the time were not a major threat (Bodger 1980, pp.56-57). The horde's relations with Khiva and Bukhara were

---

8   For the genealogy of Abulkhayir see Erofeeva 2007, central plates (not numbered).

9   Erofeeva 2007, p.216.

10 The formation of the three separate hordes (*Kishi, Orta* and *Uli Zhuz*) of the Kazakh Khanate had emerged sometime in the sixteenth century (this is still debated, Martin 2001, p.21; Frank 2009, pp.364-65; Masanov 2011, p.95 proposes the beginning of the seventeenth century.) While the composition of the Senior Horde was connected to former Moghul tribes, the origin of the Junior Horde is more obscure. It consisted of three clan confederations, the Alimuli, the Bailuli and the Zhetiru, to which the Noghay Altïulï tribes were a component. The Zhetiru was made up of unrelated genealogically unrelated clans, (Frank 2009, p.365). Junior Horde traditions trace their confederation to the third son of the mythological Alash or Kotana, who had three sons: Alim, Kadir Khoja and Kart-Kazakh, from whom stemmed the Alimuli, the Baiuli, and the Zhetiru (Frank 2009, p.365; Erofeeva 2011, p.81; Masanov 2011, pp.180-276; Tevkelev 1748, *IKRI* 3, pp.298-304; Rychkov, *Topografiia* pp.139-40). For the Junior Horde's Chinggisid connections see n.217.

difficult and volatile, and those with the Middle Horde factional and competitive, despite family ties.[11]

After the Jungar wars of the early eighteenth century unification of the Khanate broke down and Kazakh Khans increasingly acted as independent rulers.[12] Diplomatic contacts between the Kazakhs and the Tsars with talk of military alliances went back to the late sixteenth century, but the early eighteenth-century war with the Jungars had brought matters to a head. Talks began in earnest in the 1730s, with Abulkhayir promising to pay tribute. Tevkelev's diary of 1731-33 shows the volatility and complexity of the situation in the early 1730s (*IKRI* 3, e.g. pp.73, 77, 87, 94). The Kazakhs hoped to gain Russian protection against Bashkir and Kalmyk raids, to access roaming and water rights along the Yaik and Tobol rivers, to reclaim lost lands from the Jungars and to obtain gifts and concessions from the Russians (*K-R Otnosheniia* e.g. no. 25, letter from Abulkhayir 1730; Tevkelev report of 1732 ed. 2005, pp.52, 55; his diary 1731-33 *ibid* pp.68, 75-76 and *passim*; Khodarkovsky 2004, p.154). For the Russians the advantage was seen as having the Kazakhs police the western steppe and prevent raids on the Yaik, Ufa and Siberian border regions, to secure the passage of trade caravans,[13] to use the Kazakhs against Jungarian ambitions in Russian Siberia and Badakhshan (coveted by the Russians, see [p.16]), and to open new trade routes to the east (*K-R Otnosheniia* nos. 40-43, Tevkelev 1733, *ibid* no. 50 Kirilov 1734; Khodarkovsky 2004, pp.152-56). The conditions imposed by the Empress were: to serve faithfully and pay *iasak* (tribute paid by non-Christian people, Khodarkovsky 2004, p.232), later made voluntary; not to injure Russian subjects; to be protected from harm; to return prisoners; to live in peace with Bashkirs and Kalmyks; to build a

---

11 Frank 2009, p. 368. The Middle Horde was constituted of three major tribes: the Arghun, Nayman and Qïpchaq as well as smaller ones such as the Qonqrat or Qonrad, Waq, Kiräy and miscellaneous groupings such as the Tarakti (Frank 2009, p.365; Erofeeva 2011, pp.73-81).

12 Frank 2009, p.368.

13 The trade which passed through the Kazakh steppe connected Central Asia with centres on the Volga (Kazan, Samara, Astrakhan) and western Siberia (Frank 2009, p.374).

fort at the source of the Or (*K-R Otnosheniia* nos. 28, 29).

Abulkhayir's move towards Russia in order to consolidate his own power[14] was secretive as he knew it would not be popular with his own people. Castle's paraphrase—'...he [the Khan] reiterated most emphatically his hope to succeed in imposing his will and to sacrifice himself before Russia, because he had to handle his people very carefully...'—encapsulates the Khan's precarious situation. The power of the Khan was not absolute and very much dependent on the support of elders, sultans, *biys* and clan leaders,[15] who needed to be courted, assuaged or even driven out.[16] This is re-iterated in all contemporary sources (see below), although the internal workings and alliances of the Kazakhs are not truly known because of limited Kazakh sources (see below).

A nominal oath to Russia was first given by Abulkhayir, Bukenbay *batyr*, and other nobles and elders before Tevkelev in October 1731 (Tevkelev, *Diary* 1731-33, p.76). Other prominent members were subsequently co-opted by gifts (Tevkelev, *Diary*

---

14 Bodger 1980 and A. Morrison (personal communication) believe this to have been the Abulkhayir's principal motivation.

15 The social stratification and kinship of the Kazakh nomads was complex but defined by ancestry. Briefly, it consisted of Khans and Sultans of hereditary nobility (*aq söyek* or white bone) claiming descent from Chingis Khan (chiefly though the Golden Horde Barak Khan and his sons Janïbek and Kiray; Frank 2009, p.366) and commoners (*qara söyek* or black bone) organized into clans and lineages within clans. The status of clans and lineages shifted depending on the political weight of the kinship group (Martin 2001 pp. 22-23, for a summary; Frank 2009, p. 366; Masanov 2011, pp.95-268; Erofeeva 2007, pp.34-52; 2011, pp.81-99; Bardanes *IKRI* 4, pp.167-70; Rychkov, *IKRI* 4, pp.195-212).

16 According to Rychkov Abulkhayir drove Abdul Muhammed (the son of Khan Semeke of the Middle Horde) out of the Middle Horde to Turkestan, and such intrigues eventually led to Abulkhayir's own assassination (*Topografiia*, pp.153-55/183-85; see further pp.8-9, n.18). While Abdul Muhammed's presence away in Turkestan may have suited Abulkhayir, it is otherwise thought that it was due to the aftermath of another war with the Jungars (for this war see Erofeeva 2007, pp.326-49), which allowed Abdul Muhammed nominal control of Turkestan from 1743, while the stronger Sultan Ablai managed the horde from Semipalatinsk and negotiated with the Jungars (Erofeeva 2005, pp.410, 412-13; Olcott 1987, p. 40). After Abulkhayir's death Abdul Muhammed was theoretically the most senior Khan of the steppe (Erofeeva 2005, pp.409-10).

1731-33, e.g. p.85). This process was ongoing in the 1740s (Erofeeva 2007, p.313). The conditions of the oath were broken by both sides from the start (Khodarkovsky 2004, p.159). Russian designs were clearly imperial as was soon shown by the limits imposed on rights to movement and pasture (see p.59), by the proliferation of fortresses, the beginnings of the erosion of the Khans' powers and the creation of internal divisions. For Abulkhayir the alliance was pragmatic, tactical and non-binding (e.g. Khodarkovsky 2004 pp. 153-54), not foreseeing the full colonization of Kazakh lands and certainly not the abolition of the khanship. Soviet historians (Bodger 1980 for references) and others (e.g. Erofeeva 2007, pp.424-432) have argued that it was the beginning of a binding association or union and on Abulkhayir's part a statesman-like, far-sighted move to 'civilize' and ultimately protect the Horde and the steppe by negotiating with the Russians.[17]

Given this context, did Castle's mission achieve anything? Having opportunistically taken up what Orenburg had to offer, he fleetingly aided the establishment that took advantage of him. At personal risk he recorded names and places, returned with envoys from the three Hordes, conveyed messages of loyalty to Russia, briefly enhanced the Khan's standing among his own people, temporarily eased the situation between the Junior Horde and Russia and certainly created amusement among the Kazakhs. His true achievement was the record he made of it all.

Abulkhayir was murdered in 1748 by a rival faction led by Sultan Barak of the Middle Horde (Tevkelev, *IKRI* 3, pp.307, 316).[18] A long-standing rivalry had existed between the two over

17 For a detailed biography of Abulkhayir see Erofeeva 2007.
18 Barak (d. 1750) fled to the Jungarian frontier to seek protection, but denied killing Abulkhayir himself. He was acquitted by a court and went to Turkestan. His children and Janïbek-batyr continued to seek revenge (the Russians maintained that he was seen doing it by witnesses) and as a result of intrigue with the Jungars, Barak and two of his sons appear to have been poisoned in Karnak (*K-R. Otnosheniia* nos.175, 186, 187; *IKRI* 3, p.307; Fuchs 1981, p.78; *IKRI* 4, pp.293-94; Franks 2009, p.373). For a discussion of the confrontation with Barak see Erofeeva 2007, pp.324-25, 395-432). Abulkhayir is buried in Aktiube oblast, not far from the confluence of the Olkeirak and Kabirga rivers. His burial place is shown

Abulkhayir's ambitions over the hordes, and his minor ancestral status,[19] but a number of reasons have been suggested for the confrontation of 1748: arguments over trade routes and/or the robbing of a caravan destined for Barak's daughter by the Junior Horde and/or over spoils from Kazakh families travelling from the Karakaplaks to the Senior Horde. The then Governor of Orenburg, Ivan Ivanovich Nepluyev, against whom Abulkhayir had many grievances, and who believed in encouraging existing divisions between the Kazakhs in order to weaken them, may have fuelled the situation.[20]

Russian sources of the time show that Abulkhayir was considered clever and learned but hot-headed and arrogant, crafty, quick and a nuisance because of his constant demands for gifts and favours[21] (see below for Castle). Georgi, writing rhetorically after the event and wishing to cover all angles, remarks that he was 'wise and prudent, but violent and bold' (Georgi 1780-83, Vol.2, p.249).[22]

Approaches to Russia via Tevkelev by Khan Semeke of the Middle Horde had been made in 1731 (Tevkelev, *Diary* 1731-33, p.94; Rychkov, *Topografiia* pp.149-50), but it was only in 1740 that a nominal oath to the Russian Crown was taken by Khan Abdul Muhammed and Sultan Ablai, who tried to negotiate better terms than Abulkhayir's (Rychkov, *Topografiia* pp.152/182). They were in a better position to do so, being wealthier because of trade, superior pastures and a greater number of horses (Rychkov, *Topografiia*, pp.145/175). In effect Ablai remained more or less independent, maintaining a careful balance between the Russians

---

on maps of 1755 and it remained a place of pilgrimage until the mid-twentieth century (Erofeeva, 2005, p.400).

19 Bodger 1980, pp.45-46; Erofeeva 2007, p.396.
20 Levshin 1840, p. 210; Khodarkovsky 2004, pp.164, 166 on the origins of some of the different stories; Erofeeva 2007, pp.395-99.
21 Kirilov, *K-R Otnocheniia* no. 50, p.107; Rychkov, *Topografiia*, pp.153-54/183-84; Khodarkovsky 2004, pp.159-60.
22 Abulkhayir is vilified in Levshin as insolent, greedy, insincere, ambitious and cowardly; the Kazakhs themselves are described as ignorant and lazy, but as having respect for their elders and gratitude for good deeds (Levshin 1840, pp.165, 199, 209, 344, 349).

and the Qing.[23] Representatives of the Senior Horde had been part of Abulkhayir's embassy to Empress Anna in 1732-34[24] but this was more bravura on Abulkhayir's part than any true desire by the Senior Horde to become subject. In 1738, prompted by potential commercial advantages, Khan Cholbars offered himself and his Horde as Russian subjects, but he never swore allegiance nor came to court. (Tevkelev, 1731-33, p.91. *K-R Otnoscheniia* pp.36, 62, 120, 128, 129; Erofeeva 2007, pp.443-44). By the early nineteenth century the position of Khan had been abolished and Russian Imperial administration and legal structures imposed on the Junior and Middle Hordes (Khodarkovsky 2004, pp.182-83): this began the real extension of Russian control of the Kazakhs. Internal dissent had reduced many clans to such poverty that they were forced to come to the Russian frontiers and sell their children *en masse* (Levshin, ed. 1840, p.351). The final conquest of the steppe is considered to have come in the 1860s.[25]

THE AUTHOR

Castle is elusive. He is known from this diary, references to him in Russian sources,[26] including the letter he wrote to Empress Anna, and from John Cook's *Voyages and Travels...* (1770) written in the 1740s. Here Castle is described as having been born in Prussia to an English mother, and to have passed himself off as an Englishman because of England's favourable trade conditions with Russia at the time. Cook writes that Castle went to Persia (presumably after he finished editing his diary in St. Petersburg in1741) together with John Elton (see p.104), hoping to find employment with Nadir Shah. He was eventually commissioned to paint eight pictures of the Shah, but the results did not please

---

23 My thanks to A. Morrison for making this point.
24 Levshin *op. cit*, p.172. See also a letter from the Sultans and *biys* of the Senior Horde to Empress Anna, dated to 1733 (*K-R Otnosheniia*, no.45 pp.101-102. Reproduced in Chagatai and Persian script).
25 Franks 2009, pp.373-78; my thanks to Alexander Morrison for making this point.
26 RGADA, f.248, kn. 1164, ll.73-75 (the letter, seen by courtesy of TsGAZ); from Matvieski 1958 pp.134-38, 140 : TsGIAL (now RGIA) f. 1329, kn. 89, ll..150-51; 410, 421 ob.; GAO f.2, d.9. ll.20-21; ABPR f k-k *dela* 1736, d.3. See Editorial Note.

the Shah, who ordered Castle to be strangled. Elton intervened, apparently successfully (Cook 1770, Vol.2, pp.414-15). The trail then goes cold. Castle is not mentioned in association (mercantile or otherwise) with Elton in any of the Russia Company Minutes[27] or in Hanway's account of Elton in Russia and Persia (*idem* 1753). This confirms Castle's independent adventurer status. If he had stayed in Persia in Elton's circle, he might well have suffered the same fate as him: shot in 1751 in the chaos following Nadir Shah's death (n.162). Other merchants, however, extricated themselves safely from Ghilan at the time. The diary mentions that Castle had a brother (on commission) and a father in Moscow in the 1730s[28] (see Editorial note). The family may have been from from Hamburg.[29] It is worth noting here that Castle's German is colloquial and pedestrian, with French words used for effect and to supplement his vocabulary.[30] This may indicate some education but with pretensions to more.

THE TEXT

This edition is a translation from the German of Castle's diary as published in Riga in 1784, as an appendage, with its own pagination and no key to the prints, to *Materialen zu der Russischen Geschichte seit dem Tode Kaisers Peters der Grossen, Zwieter Teil*.[31] This suggests that the text, glossary and plates were printed separately, possibly earlier. The German text of 1784 is the result of several editorial stages: the original diary, presumably in note form (cf. pp.20, 81); two signed copies written up and submitted in Simbirsk in 1737 (Matvieskii 1958, p.138);[32] a further edition made in St. Petersburg in 1741 (possibly anticipating publication) added an Introduction, pp.1-2 of the Diary, a recapitulation of

---

27 LMA: MS 11,741/6:pp.150, 218, 224, 281, 372, 375.
28 No other references to Castle's family have been found by me so far. See below Editorial Note.
29 This is how he is referred to in Russian catalogues: Eduardovich, 1995, p.298; Singaevskii 2006, p.56. My thanks to Neil Jeffares for these references.
30 My thanks to Sarah Tolley for pointing this out.
31 A Russian translation by V. Starkenberg appeared in 1998. This is so far unobtainable in Europe.
32 ABPR, k-k *dela* 1736, d.3.

salient points of the adventure and subsequent events until Castle's decommission (pp.81-116) and a section in three parts on the Kazakhs (pp.116-144); and finally a Glossary and thirteen prints, which were added at the time of publication. Judging by the extremely lengthy references to the author's deeds in the Glossary, it is likely that Castle himself or a member of the family prepared the Diary for publication and published it at their own expense. The two signed copies (referred to in Matvieskii *op. cit* above) have to my knowledge not been seen or worked on since 1958, and are presently inaccessible.

As well as keeping a record for his Russian patrons as was expected of him (as was *de rigueur* for merchants, envoys and officials of the State, as well as for Academicians on official expeditions) in a climate of 'political ethnography', Castle was also conscious of the singularity of his journey and probably of the popularity of travel writing in Europe at the time. Castle does not mention previous famous travellers of the time such as N. Witsen (*Noord en oost Tartaryen*, Amsterdam 1692), or P. J. Strahlenberg (*An Historic-Geographical Description of the North and Eastern Part of Europe and Asia, but more particularly of Russia, Siberia and Great Tartary*, London 1736;); neither does he refer to J. G. Gmelin who was at the time officially travelling and observing in Siberia[33] or to articles in *Sammlung Russischer Geschichte* (St. Petersburg 1732-64). Yet the addition of a section on the Kazakhs (on the land and natural resources; on physical attributes, character and customs; and on the position of the Junior Horde and the Khan) shows a desire to emulate the information-gathering and 'scientific' expeditions of the time, with an expectation of recognition and publication. Castle's comments on the Kazakhs in the diary are a mixture of exasperation, superiority, irony and disgust (for example, at what he was given to eat). Yet his comments never seem overly censorious or vicious, and at times they are appreciative or relaxed and matter of fact (e.g. pp.52, 64, 78). In his three-part observations on the Kazakhs, added in 1741, Castle does use denigrating labels characteristic of contemporary Academicians

---

33 *Reise durch Sibirien von dem Jahr 1733 bis 1743*, 4 Vols. Göttingen, 1751-52 (edited trans. into French, 1757).

and officials to describe the Kazakhs (crafty, uncouth, rapacious)[34] but he also states that 'when one shows them that one is upright, they too will be trustworthy and not nearly as terrible as they have been described' (p.126). Here Castle may have been intent on showing up Russian officialdom. The Khan[35] is described as being 'of large and distinguished stature' with an amiable face, strong and forceful, and probably being held back by his subjects (p.144). Castle shows no desire to emulate Academicians or other officials in trying to shed light on Kazakh history. He never mentions, for example, Ebulgazi Bahadir Khan's then well-known *A General History of the Turks, Moguls, and Tatars...* (London 1729-30).[36]

Other additions to the text, such as the Introduction, attempts a vindication *vis-à-vis* the Russian authorities, possibly with the hope of a reward from the Crown. We do not know whether this came about: the treatment of many foreigners serving the Russians was frequently exploitative, cavalier and callous, with payment often deferred or never honoured (Teissier 2011, cf. e.g. Bruce, Cook, *passim*).

SOURCES

The principal primary sources for this period against which Castle's observations have been checked, are P. I. Rychkov's *Istoriia Orenburgskai* (1759, ed. 1896) and *Topografiia Orenburgskaia* (1762, ed. 2010); the comparatively recent editions of Tevkelev's writings, notably his diary of 1731-33 (*IKRI* 3, 2005), the miscellaneous writings of Rychkov (*IKRI* 4, 2007); the letters and documents in Dobromyslov 1900 (Vol.2 only accessible) and in *Kazakhsko-russkie Otnosheniia*, and crucially for the Bashkir rebellion of the 1730s, Demidova's *Materialy po Istoriia Bashkortostana*, Vol. 6; and the later writings of Academicians and ethnographers such as P. S. Pallas, Ch. Bardanes, J. G. Georgi, A. Levshin, Ch. Valikhanov and I. A. Castagné. These were written on behalf of the Russian State, and while not all biased, do present, with the

---

34 For a discussion of this subject see Slezkine 2001.
35 Pl.13, p.141.
36 e.g. Rychkov, *Topografiia*, pp.131/161-134/164; Pallas 1788, Vol.1 pp.610-11; Georgi 1780-83, Vol.2 pp.242-43.

---

partial exception of Valikhanov, the official position. Except for a few official letters from Abulkhayir published in translation from the Chagatai (e.g. *K-R Otnoscheniia* nos. e.g. 26, 27, 36, 41, 42 and ff.)[37] the true position of the Kazkahs, their relations with their neighbours and among themselves remain partially known. This will soon be partially redressed by the publication of Abulkhayir's correspondence with the Russians, although this again is official material.[38] Of the secondary sources written in English, Alton Donnelly (1968) and Khodarkosky (2004) are still fundamental. In Russian the works of Erofeeva, Masanov, Fuchs and Zimanov are particularly important. Matvieskii's 1958 article is the only proper Russian study of Castle's diary.

NAMES

The ethnonym Kazakh is used in this text, instead of Kirghiz or Kirghiz-Kaysak as used by Castle. The latter was standard Russian practice at the time. The name Kirghiz is taken from a Turkic people from around the Yenisei and in Mongolia, who in the seventeenth century had been ruled by the Kazakhs (Barthold/ Hazai 1986, pp.134-35). The name Kazakh (more correctly *Qazaq*, also written *kazach, kazax*) is found representing the nomads of Eurasia or the eastern Qipchaq steppe in the fifteenth century (Bregel 2003, p.50). The two names were conjoined in the Russian sources to avoid confusion with *Kazaki/Kasaki* or Cossacks.[39] The actual Kirghiz were known as the Kara-Kirghiz.

EDITORIAL NOTE

Matching personal names, particularly in the case of Chagatai, has been problematic due to the series of transliterations: from the original via an interpreter to German, and from German to English. Names in the main text that can be recognized or matched from contemporary sources have been noted, others

---

37 See also Erofeeva 2001, pp.38-39, for examples of Abulkhayir's seal and other letters.
38 Personal communication from Irina Erofeeva.
39 The Kazakhs themselves thought the name Kirghiz-Kaysak meant 'soldiers of Khan Kirghiz' (Pallas 1788, Vol.1, p.611).

have been left in transliteration. Place names have been checked against maps of 1755 (published with Rychkov ed. 2010) and contemporary texts, but again not all of these have been found. This is due partly to the use of local names for places or rivers, and to changing names.

The translation has tried to convey the style and content of the original as much as possible. To give a sense of the original, the glossary has not been edited and names and interchangeable tenses (present when the author refers to himself and perfect for the narrative) have been left as written. The page numbers of the diary as printed in 1784 have been left in square brackets in the text to guide anyone wishing to check the original.

The aim of this work has been to make available the translation and edition of Castle's diary without undue delay. While new archival material (courtesy of TsGARKaz, Almaty) has informed this publication, checking the archival material on Castle in Russian archives referred to by Matviesky 1958 has been postponed until the archive of the Foreign Policy of the Russian Empire (AVPRI) that holds the original diary is opened. I then hope to be able to check all the relevant material, including potential new sources and drawings,[40] and report any findings in a supplementary article.

---

40 See e.g. Dictionary of Pastellists before 1800 (Neil Jeffares, online), a watercolour of the head of a young Bashkir signed J. Cassel Fe. 1735, in the State Russian Museum, St. Petersburg, inv.Ж-163.

JOURNAL

of
an extremely necessary and happily completed
journey
undertaken on
ao 1736 from Orenburg
to the
ABUL GEIER
Khan of the Kyrgyz Kazakh
Tartar Horde
of my own free will and purely for the best advantage of
the Russian Empire

presented
by
John Castle
an Englishman and artist serving on the
Orenburg Expedition

To the

Most illustrious and mighty
Prince and Great Ruler
Lord John the Third[1]

By the Grace of God Emperor and
Protector of all Russia, Moscow, Kiev
Wolodimir and Novogrod, Tsar of Kasan
Tsar of Astrakhan, Tsar of Siberia,
Lord of Pleskow and Great Prince of Smo-
lensk, Prince of Esthland, Eiesland, Carelien,
Iwer, Jugorien, Perm, Wiatka, Bolgarien and
further, Lord and Great Prince of Novogrod,
the Low Lands, Tschernikow, Resan, Rostow,
Jaroslaw, Bieloserow,
Udorien, Obdorien, Rondin and the whole
Regions of the North Side, Lord of the Iwer
Lands, of the Kartalin and Grusini
Tzars, the Kabardin Lands,
and of the Tscherkas and Boris
Lords and hereditary Lord and Ruler
of many other lands

to whose
gracious and illustrious favour

this little work is dedicated
with profoundest humility

by
the author

---

1 Confused with Ivan VI (Ivan Antonovich) 1740-64, nominal Emperor
of Russia from October 1740-November 1741. He was the son of Anna
Leopoldovna, the niece of the Empress Anna (1730-40), who briefly
became regent after Empress Anna's death. The child was incarcerated
and murdered in 1764, and Elizabeth, Peter the Great's daughter, became
Empress in 1741 (-1761).

MOST GRACIOUS EMPEROR
AND GREAT RULER

Your Imperial Majesty's inherent and utmost graciousness and concern for the happiness of his people embolden me to lay this present journal at your most sanctified feet with the utmost humility. Although I seek hereby to gain no glory for my unworthy services, since the respect I feel as a foreigner for the Russian Imperial Monarch inspires me to leave this for Your Imperial Majesty to determine, since this may not yet have been effected by the Orenburg Chancellery with regard to my person, given that I am wholly unaware as to whether the true report of the circumstances of what I undertook to the true advantage [VIII] of this Empire, as set out in the *relationes* of these which can be found in the Orenburg Chancery, which involved diverse and very dangerous expeditions entirely at my own expense and without support or assistance from anyone, has been conveyed to Your Majesty, or whether anything of that nature has been sent here? It is with this intent that this present *journal* is supplied to give public witness to that loyalty which I have sacrificed with profoundest submission to your Imperial Majesty and the Empire, on account of which State Councillor Iwan Kiriloff[1] has not only praised me highly many times and promised to reward my loyal services, by sending an account of my achievements to Your Imperial Majesty, he also presented my person on various occasions to many staff and other esteemed officers, and urging them to model their achievements on my example, and saying may times to these people that he would never be able to provide

---

1 Ivan Kirilovich Kirilov (1689-1737), state councillor, economic geographer, head of the Orenburg expedition 1734-37, responsible for policy-making in Bashkiria. His time as the head of the Orenburg expedition was mostly spent in brutally suppressing the Bashkir uprising and constructing defensive forts along the Yaik/Ural and Samara rivers. This interfered with his diplomatic work with the Kazkahs and with the development of Orenburg. Castle found Kirilov the most difficult of all the Russian officials he dealt with. Main works: *Tvetuschee sostoiane Vserossiiskogo gosudarstva* (The Flourishing Condition of the All-Russian State), St. Petersburg, 1727, and *Atlas Vserossiskoi imperii* (Atlas of the All-Russian Empire), St. Petersburg, 1734.

a sufficient reward for my loyalty!

[IX] However, in that I have to date not succeeded in gaining what has been promised me, and have consequently been subjected to no little inconvenience, since, instead of receiving much-vaunted reward from Iwan Kiriloff, after further unnecessary losses were subsequently inflicted on me, for which reason I was indeed obliged for this very reason to request my decommission on 14 January 1737 and to send my brother[2] here on this business, whose commission was happily effected, and, in that following his representation the order was given from the High Cabinet, that the truth of my very varied account should be investigated and if I was no longer required, my request for a decommission should be granted. However, it appears that despite all these circumstances, State Councillor Iwan Kiriloff was not prepared in the slightest to meet the assurance he had given me, since the former had merely approved a service report [X] about my Bashkir and Kyrgyz travels, and did not convey the slightest detail about my fine achievements for the Empire in those places, and indeed he went so far as to take a noble stone weighing 62lb that I had found in Tartary, and which I had conveyed through hostile Bashkir Tartars, who I induced through my good offices to adhere once again to the Russian side, sending 200 lb meat to Orenburg during the famine in March *an* 1763,[3] in order to deliver this stone to my commissaire there, the Surgeon Rodet, with the Pensich Regiment,[4] which however was retained along with myself by the

---

2 See Editorial Note in the Introduction.

3 Typographic error: 1736. The continuous fighting and harsh suppression of the Bashkirs had a devastating effect not only on the local population but on the economy and transport of the region, leading to starvation and rationing (Demidova 2002 e.g. nos. 94, 61, 94, 125: famine on the Yaik/Ural nos. 136, 144). This, together with extreme cold of the winter of 1736 severely affected Russian troops and garrisons, who lacked provisions, fodder, clothes and funds. In 1736 Orenburg was in a critical condition (Donnelly 1968, from primary sources, pp.73-75). It cannot be proven, but it is perfectly possible that Castle sent meat to Orenburg, given that he had lived there for almost a year (see p.24). Whether the supplies would have got to Orenburg is another question.

4 Penzensk/Penza regiment from Kazan, one of the units brought to protect the Orenburg project.

Commandant of Orenburg,[5] yea, and subsequently removed by Iwan Kiriloff from that above-mentioned Commandant, and s*ub dato* 14th March 1737 on orders from the High Cabinet, was sent here, for which [XI] and for my other loyal services I have not to *dato* yet received the slightest payment.[6]

May Your Imperial Majest. be moved to view with the greatest *clemence* my unfalsified description in this present journal, which only differs from the journal that is found in the Orenburg Chancellery in that the one contains merely my journey and my achievements thereby, whereas in order to explain the circumstances and other occasions that arose, the present one includes many *specialia* and remarkable curiosa as they occurred from day to day, which gracious *clemence* to observe how, , in the course of time, I have inserted comic instances among the grave concerns and have added other instances that occurred to me quite *naturellement*, so that I am offering, on the one hand a romance that I did not invent, and on the other hand, an unfalsified monument to my [XII] honest loyalty to your Imperial Majesty, whereby, contrary to Your Most Elevated orders and wishes, a loyal servant may at times, wholly undeservedly, be dismayed and chagrined on account of his good intentions. In that now I dwell on these matters in this work, which are all well-founded, so the truth of all this will be revealed all the more clearly since the bulk of it corresponds perfectly with the journal that is located in the Orenburg Chancery, whereby I regret simply that I was not able to include the original drawings of the Oriental peoples and other remarkable things that pertain to it, since I have already submitted these to the oft-mentioned Orenburg Chancery. However, grant me Your Gracious permission to present, with profoundest submission, along with copies of these, 5 original portraits, one of Abul Geier Khan,[7] another of his son, Eraly

---

5 Yakov Fedorovitch Chemodurov was made governor by Kirilov in 1735, and replaced by Major B.L. Ostankov in 1736 (Rychkov, *Istoriia*, pp.22, 26; Donnelly 1968 pp.72, 86). See p. 92 and references to 'Lieutenant-Colonel'.

6 Castle's problems with Russian officialdom and his sense of injury pervade much of the diary (see Introduction).

7 Abulkhayir (c. 1680-1748) became Khan of the Junior (*Khsi Zhuz*)

Sultan,[8] who is currently in Orenburg, [XIII] the third of the very renowned Bashkir war leader, called Aldar, the fourth, of the daughter of said Aldar,[9] and the fifth, of Mursa, a Tartar, who is an interpreter, represented in their true likenesses, and thereby simply to show how I was also able to promote the well-being of the Russian Empire among these wild people too, and thereby achieve *insinuence* to them and paint their portraits freehand just with my finger, to their great enjoyment and astonishment.

And as I attest to Your Imperial Majest with the profoundest submission that I have never faltered in the *continuation* of my most submissive loyalty, and appeal passionately to God that he shower unceasing blessings from on high and grant Your Imperial Majesty a steady increase of power and strength [XIV] unto a very great age, and also that Your Imperial Highness the most excellent Lady Regent and Loftiest Consort of Your Imperial Highness, be filled with all the *contentement* that she desires, and that your Eminent selves be eternally disposed to confer blessings, so may I die professing such devoted wishes in the profoundest submission,

Your Imperial Majest

St Petersburg
--- Ao 1741

Kazakh Horde in c. 1719. See Introduction. For a detailed biography of Abulkhayir see Erofeeva 2007. These portraits, with the possible exception of the Khan's, were not reproduced in the printed diary.
8 Erali Sultan, the second son of Abulkhayir c. 1721-94, by his wife Bopai. Khan of the Junior Horde from 1791-94.
9 Aldar Siangeldin (Iskiev) c. 1670-1740. A Bashkir *batyr* (warrior of repute) and *tarkhan* (tribal or clan leader who pays no tribute or taxes in return for military service) with close ties to Abulkhayir. See p.64, n.109.

CASTLE'S DIARY

[1] In that the **glory** of the Russ. **Imperial** Empire succeeds in drawing countless people in all the countries of **Europe** to pay peculiar respect and devotion to itself, so I too as an Englishman been quite unable to resist sacrificing myself in abject subjection to the high **monarchs** of this blessed Empire, and to engage my insignificant self with the **Orenburg Expedition**.[1]

However, given that I have from my youth onwards constantly adhered to the opinion that the efforts of an upright servant and subject should be directed chiefly to this purpose, that his honest loyalty may be realized in his deeds: Thus, it was with this intention that, following my arrival at the **River Or**, where **Orenburg** is situated, when I was absolutely denied the opportunity to cultivate this place, on the pretext of sickness, in that I received no horses and so had to remain there, my most precious concern being directed at making myself worthy of my service, to put the interests of the Empire before all other things, and thus to constantly achieve more than my regular function actually required. Although the circumstances that I have just mentioned caused an envious Momo to accuse me frivolously [2] of seeking my own glory, although I sought only to acquire merit by these means; my intention being directed not towards my own glory and use, but being aimed simply at encouraging steady imitators, as opposed to those others who prefer their own *commodité* to the true zeal of an honest undertaking, and so are not the slightest use to the world; so hopefully I am committing no sin or anything reprehensible, by presenting these deeds that actually took place as an example to others, the more so since my high *Commandeur* and all those other persons on the Orenburg Expedition, of whom I can find a good number here in St Petersburg, are exceedingly well aware of how I on various occasions without anyone's advice or command made the greatest effort to put the Imperial Interests before my entire wealth and

---

1 See Introduction.

my own life too; further that I did not otherwise experience the slightest assistance from anyone. The evidence for this I will show more clearly, when I simply present the Commerce in which I engaged, not as part of a merchant consortium,[2] but simply to serve the Russian Empire by consorting successfully with very rough and wild peoples, such as the Kyrgyz and Bashkir Tartars,[3] by presenting these matters in this journal, and relating the true circumstances of these events in the following form.

Anno 1736 (June 14)

[3] Two envoys along with a *Besaul*[4] or Adjutant from the Kyrgyz Abul Geier Khan and from Iambeck Batur[5] (this last word means a hero), likewise an envoy, came to the Orenburg fort with a letter

---

2 Castle refers to British merchant consortia, such as that of George Napier in St. Petersburg, which included Mungo Graeme and Reynold Hogg, associated with John Elton see p.104, n.162 or Jonas Hanway of the Russian Company. The Russia Company (the old Muscovy Company, the British-Russian trading company established in 1555), had signed an advantageous commercial treaty with Russia in 1734, which included a concession to trade to Persia via Russia (Hanway 1753, Vol.1, pp.1-8, 13-82; Vol. 2 pp.70-99, 102-5; Teissier 2011, pp.140-41 and *passim*; see p.104 Elton). Britain was to export wool and luxury goods in return for iron, timber, hemp, flax and other commodities. These treaties had to be renegotiated and could even be suspended (1741) but covered most of the Company's Golden Age (the eighteenth and early nineteenth centuries, Cross 1997, p. 46). Merchants and traders were a wealthy and significant part of the British community in eighteenth-century St. Petersburg (Cross 1997, pp.10-11; 44-89).

3 For a study of eighteenth-century British and St. Petersburg Academicians' labelling of frontier peoples such as the Kazakhs (Kirghiz), see Slezkine 2001; Teissier 2011.

4 *Yasayul*: an official whose functions included collecting rents and delivering letters and messages between Khans, Sultans and elders (*IKRI* Vol. 3, p.417).

5 Janibek Koshkaruli, d.1751. An important *batyr* (warrior of repute, hero) and *biy* (or *bek*, noble, customary law (*adat*) judge) of the Middle Horde (Shakshak clan, Arghyn family/lineage). He was an advisor to and ally of Abulkhayir, and involved with Tevkelev in negotiations over the Middle Horde's becoming subject to the Russians: Tevkelev *Diary* 1731-33, ed. 2005, p.117 and *passim*. (For the Middle Horde's negotiations, attitudes to this and rivalry with the Junior Horde, see Introduction and pp.8-9). Janibek was made a *tarkhan* by the Russians in 1742. *IKRI* Vol.3, pp.411-12. His closeness to Abulkhayir is reflected by his frequent mention in Castle's diary.

for the Commandant there, Lieutenant-Colonel Jacob Foedrowitz Tshemaduroff,[6] with instructions to discover whether the town of Orenburg had already been abandoned or was still being held,[7] to request in the Khan's name a Russian envoy, with regard to many tokens of its prosperity, but, for reasons entirely unknown to me, the Commandant did not send one.

Given I had by now already befriended the Khan's son, Eraly Sultan,[8] for a considerable time, he having been left behind in Orenburg[9] as a hostage, and to whom I had during my stay of almost a year rendered various friendly services and had drawn him to me, thereby rendering him obliged to me, so on the 14 June I allowed him to invite him and the envoys and the various Kyrgyz with him, together with the Buchar priest or Agun[10] called

6 Yakov Fedorovitch Chemodurov was made governor by Kirilov in 1735, and replaced by Major B.L. Ostankov in 1736 (Rychkov, *Istoriia*, pp.22, 26; Donnelly 1968 pp.72, 86).

7 This is a reference to the desperate state of the garrison in Orenburg in late spring as well as to possible threats from the Bashkirs, even though the centres of insurrection were further north, in the Kazan, Noghay and Siberian *dorogas* or districts.

8 Erali Sultan, the second son of Abulkhayir c. 1721-94, by his wife Bopai. Khan of the Junior Horde from 1791-94. He participated in Abulkhayir's embassy to St. Petersburg in 1732 and returned with the Orenburg expedition in 1734. He was held hostage (*amanat*) in Orenburg from 1736-38. After his father's death he left with his family for the Syr-Darya region, and became Sultan of the Shomeki and Tortkara of the Alymuli tribe. He was involved in the suppression of a Bashkir rebellion in 1755 and fought against the Jungars and the Volga Kalmyks in their exodus from Russia in 1771. Together with his brother Khan Nurali he opposed the Russian policy of abolishing the title of Khan in the 1787, but became the Russians' candidate and was eventually made Khan by the Russians in 1791 after Nurali's death. This precipitated a rebellion against the Russians by the Kazakh faction who wanted to appoint their own Khan. After his death he was replaced by Esim, Nurali's son in 1795 (Khodarkovsky 2004, pp.180-81; *IKRI* Vol.3, pp.417-18). Erali played a pivotal role in enabling Castle's visit to his father: he negotiated with the commandant Chemodurov and assured Abulkhayir of Castle's viability, thus demonstrating his usefulness, even as a hostage.

9 See pp.88-91, n.147 for Castle's description and Pl.7, p.89.

10 *Akhund*, a very high-ranking member of the Islamic clergy and specialist in Islamic law. This reference to a 'Buchar' (most probably from Bukhara, or otherwise from Central Asia, possibly Tashkent, Turkestan, the Ferghana Valley or Khorezm) *akhund* in Orenburg accompanying the envoys of the Kazakh Junior Horde shows the link

Monsur, who had also stayed in Orenburg, to my house.

At the time, I did not lack for anything, and was able to them show every kindness and hospitality and I know according to 5. Matt. Ch. II[11] that at the same time, [4] I gave you everything that I possessed. I thereby obtained their good will and they revealed to me in confidence how the Ottoman Pforte[12] had incited 40000

1736
(June 14)

---

between élite Kazakhs and orthodox Islam. For coexistence with steppe Islam see pp.33-35 n.38. Bukhara's prestige as a holy city and centre of culture and religious teaching, which was renowned among the Muslim of the Russian Empire, the Tatars of Kazan, the Bashkirs and Siberian Muslims, had also permeated to the steppe through caravan routes and rich merchants. It gathered momentum from the mid-eighteenth century onwards (Frank 2012, pp.43ff.) in major trading centres such as Orenburg, Astrakhan and parts of Siberia, where Bukharan merchants held a privileged position (Frank 2012 p. 45). It is not possible to investigate here the intriguing nature of the relation between Khans and *akhunds*, the measure of influence an *akhund* would have had on the Junior Horde, and what the thoughts and plans of the Islamic ulamā from orthodox centres such as Bukhara were regarding the Kazakhs. It is worth noting that by the 1740s the Russians had become actively involved in trying to control Islam in this frontier area: the Mufti of Orenburg (Ibrahim b. Muhammad-Tulak) was appointed by them in 1744 (Franks 2009, p.376).

11 The pages of the Diary (and the Glossary) are interspersed with references to Matthew's Gospel e.g. p.58. The references printed (Chapter 2, verses 3 or 5, from the Life of Jesus) do not make sense in this context. The reference Castle appears to want to quote from here is Matthew Chapter 19 v.21. Thus he either misremembered the quote, the error was a consistent typographical one or the printer was using remaindered sheets from another text (a Bible or New Testament).

12 Ottoman and/or Crimean Tatar involvement in Muslim affairs within or at the frontiers of Muscovy and of the early Russian Empire, whether real and tactical or for purposes of intrigue, had been a threat to Russia since the expansion of Muscovy and the conquest of the khanates of Kazan and Astrakhan by Ivan IV in the seventeenth century. The Treaty of Constantinople between Russia and the Ottomans in 1700 had stipulated mutual respect of borders, but yet another Russo-Turkish war had broken out in 1736-39, occupying the Ottomans with their northern (Black Sea, Azov) and eastern (Persia, Caucasus) fronts (Aksan 2012, p.318; Davies 2011, pp.13, 19, 180-241). Overt Ottoman involvement within Russia's frontiers itself at this time would have been unlikely, yet there is evidence of dissent and support given, for example, to Bashkir raiders on the Volga by other disaffected groups of Tatars and others from the Caucasus in 1707 (Davies 2011, p.19) and of Bashkir rebel leaders petitioning the Crimeans for a Khan in 1708 and 1736/7 (refused both times, Donnelly 1968, p.126; Demidova 2002, no.

---

angry Kyrgyz who were now standing ready, and had combined with the Kilmeck[13] Kyrgyz rebels, to attack the Russian Imperial State Councillor Iwan Kiriloff and his forces and to engage battle, and thus to lay waste the entire country from Ufa and Casan, though they merely intended to subdue Orenburg though starvation; to prevent this, therefore, their Khan was for this very reason requesting a Russian envoy, to soften his wild people[14] with his presence, whereby they also commented that should they, namely the Kyrgyz envoys, be disappointed and forced to return alone with no Russian envoy, they would immediately combine with the Kilmecks, and would themselves be viewed as traitors and would be killed on that account.[15]

This unexpected news appeared to present great danger to the Russian Empire and aroused no little alarm in my mind, given

---

216, p.369). Ottoman spies were supposed to have been in Bashkiria in 1739 (Donnelly 1968, p.126). Given the context it is very possible that rumours of Ottoman involvement with the Bashkirs and indirectly with Kazakhs opposed to subjection to Russia were circulating at the time. Castle certainly plays up to them (for Kazakh involvement with the Bashkirs, see p.30, nn.15, 31) The numbers supposedly involved, probably inflated, are impossible to gauge (compare the changing estimates and numbers of Bashkir rebels see n.110).

13 Kilmiak Nurushev (*abyz, mullah*) from the Noghay district, was one of the main leaders of the Bashkir rebellion from 1735. He was captured in 1737 (Demidova 2001, e.g. nos. 69, 107, 182). Castle has mistakenly conflated the name of the rebel Bashkir with the Kazakhs. Other major leaders of the Bashkir rebellion at the time were Yusuf Arikov (*batyr, mullah,* Demidova 2002 e.g. nos. 125, 128, 188); Bepen Trupbergun (*abyz, mullah,* Demidova 2002, e.g. nos. 188); Isyangul *abyz* (Demidova 2002, e.g. nos. 125, 188) from the Siberian district.

14 Wild people or *dikie lyudi* was indeed a term used by Abulkhayir himself about his people (e.g. in a letter to Empress Anna, 1736 (*K-O Otnoscheniia,* e.g. no. 42, p.98) in order to ingratiate himself. In this he was echoing the words used by the Empire about the Kazakhs (e.g. Tevkelev 1731-32, pp.58-59; Kirilov, 1734, *K-O Otnoscheniia,* no. 50)

15 Whether the Kazakhs of the Junior Horde who were not in agreement with Abulkhayir did actually collude with the Bashkirs in 1736 to fight against the Russians is not proven; but it was not out of the question and a useful threat for purposes of agitation. In 1737 Abulkhayir himself interfered in Bashkiria, first on behalf of the Russians, then on the side of the Bashkirs, but reluctant to fully antagonize the Russians and fearing the military, he eventually renewed his oath (Donnelly 1968, pp.109-116).

that I was considering how the aforementioned Commandant did not wish to send an envoy, and how at the same time the greatest speed was required, in order to avert this great disaster, yea, to divert harm and disadvantage from the Empire [5] and so I determined that it was my duty to go and present myself to the young Eraly Sultan, and explain that I was thinking of going on a journey to his father, with the intention of travelling to Samara on the way back, to the State Councillor Iwan Kiriloff, with a view to reporting back to him, a suggestion which cheered them up considerably and was approved on all sides and was considered extremely necessary. However, in order to enable this business to be expedited as quickly as possible, the young Eraly Sultan went to the Commandant and asked him to permit me to travel to his father for a while, under the pretext that I should paint the latter and bring his portrait back with me.

1736
(June 14)

Once the Commandant had consented to this, the young Eraly Sultan immediately wrote a letter to his father, with the assurance that he had confidence in me in all things and that he could confide totally in me, whereupon I prepared for the journey, and left my possessions in the care of *Chirurgo* Rodet of the Pensich[16] Regiment, with the request that if I did not return alive from this journey, he himself would convey them to my father, because I had to start my journey that very afternoon, having received the above letter from Eraly Sultan; Now for some details about my companions on this journey; I took with me a German apprentice called [6] Dietrich Luftus aged 14, next, a Tatar servant, called Kulben, who belonged to Colonel Teffkeleff,[17] and who proved

1736
(Juune 14)

---

16 Pensensk/Penza regiment.
17 Tevkelev, Alexei, Ivanovitch (Kutlu Muhammed) 1674-1766, Muslim interpreter, diplomat and government official, first served under Peter the Great. He was a major architect of Russian policy towards the Kazakhs (e.g. the building of forts, development of the steppe etc. *IKRI* Vol.3, 1731, pp.51-64) and successful envoy to Abulkhayir to negotiate his oath of subjection to Russia (*IKRI* Vol. 3, *Diary* 1731-33), pp.65-142). He was duly made Colonel (Rychkov, *Topografiia*, Vol.1 p.48/178 and as such accompanied I.K. Kirilov as second in command of the Orenburg expedition. He was an influential aid to I.I. Nepluiev, the Governor of Orenburg (1744-58) and was appointed Major General (Rychkov, *Topografiia*, Vol.2 p.45/405). He was an expert on Kazakh

extremely difficult to persuade to come on the journey, and I used both of them as my interpreters, since the former had to turn what I spoke in German into Russian, so that the latter could continue to interpret into the required speech. Thus, my journey started in this well-considered way on that very same 14 June in the afternoon in the Name of God, along with the above mentioned envoys, two from Abul Geier Khan, whose names were Beybeck Augluck,[18] and Schag Bey,[19] along with their *Gesaul* or Adjutant, called Kalbeck,[20] along with Afan Abuys,[21] Jambeck Khan's[22] third envoy, and alongside these, three further young Kyrgyz merchants who had travelled with the Khan's representative Bey Ian Bey[23] during the previous winter and had been robbed by Bashkir Tatars, and we rode about an hour from Orenburg[24] and swam the River Or,[25] and then set our course

customs and genealogy, and generally trusted by the Kazakhs, but colluded in Kirilov's brutality towards the Bashkirs in their rebellion of 1735-40. There is disagreement about whether Tevkelev converted to Christianity to allow his advancement (cf. Khodarkovsky 2004, p.204; Chibilieva ed. Rychkov, *Topografiia*, Vol. 2, p.91) and Erofeeva who asserts that he was the first Muslim to become a Colonel in the Russian army (*IKRI* Vol. 3, p.42). Rychkov does not mention Tevkelev's conversion, and continues to give him the title *mirza* (noble). If he did convert, his fellow Muslims seemed unaware of it (Khodarkovsky 2004, p.204). It should be noted that after his return from his mission to the Kazakhs in 1733 and becoming a Colonel, Tevkelev's signature changes from Memet Tevkelev to Alexei Tevkelev (cf. *K-O Otnoscheniia* no. 35, 1732 and no. 56, 1734).

18 Beybek Aglik, *batyr, biy*, the Khan's envoy and guard, who plays a principal role in the journal. He is frequently mentioned in Tevkelev's papers (*IKRI* Vol.3, Index).

19 Shak, Shakir *biy*.

20 Kal *biy*, Kalbek.

21 Asan *abyz* (an *abyz* was a literate person acting as a scribe, secretary, interpreter, teacher, cleric), Janibek *tarkhan's* scribe (*IKRI* Vol.3, p.442).

22 Despite calling him khan this is a reference to Janibek Koshkaruli *tarkhan, batyr* (d. c. 1751). An elder of the Middle Horde of the Shak-Shak clan, Arghyn lineage/family (*IKRI* Vol.3 p.411-12), and close associate of Abulkhayir (see p.3 n.5).

23 Bayanbai, Bayanbiy.

24 Orsk, the first Orenburg, established as Orenburg in 1735 (see pp.88-91, n.147). Its name was changed to Orsk in 1740 (Rychkov ed.2010, p.182).

25 A tributary of the Ural river, 332 km. long, between the Orenburg *oblast* (region) and the Kazakh Aktiube *oblast*.

to the South, and travelled on through the wilderness, with no trees or water, until the middle of the night, whereby nothing especially **remarquable** occurred.

On the 15th *huius* I encountered many wild horses, and I brought down a foal with my flintlock and my people killed another with bow and arrow [7] and we took the flesh for food, which we then, having no pot to hand and *manquement* of water, roasted this utmost delicacy on wild horse dung as in our haste we had not brought anything from Oldenburg.

1736
(June 15)

On the 16th *dito* I marched the whole day[26] with no water, until I finally encountered the Or River again,[27] which I then swam across with the horses, with on my left hand, to the east, the *rudera* of an old Mungalish town,[28] which gave rise to a great

---

26 It was common at the time to give distances in terms of days and hours travelled by horse. Distances covered were clearly dependent on terrain, numbers travelling, state of the horses, potential threat, heat and the like; but based on precisely annotated itineraries from the region (e.g. Meyendorf, Nazarov, Putimtsov in Levshin ed. 1840, pp.99-107), the norm was to travel anything from 49-18 *versts* (or 51-19 km. 1 *verst* =1.066km.) a day, with an average of c. 35km. (but see pp.81, 86 for Castle's claims to have travelled 95 and 106 *versts* in one day).

27 One of Ryckkov's maps (*Topografiia*, ed.2010 Map X, 1755) shows commonly used tracks southwards: an immediate crossing over the river from the fortress of Orsk (then Orenburg), with two main re-crossings in a south-easterly direction, one leading south (c. 58 km. from Orsk) and others (c. 68 km. from Orsk) leading eastwards, one branching to Lake Aksakal.

28 There is no record of the remains of a 'town' in this area from contemporary accounts or nineteenth-century records. Remains of mosques were recorded by Pallas to the south-west of Orsk (Pallas, *op.cit.* Vol.1, p.424, and by Falk on the site of the 3rd Orenburg (Egorov 1985, p.124). There is, however, evidence of numerous mausolea in the region (Rychkov, *Topografiia*, pp.269/292; Castagné ed. 2007, e.g. p.85; Egorov 1985 pp.124-25; Fyodorov-Davydov 1984, pp.203-210, for the typology of the mausolea).Castle may probably be referring to one or a group of these, or to what is marked as a 'former mosque' (*byvshaia mechet*), three-quarters of the way down the east bank of the Or, as shown on Rychkov's Map X. This would have indicated an old settlement. These stone and baked clay remains are of fourteenth-century Golden Horde date and are to be differentiated from kurgans (or burial mounds, see p.67, nn.117-8), which were also characteristic of the Orenburg region (e.g. Rychkov, *Topografiia*, pp.269/292. Pallas, *op. cit.* Vol.1, p.417-19; Falk, from Castagné *op. cit.* p.17; Castagné *op. cit.* pp.27-33, 85ff.), some of which date from the late fourth and third millennia to the Iron Age

deal of talk and has some meadows and woodland nearby, and leaving it on one side, whereupon I passed by many lakes, one of which led strangely enough to a white sky-blue water, with a sweet taste.[29] It was here that the envoy of Iambeck Batur, who was called Asan Abuys, and who uttered his farewell speech in a learned manner, took his leave of us to travel to his horde, but said that his leader would undoubtedly expect me to visit him, and would I care to go there; whereupon I made my excuses, because I did not have the appropriate gifts with me, and consequently simply asked him to present my compliments and if his leader deemed it necessary, to inform me of this and that I would then present myself to the Khan.

1736
(June 17-19)

On the 17th I marched over mountains and hills and on the 18th *dito* in the morning at 9 o'clock, encountered the first Kurds [8] who slaughtered a sheep on account of my arrival, and while we were eating it, we toasted Your Imper. Majesty's health, whereupon my host, whose name was Guder Bey, gave me his express assurance that had I not come, they would without fail have attacked us along with the Bashkirs in a few days' time. Consequently, they viewed me as an envoy and rejoiced heartily that I had come, since now everything would be made right and all the misunderstandings among themselves would be appeased.

There was this gentleman among the Kyrgyz people, a very great man, to whom I undertook to show the greatest respect, on account of his very poor eyes, and I recommended a substance that he could use and gave him a white powder, a small quantity of which I had in my possession, which consisted of a not very finely ground *sacharo camariensis*[30] and I administered a quill full of this to Guder Bey, in his red eyes, and he was very amazed

---

(e.g. Morgunova and Khokhlova 2006, p.311 and *passim*, but rarely of the Medieval period). The Kazakhs considered old burial grounds as sacred, and continued to bury their dead on tops of mountains and isolated spots in a similar manner (Pallas, *op. cit.* Vol.1 pp.417-19, 379).

29 The only lakes on Rychkov's Map X are to the south-east of Orsk between the two routes described above. It would have been possible for Castle to have reached these, and even the drying up rivers further south, in the timeframe he gives. The 'sweet' water may refer to pools of river water.

30 Canary sugar.

---

about it and in consequence took me for an extremely skilled *medicus*. Whereupon I set off again that very evening and after riding all night through a great many yurts finally came on the 19 *huius* to the Khan's yurt, though he was not at home, having gone on a journey of about 2 days to Jambeck Batur in order to [9] consult with the latter about the arrangements against Russia.[31] He was immediately advised of my presence by two couriers and they erected a Buchar tent of white cotton for me.[32]

In this place I received countless visitors, because the people there found my person and German dress very strange. Some of them examined my body and my clothes, nor did my leg-clothes escape, and they laughed immoderately at my tight-fitting clothes and large eyes, while others demanded to see the things that I had with me, which were rather spoiled by their excessively keen examination. They were not content with viewing things from outside and insisted on knowing how they were put together as well.

And, because my things were being passed through so many hands, many of them simply vanished from sight. I was wearing English boots, with Bernkleder leggings beneath, which they drew off me completely with the greatest politeness.

Some of them admired my leggings, others my shoes and buckles, while others visited my remaining things, among which they found my watch, and thus wished me to tell them what sort of creature it was. Although I informed them that it was no living creature but had been made by human hands and told the time, they were unwilling to be satisfied with this, and [10] were much keener to place my watch on the ground, being of the opinion that it was the devil, and that my watch had to be destroyed. I hid

---

31 Given the ongoing Bashkir rebellion and their desire to enlist some Kazakhs, it was highly likely that the Horde needed to deliberate over what action would be to their advantage. See p.6 n.15 for the attempt at collusion with the Middle Horde (Demidova 2002, nos. 131, 216).

32 The whiteness of the 'tent' or yurt is significant: this was used only by the nobility (ordinary people had grey felt tents) and was given to Castle as a sign of respect. The former also sometimes used a red covering on the yurt (Levshin *op. cit.*, pp.309-10). For a description of Kazakh yurts see Levshin, *op. cit.* pp.309-10; Pallas, *op. cit.* Vol. 1, pp.611-12; Georgi 1780-83 Vol. 2, pp.277-78. See Pls.3 and 4 for further details.

---

my flintlock, which was loaded, under a carpet and sat on it in the Turkish manner, but it did not remain concealed from their sharp fox eyes for long, since the Khan's little son of about 12 years old spotted the lock on the gun barrel while I was talking with the others, and, since these people know nothing about locks of this kind,[33] and don't understand anything about shooting without fire or a fuse, the young gentleman fiddled with this lock, which set off the flintlock that was under me and shot a horse that was grazing 200 paces away and broke its leg, which caused no particular damage, and was an immediate cause of entertainment. My patience induced them to love me very much, and they were almost ready to think me a great magician, since it so happened that their many impertinent gestures caused my wig, which was clubbed, to shift from its correct position.

1736
(June 19)

Given that those present thought that I had changed my own growth of hair this way, and were therefore afraid that I was able to change my whole head, they [11] withdrew and wished to run away, which seemed very strange to me and I was obliged to ask my interpreter about it. He explained the reason to me with a great deal of laughter, whereupon I was unable to find any other way of reassuring them than that of removing my wig from my head and showing them this circumstance whereupon they became so confident that they took the object in their hands and viewed it as something rather foolish, and tried it on each other with hearty laughter and afterwards I was frequently asked to show them this wig which they would then try on each other while laughing heartily and deriving a great deal of pleasure thereby, which provided me *justement* with the means of insinuating myself among them.

---

33 According to Pallas, most wealthy Kazakhs owned guns (cf. cover; Pallas *op. cit.* Vol.1. pp.614-15), but these were without locks, and fired with a match (Georgi, *op. cit.* Vol.2, pp.259-60). They were not handy with guns, and could only use them when dismounted, which lost them advantage in battle (Georgi, *op. cit.* Vol.2, pp.259-60). The Kazakhs manufactured gunpowder, with saltpetre taken from old tombs in the desert, which was then mixed with carbon and sulphur (Pallas, *op. cit.* Vol.1, p.615). Georgi says the quality of the gunpowder was bad (*op. cit.* Vol.2, p.269).

What they required, in needles, knives, mirrors and other small items that I had brought with me for this purpose, I was obliged to give them, and neither could I preserve the buttons on my jacket from their curiosity.[34] That afternoon I was invited to supper with my host, Ellnaitscha,[35] in his house or rather yurt, on which occasion the brother of the Khan[36] and the elders congratulated me on my arrival, and the mares' milk that is the Kyrgyz people's nectar was poured unstintingly.[37] That very evening, they took their farewells of me once again with many compliments, with the consoling news that the Khan [12] would soon be here again. The following night a one-year-old lamb was slaughtered and they practised their customary magic, whereby the lamb's bones, once I had helped to consume the flesh on them, were laid out in the following manner. The bones were heaped together in a copper pot, with the skull on top. A small stick with a little red flag of red taffeta, like a ship's pennant, hanging from it was inserted the *sutura saggitali* of the skull, after which lights

1736
(June 19)

---

34 These items are characteristic of the smaller trade goods brought by Russians to centres such as Orenburg in exchange for Kazakh sheep, horses, lamb-skins, felts, leather items and other goods obtained through the Kazakh Central Asian trade (see Introduction n. 13 and p.91, n.147 for Orenburg town).

35 On p.35 Castle gives a different name (Yungitscha) to his host. He may have confused the name with the function of the host, who may have been a type of diviner, whose names ended in 'scha': eg. *faltsha* (astrologer) *baqsi/shi* (a type of shaman); *kamsha* (flame reader); *diagsha* (rain and fair weather makers); *yaruntischi* (reader of animal bones) (Pallas *op. cit.* pp.619-21; Georgi *op. cit.* pp.302-303). See Pl. 2.

36 Nyaz-sultan (see p.46).

37 Kumiss: fermented mare's milk. This staple drink of the Turic and Mongol steppes was known in Europe from early histories such as Herodotus (ed. Marincola 1996, Book 4, p.234) and travellers such as William of Rubruck (ed. Jackson and Morgan, 1990, Chapter 4, n.1 for other early references). Academicians continued the tradition of describing this drink among the Kazakhs (e.g. Pallas *op. cit*, Vol. 1 p.624, trans. of 1771-76; Georgi *op. cit*, Vol. 2 p.282), and its preparation and medicinal properties were the subject of a scientific paper in Britain (J. Grieve, *Papers of the Royal Society of Edinburgh*, Vol.1, 1788, pp.178-90, including other references). Kumiss remains a staple drink with reputed curative properties in parts of Russia and Central Asia. See Pls.3 and 4 for an illustration of kumiss being served in the Khan's yurt and p.135 for Castle's description of how it was made.

Pl.2

A purification and divination ritual performed by a *baqsi* (a type of shaman).
Castle's host is wrapped in a white sheet, with nine burning lights placed
on him. The *baqsi* (priest or mullah in text) holds a book of spells and a
whip. A pot on the right contains a lamb's skull with two burning lights
in its eyes and a pole with a flag in its sigittal suture. The rest of the lamb's
bones are also in the pot. A soothsayer prophesied from the bones once
they had burned down.

were placed in the eye-holes.

My aforementioned host, called Iungitcha, was wrapped completely naked in a white cotton cloth and then made to lie on his back, with his feet against the doors, without moving at all. 9 burning lights were placed on him, one on his forehead, one on each upper arm, one on each foot, one on each knee, one on his breast and on his stomach, too, there was a light, and these lights were made from the hoof bones that had been struck in half so that each bone produced two lights, so that all these 11 lights were made from the lamb's fat, wherefore they used some rags from old ripped cotton shirts to make the tapers. The priest or Mulla then performed the ceremony in the Arabic tongue, [13] kneeling on the ground, holding in one hand a whip and in the other a book with strange characters and thus, after much whistling, warning the devils to keep away from all right-minded Muslims by uttering yells and pulling dreadful faces, they sought to discover forthwith whether or not my person and my arrival would bring them good fortune or not? After the lights had burned down, the bones with their pot were taken outside and all the burnt stuff and the ashes were removed, and the Mulla began to prophecy extensively from these, but I was not able to determine what the prophecy actually contained, because they consider this a great secret, thought their joyful expressions allowed me to presume that the Devil was not against me in this place either and that the prophecy must be to my advantage.[38] In this place, a girl of about

1736
(June 19)

---

38 This eyewitness account of a lamb sacrifice and consequent purification and divination ritual in which a mullah, amongst others, officiates is extremely rare for this period: it clearly demonstrates the assimilation of the animistic, spirit beliefs of the nomads, which included shamanism, with Islam. Other descriptions by travellers of this period further east only refer to the shamanism of Siberia (e.g. Bell 1753, pp.221-22 (obs. 1716); Gmelin 1751-2, Vol. 2 pp.491-99, 502, but see Rychkov quoted in Levshin, *op. cit.* p.334). Islam was introduced more gradually into the steppes after the Arab conquest of Central Asia in the seventh and very early eighth centuries, and the adoption of Islam by its sedentary centres in the eighth-ninth centuries (Akiner 1996, pp.92-94; Alan Jones, verbal communication). The Kazakhs, among other Turkic people of the steppe, were the heirs of the official adoption of Islam under Özbek Khan of the ulus of Jochi in the early fourteenth century (de Weese 2009, p.125). They were thus Muslim before being Kazakhs

20 years came up to me, addressed me in the Tartar tongue, and fell at my feet saying she was a Russian Christian, since her father had been a smith in the town of Jaick[39] and that she had been

---

(my thanks to Alexander Morrison for this observation). Itinerant Sufi shayks travelling with merchant caravans (rather than organized Sufi orders) were initially responsible for the spread of Islam to the Golden Horde, as well as other influences from Crimea, Khorezm and Bulghar (de Weese 1994, pp.135-9; idem 2009 p.125-6). This was later sustained through mullahs from Turkestan and Kazan (Georgi *op. cit,* Vol.2. p.301; Akiner 1996, pp.94-96; Privratsky 2001, pp.46-47; Uyama 2004, p.519). The Sunni Islam of the steppe was far less orthodox than that in urban centres and was combined with customary steppe traditions. It also varied locally, in relation to proximity to Central Asian urban centres, and in proximity to the Khan, whose scribes were mullahs or other clerics (see pp.136-7, 139 for Castle on Islam and superstition among the Kazakhs and the cover illustration showing a mullah). The mullah in this account also functions as a shaman (*baqsi*), treating the host as a patient potentially threatened by evil spirits (brought by Castle's presence) who need to be frightened away, through the use of a whip, whistling and yelling (cf. Pallas *op. cit,* p.620; Levshin ed. 1840 reprint, pp.335-9, p.339 for mullahs acting as *baqsi*). The 'mullah' here is not dressed as such (cf. the cover illustration). The book the *baqsi*-mullah holds is possibly the Koran (even though this is not specified) because he speaks Arabic and mentions Muslims, or a book of special verses copied from the Koran for use in healing, an imitation of such for the mullah's personal use or simply a book of spells. He may not even have known what the verses in Arabic signified exactly (Bardanes 1770s *IKRI* 4, p.180; see n.92). No other books appear to have been known to the Kazakhs at the time. The setting up and reading of the bones, corresponds more to the role of the *yaruntchi* soothsayer (Pallas *op. cit,* p.619, Georgi *op. cit,* p.303; Levshin *op. cit.* pp.333-4; Valikhanov 2009 ed. pp.473-4).

Contemporary accounts of Kirghiz religion by Academicians from St. Petersburg and others (see Introduction) stress their belief in and respect for Islam (in contrast to certain nineteenth-century sources e.g. Valikhanov ed. 2009, which emphasize shamanism) but that it was ignorant and lax (rather than just different, as argued by de Weese 1994, p.58) due to lack of mullahs, and conjoined with practices of 'sorcery' (e.g. Pallas, Georgi *op. cit,* Bardanes *op. cit*). For Kazakh belief in the devil (*shaitan*) in contemporary sources see Bardanes, *op. cit.* p.180. See Valikhanov *op. cit.* pp.477-91 for an account of shamanism and customary religious beliefs among the Kazakhs. A similar mixture of beliefs in healing practices exists in Kazakhstan today (Privatsky 2001, pp.193-236, 243).

39 The administrative centre of the Yaik Cossack host (established in 1613) on the right bank of the Yaik or Ural river. It was renamed as Uralsk in 1775. See n.156 for Castle's description of the town. Although this story

stolen away by these Kyrgyz people about 10 years ago and had since then entirely forgotten the language of her own people, and for this reason she begged me to release her from her captivity.[40] My sympathetic heart would gladly have granted her wish but for various reasons could not do so, on the one hand because several Russian captives were present who would have petitioned me in the course of [14] this whole business and on the other hand, I could have drawn the hatred of the entire Kyrgyz nation on myself by this means. So, through my interpreter, I told her about the locality of Oldenburg,[41] itemizing the rivers and other landmarks which she would have to pass, and I showed her the way to escape from her captivity, which she took good notice of; a year later she arrived in Oldenburg with two fine horses and soon married a Russian sergeant in the Pensich regiment.[42] Otherwise, at this point I should mention that this place beside the Khan's horde was where the River Deen[43] flows which takes its source

1736
(June 19-20)

---

    sounds like a literary 'damsel in distress' trope, the incident was quite plausible.

40 The taking of Russian (and other, notably Kalmyk) prisoners (*yasur*) during raids on settlements or caravans was customary for the Kazakhs. The prisoners served as slaves or wives, and could be sold on, exchanged for cattle and used as bargaining tools. Among the conditions stipulated in Empress Anna's 1734 edict accepting Abulkhayir's Horde as subject, was the release of prisoners and the protection of caravans. The practice of taking prisoners continued, however. Pallas (*op. cit.* Vol. 1, p.623) and Georgi (*op. cit.* Vol.2, pp.275-76) state that the Kazakhs treated their slaves well as long as they conformed and did not try to escape.

41 Orenburg.

42 There is no means of knowing whether this happy ending did in fact occur, but it is not impossible.

43 There is no mention of a River Deen (or any sounding similar in the area where the Junior Horde moved) in Rychkov and the 1755 maps in *Topografiia*, ed. 2010 in Pallas (*op. cit.*) or Bardanes (*op. cit*). He may be referring to one of the several rivers flowing into the Temir at its head; the Temir then flowed into the Emba (Iemm), which flows into the Caspian (Rychkov, *Topografiia*, ed. 2010 Map X) or more likely to a river that used to flow into the Emba from the east, closer to the Mugodhzhar range. Maps of the day show the number of drying river beds in the area (cf. Rychkov, ed. 2010, Map X; *Atlas Russicus*, Pl.13).

    Rychkov lists the places used by the Kazakhs of the Junior Horde in the summer and winter. Their summer grounds were to the south-west and east of Orsk, on the rivers running into the Or, and in between the Or and the Ural/Yaik and its tributaries (e.g. the Kobde, Ilek, Temir,

in the Mahaschell Anruck Tau[44] or mountain and divides into 3 branches, and that the Kyrgyz people customarily move along it for the fodder, although this river ends by flowing into the Iemm River, which springs from a high mountain with two peaks that lies four and half days' journey from Orenburg and joins the River Iack beside the little town of Burioff,[45] which river then subsequently flows into the Caspian Sea. That night, we slept very close to the Khan's horde.

On the 20th I had to set out very early with the Khan's three sons and ride onto a mountain,[46] where the oldest of them told me to get off my horse, which I did. But, when they remained on their horses [15] and wished to talk to me from that position, I demanded that they too should get down from their horses if they wished to talk to me, whereupon I climbed back onto my horse, leaving just my interpreter standing.[47] After observing this

1736
(June 20)

Emba and their tributaries) and along the rivers north of Orsk flowing into the Ural/Yaik, up to where the Ural/Yaik branches into two, in the region of fort Kizilkaya. In winter some of the Horde moved also moved east to the region of Lake Aksakal (seven days away from Orsk, now virtually dried up), and closer to the Sïr Darya. Some areas could be shared with the Middle Horde, such as the Lake Aksakal region and the rivers falling into the Or (Rychkov, *Topografiia*, Vol. 1, pp.136-9). See also Levshin 1840, pp.506-507, for the use of specific areas by tribes within the Horde in the nineteenth century. The restriction of pastures on and over the Yaik by the encroaching Russians and competition with the Kalmyks over pasture led to much aggravation and hardship for the Junior Horde. See Introduction.

44 The Mugodhzhar range of mountains, a continuation of the Urals southwards.

45 Guriev (modern Atyrau), a small garrison town at the mouth of Ural/Yaik river on the Caspian. Despite a noxious climate and liability to flooding, it had good fishing and seal hunting resources and was used, when possible, as a route across the Caspian to Astrakhan (Rychkov, *Topografiia*, pp.196-97/226-27, 199/229, 202/232, 223/253, 297/327, 12/372, 24/384).

46 The Khan's oldest son (from his second wife, Bopai-Khanim, see n.69, was Nurali (1710-90); the second was Erali (1721-94); followed by Kojah Ahmed (1722-49); Aichuvak (1723-1810); Adil (?-1756). His third wife bore him one son, Chinghiz (c. 1720-50/60), and his fourth wife another, Karatai (1738-1830, born after Castle's visit) (Erofeeva 2007, pp.383-92). Castle only specifies the oldest son.

47 The Khan's sons are insisting on the sign of respect (dismounting) that would be due to them from the Kazakhs themselves (Georgi, *op. cit.* Vol.

---

ceremony, the oldest son began to enquire after Your Imperial Majesty's well-being, and also after the health of State Councillor Kiriloff, whereby they expressed at length their willingness to loyally keep the promises they had once made to Your Imperial. Majesty. In return I thanked them and assured them of every high Imperial favour. On our return, once again a sheep was slaughtered at midday, it being led before me, alive, in accordance with their custom, to show that it was healthy, and God was called on by all those present, that a thousand blessings might be conferred on the giver. Whereupon Nyas Sultan, a brother of the Khan's, ate with me. That very day, I had to move to different quarters, and got an old man for my host, who told me that he was obliged to make cool air today, because the Khan was travelling.[48] However, I realized that this old man's skills in this respect were not excessive, and had to laugh at his proposition, having all the more reason to do so since I anticipated that when the Khan arrived [16] it would be extraordinarily hot, whereupon I asked him why he had not made any cool air? Whereupon he answered that he had been sleeping at the time on account of his great age. This reply also appeared comic to me, so I asked him to reveal this skill to me, while offering to give him whatever he asked in return, whereupon the old man replied that it was no such great art, that many of their people knew it, but that he was unable to teach it to me, because I was no Muslim, and so such arts would never work with me, unless of course, I was resolved to become a Muslim (which means something like True Believer).[49] Although I responded by claiming I was already a Muslim, the old man was not prepared to believe this, so he did not teach me his art.

1736
(June 20-21)

2, p.290; Levshin, *op. cit.* p.375), but in this instance there was probably an element of playful goading in it as well.

48 A spell or exorcism to facilitate travel and avoid fatigue or illness caused by stuffiness and low pressure in the mountains (Valikhanov, *op. cit.* pp.286-87). According to Georgi, 'rain and fair weather' makers were called *diagsa/diagsha* (*op. cit.* p.302).

49 This example of a Kazakh spell-maker invoking the protection of Islam, thus identifying himself as a Muslim while practising steppe traditions validates eighteenth-and nineteenth-century observers' comments on the mixed beliefs and rituals of the Kazakhs (see n.38). See pp.136-139 for Castle's account of law giving and burial practices.

That evening a courier arrived with the news that the Khan would arrive early the following day. Immediately afterwards the Beybeck who had returned with me as an envoy from Orenburg, arrived and conveyed the Khan's greeting to me and enquired after my health, advising me at the same time that the Khan had already arrived.

On the 21st I observed a rather large but unpolished Palle ruby on my hostess's headdress.[50] I asked her where this kind of stones come from, and what such a one would cost? But she had no information to give me, [17] except that she had heard that there are many such stones in Bucharia, and she exchanged the stone for a little clasp knife. That same day, the Beybeck visited me very early, greeted me from the Khan, and explained that the Khan wished to see me in German dress on horseback, so I accordingly rode to him wearing such clothes. Immediately upon my arrival a white Buchar tent of cotton was erected for me, and I was instructed to remain there until the many people who currently found themselves with the Khan had dispersed among themselves again. Every few minutes the Khan was constantly sending someone from this company to me to enquire as to my health, whereby they also brought small pieces of horseflesh and mares' milk, with which I regaled those present in the tent with my hand according to their custom.[51] Whereupon I was asked if I would make my compliments to their Khan in their manner? When I responded to this by saying that I did not know how, they were immediately ready to teach me the same and instructed me to go down on my knees and touch the ground three times with my forehead. Since this form of greeting did not please me, I pretended to be unable to learn it so quickly, and wished to make the Khan a bow [18] such as it is our custom to pay to a great Lord in Russia. After half an hour had gone by, I was conducted to the

*1736
(June 21)*

*1736
(June 21)*

50 'Balas' (i.e. from Badakhshan) ruby or pink/red (Persian *lal*) spinel. Badakhshan, historically part of Tajikistan and Afghanistan, was renowned for its mines: for Kirilov control of its resources (gold, *lal* stone, lapis, lazurite) was one of the Empire's aims (*K-R Otnoscheniia* no. 50, 1737, p.111; see also Rychkov, *Topografiia*, pp.235/265). Such stones were part of Bukharan trade.

51 See n.55.

Khan in the midst of a great crowd of his people, whereupon the Beybeck and another man grasped me beneath both my arms and bore me away. Ten steps away from the Khan's yurt, they asked me to stand still for a minute, whereupon the Adjutant or, in their language, the *Gesaul*, informed me that I would be conducted a further six steps, and would then keep silent for another minute, until the Gesaul came back again, whereupon they brought me to the doors, and finally, after some standing around, demonstrated their usual *manners* by giving me a little shove as they pushed me into the Yurt.[52]

The Khan was sitting right opposite the doors to the yurt, dressed in striped cotton, with his brother, Nyas Sultan and his two sons, along with many elders seated beside him. On entering, I removed my hat, and after bowing three times to the Khan in the French manner, and greeting all the other persons present, and replacing my hat, I was required to sit down, whereupon I addressed the Khan as follows: that since the State Councillor Iwan Kiriloff had conveyed me to Orenburg last winter, and the Khan had granted me the honour [19] of forming an acquaintance with his son, Eraly Sultan, who was residing there, along with many other respected Kyrgyz gentlemen, I had therefore come to this place to have the honour of seeing him, the Khan, as well and to enquire as to his well-being, with the request that, should the Khan be disposed to send a greeting to Your Imperial Majesty or to the State Councillor, I would be very willing to convey it. The Khan expressed his thanks and those of all present, whereupon this esteemed leader also made enquiries concerning Your Imperial Majesty's health and the condition of State Councillor Iwan Kiriloff and Colonel Teffkeleff, and commented on the heartfelt joy he was experiencing on seeing me, a Russian envoy, since he was not only obliged to dispossess his subjects of the impression they had gained in Orenburg, that the latter was about to be abandoned by the Russians, but he also said openly, as is his preferred manner, that my assertion that this news was unfounded would give him cause for forbidding

1736
(June 21)

---

52 This elaborate protocol for approaching a Khan is not, as far as I am aware, described in any other contemporary report.

Pl.3

A feast in the Khans' yurt. The Khan, beseeched by a kneeling Kazakh, is in the centre below a canopy. One of his sons is beside him. Castle and his two companions are to the left, with a Kazakh bowing before them. The rest of the yurt is full of elders and other Kazakhs. A man serves kumiss from a central vat.

his subjects from joining the conjunction that they were planning with the Kilmeck rebels.[53] I made the Khan yet another bow and lost no opportunity to vaunt Your Imperial Majesty's fortunate arms and advances due to Assow, and in the Crimm, and due to their Cubans, not stinting my praise, [20] and to inform him how all these had been obliged to bow before Your Imperial Majesty's sceptre. During this recital, the Khan did not allow his attention to deviate in the slightest and then, after engaging in further discussion, showed that he was somewhat pleased with it by feeding me with his own hands, whereby he not only placed the sheep flesh in my mouth, but handed me their drink, kumis or mares' milk.[54] After a period of 3 hours had passed, I was dismissed after receiving a sign of honour, which the Khan awarded me by touching my right shoulder with his right hand,[55] which is a sign of great favour among them, and returned to my tent, whereupon an escort of 20 men was assigned to me, which however, was proved unable to prevent the spectators, under the guise of paying me a respectful greeting, from touching my body after their own fashion, whereupon my clothes were handled by the generality of Kyrgyz, and, given that they have no spoons, knives or forks, and just eat with their fingers, and so possess five greasy fingers, they became horribly smeared, and what's more, torn.

On the 22nd I travelled with the Khan beside to his favourite[56] whose name is Teberde, and we ate and there was bolalaika music during the meal.[57] On the way [21] the Khan diverted me with the chase, which consisted of this, a bird that is even stronger than an

1736 (June 21-22)

1736 (June 22-23)

53 See p.26, n.13; p.83.
54 Handing food to a guest by hand was a sign of great favour (Tevkelev, *Diary* 1731-33 p.107; Georgi *op. cit.* pp.285-86). See further p.135
55 Saluting by touching a shoulder was a gesture used by the Khan and other eminent people with commoners. Hands were shaken with someone esteemed and friends were embraced (Georgi, *op. cit.* p.290; Levshin, *op. cit.* p.373). Pl.10, p.128.
56 Presumably a concubine.
57 The Balalaika was a Russian instrument in use among the Kazakhs, together with the traditional *kobyz* (3 string fiddle with cavities filled with goat leather) and the *tchibyzga* (a flute) (Levshin *op. cit.* pp.370-84; Valikhanov *op. cit.* pp.464-65, and also pp.463-69 for Kirghiz forms of song).

eagle and is called Pickurt[58] in their language, for which a stand was set up on the front part of a saddle, on which it sat, and when the occasion arose, given that we encountered many wild goats and horses, it would be released at different times and achieve this effect, whereby as soon as it reached just one of the wild prey, it would attack its eyes with its talons and blind it, and thereby furnish the occasion for killing it easily. And, although this bird was clearly unusually fierce, I felt even greater admiration because the Khan would straightway ride off on his horse, which he subsequently gave me, at those wild goats, and approach them at full gallop with the whip that he kept beside him and whip them off.

On the 23rd we rose again before dawn and marched with the horde a further 3 hours. As I was riding on my own beside the Khan at the time, he showed me a mountain and assured me that should Your Imperial Majesty be moved to allow a fort to be erected on this mountain, then he would be capable of repelling all enemies.[59]

Nor did he forgo informing me at the time, how advantageous it would be for Your Imperial Majesty with regard to the same matter in this region to erect a fortification against the South East *1736* [22] and on my enquiring the reason, the Khan then indicated *(June 23)* that in this region there is not only gold but also many precious stones to be found.[60] However, I pretended not to give these

---

58 The Birkut or Biurkut eagle (*falco fulvus*). Pallas writes that this eagle, which was exported to Russia, was trained to hunt wolves, foxes and gazelle. The Kazakhs apparently spent hours assessing the merits of an eagle, which could be exchanged for a very good horse, but not for a sheep or small copper coin (Pallas, *op. cit.* Vol.1 p.342). Rychkov writes that there were many varieties of eagles in the region, especially Bashkiria (*Topografiia*, p.301). See Levshin *op. cit.* p.304 for a description of the extraordinary strength of this eagle.

59 There is no means of knowing which mountain the Khan is referring to, but after the Khan's request for a fort to be built at the site of Orsk, the first Orenburg (an idea planted in his head by Tevkelev and Kirilov, see n.96), Abulkhayir boasted that with the help of Russians and other forts he could control her enemies (and his own people).

60 Although the Russian search for mines and minerals in the Urals goes back to the sixteenth and seventeenth centuries, the emphasis on finding gold around the Amu Darya, and in Badakhshan and Yarkand gained

matters any consideration and when the Khan noticed this, he grew a great deal more confiding and went on to consider how his forefathers had secured great wealth from this,[61] and that their successors had not laid in a store of these, whereby the matter had come to be disregarded, however, I continued to pretend to pay no attention to this, and by and by I asked in a very light-hearted way whether timber and water could be found in that region; whereupon he praised the peculiar superfluity of these things there. Then an old man called Beymaratheyla Batur[62] came up to us, and assured me that if the State Councillor were to give the order, he was ready to send 1000 sheep to Orenburg, to which assurance the Khan added that there was yet another who would be able to despatch 2000 sheep, and the State Councillor had only to announce that he required these. After this conversation, I rode with the Khan to the other horde, and dined with him. Towards evening, I returned with the Khan and the brother of

---

momentum from the reign of Peter the Great onwards, activated by local rumours and people wanting to find favour with the Tsars (Hennin ed. 1992; Rychkov, *Topografiia*, 272-73). For the riches of Badakhshan see p.40, n.50, p.123. At the time of writing Rychkov stated that there was no gold and silver in the Orenburg region, and that prospection was still needed, but that gold was reliably reported to be in the Bukhara and Tashkent mountains (Rychkov, *Topografiia* pp.272-73). The Kazakhs knew of the Russian interest in the mineral and precious metal resources in the Urals and Central Asia. They exploited this by promising to show them choice sites in return for favours. The Russians first exploited gold in the Urals (around Ekaterinburg) in the 1740s, with a sluicing centre established at Berezovzky. Other mines were at Pichma, Iset, Nieva and Tagil. Berezovsky remained the most profitable (Pallas, *op. cit.* Vol.2, pp.21-219, 222-24, 226-27).

61 See Rychkov *Topografiia* p.70 for the gathering of gold and precious stones by native peoples. The exploitation of mines in the Urals goes back to antiquity (e.g. Chernykh 2005; Epimakhov 2009, pp.77-81). Summarizing the Russian point of view, Georgi stated that the natives had neither industry nor sufficient knowledge in the art of working mines, but were expert at discovering mines, and made money by carriage from one smelter to another. An exception was Perm, where they sold ore (*op. cit.* Vol.2, p.196). For the establishment of copper factories in the Urals by Kirilov (one site abandoned by the Bashkirs), Tatischev and at the request of Berg Kollegiia (the College of Mines) see Rychkov, *Topografiia* pp.273/303-275/305.

62 Beymurat Tiole. Possibly the 'well meaning' Tiole *batyr* of the Middle Horde, mentioned in Tevkelev's *Diary* of 1731-33, p.119.

---

the Iambeck Batur back to our yurts, since the Khan had drawn me aside during the journey and had thanked me for visiting him since he hoped all the more to succeed 23 in imposing his will and to sacrifice himself before Russia, because he had to handle his people very carefully, and he requested me at the same time, that for his own person's sake, I should take their rough treatment in good part. Whereupon I bowed and assured him that I would do the latter, notwithstanding that it was actually the case took place was that his people not only incommoded me very frequently in the course of the day, but that they even woke me from my sleep at night time, just to view me, which I would endure, *en egard* for the Khan, who was firmly insisted on my presence to succeed in his undertaking with his subjects, so, to gain their love, I would present a gift to all those who came to me, to some a mirror, to others scissors, and to the majority needles and other small objects. That evening, a tent was erected for me, where I dined with the Tulek[63] and the brother of the Khan, Nyas Sultan. The food came from the Sultaness' kitchen, and was borne by her maids in porcelain dishes. The food consisted of chopped horsemeat, rice cooked with sheep's milk and covered with sheep's butter. However, since the latter dish was rather well decorated with hairs, I very strangely lost any appetite for it.[64]

On the 24th *hujus* the Tulek Batur came once more to me at dawn, to take his leave, because his wished to ride back to [24] his own horde.[65] At our leave-taking, he asked me to convey his and his brother's best wishes to the State Councillor,[66] with his assurance that in two days' time he wished to send elders to Abul

---

63 Tulek *batyr*, the brother of Janibek *batyr* of the Middle Horde (Castle's Glossary).

64 This food, coming from the Sultaness's kitchen, must have been among the best that could be offered. Rice and horsemeat (or hams of smoked horsemeat) were reserved for the rich. Otherwise billy goat, sometimes camel and (very rarely) beef was eaten. Staple foods for the poor were mutton and cheese made from cow's or sheep's milk. Salt was uncommon, but fat as butter or suet, was greatly appreciated. Flour and meal came from Russia. Food preparation was not considered clean (Georgi, *op. cit.* Vol.2, p.282; Levshin, *op. cit.* pp.320-21).

65 The Middle Horde.

66 I.K.Kirilov.

Geier Khan, to allow them to consult further with the Khan. That day, the Khan stayed all day with the other horde, but when he returned, he summoned me in the evening to an audience with the Sultaness[67] and at the same time to see him eating with his wives. The yurt that he was in was well supplied with fine Persian carpets lain on the ground, and he was sitting on his knees, beneath which lay a fringed cushion of Buchar velvet. Above him hung a canopy of silken gauze, showing three-fold colours of red, white and gold. On the Khan's left hand sat his three wives, beneath a four-cornered hanging of this same gauze material.[68] His oldest and true wife,[69] the Sultaness, sat above them, dressed in a red silken cloth, richly decorated with golden flowers, in addition to which she wore a high ornament on her head, which resembled a Turkish cap and was embroidered with gold. The other two wives were dressed in red Buchar velvet, and each of their heads was embellished with a fine white cotton scarf, one of which in my estimation must have been at least 20 arsines[70] long.[71] [25] On their feet they all wore boots of green and very

1736
(June 24)

---

67 Bopai Khanym (?-1780), the Khan's second and principal wife. (*IKRI* 3, pp.413-14). See n. 69.

68 This detailed description of the inside of the Khan's yurt, and of the seating arrangement within it, is rare (cf. Georgi *op. cit* Vol.2, pp.277-78) and more fulsome than that of Pallas (*op. cit.* Vol.1, pp.609-10). Cf. Levshin *op. cit.* pp.309-10. See Pl. 3.

69 The Khan had had four wives. The first one had been a Kazakh, taken captive in wars with the Jungars. She is thought to have died in captivity. His second, then principal wife, Bopai Khanim (the Sultaness Castle describes) was, according to one source, of Chinggisid blood. She was a strong minded, popular woman, who participated in political affairs, having her own seal (Levshin *op. cit.* p.213). Abulkhayir's third wife was a Volga Kalmyk (Baina/Bayana. See n.84); and his fourth a Bashkir. One of his concubines was a Kalmyk called Tsoiroshi (Erofeeva 2007, pp.383-90; *IKRI* 3, p.413-14).

70 An *arshin* = 71.12cm.

71 The rich materials, including silk and velvet, and the very high, almost cylindrical shaped fine cloth woven round the head (*tshauluk*) and hair ornaments such as feathers or silver plaques and coins were customary for high ranking ladies (Pallas, *op. cit* Vol. 1, pp.616-17, Vol.6 Pl. XIX b; Georgi, *op. cit* Vol.2, p.281, Pls 39-40; Levshin, *op. cit.* p.325-27). A number of these materials (e.g. silk, cotton velvet) including actual garments (the *chalat*, a long robe, or the *tshadsbau* a long hairpiece) were Bukharan (Pallas, *op. cit.* pp.616-17, Vol.6, Pl. XIX b, and see *idem* p. 615

---

fine chagrille.[72] Beyond the hanging a Kalmuk girl sat dressed in black sammet[73] and playing Russian songs on a bandoir.[74] In front of the Khan himself, an old man was sitting beside a youth; the old one was playing on a Turkish bolalaika,[75] and the boy on a Nogais violin with two strings. Three paces from Khan sat his elders, with a burning lamp of sheep fat set before them, in the centre. In the centre of the yurt stood a wooden container in the form of a washbasin, about 4 buckets in size, in which their drink, namely mares' milk, or kumis, was to be found. When I entered the yurt, the Khan gave me to understand that I should be merry that evening, and that he had invited me to his tent for that purpose, and he required me to sit down and gave me a drink out of his own hand.

Whereupon, I handed over the gifts that I had brought with me, which were

In the first place,

    a portrait of Eraly Sultan who was currently in Orenburg.

2) a gold-embroidered cloth for praying on

3) a silver box filled with balsam

4) a gold-edged money bag, containing a

    burning glass

    and 1000 sewing needles.

1736
(June 24)

5) four pairs of English knives and [26]

6) four mirrors.

Of all these presents the first two gave by far the most pleasure, and it as remarkable how the mother could not gaze sufficiently at the portrait of her son, or kiss it without tears, once I had indicated that I had painted it on the express orders of Your Imperial Majesty, which was considered a very gracious action, and caused

---

for Bukharan mens' boots).

72 Shagreen leather, probably made of donkey (Pallas *op. cit.* Vol.1, p.615). These soft leather boots (*masi*) were worn under high-heeled boots with pointed toes (*kebi*).

73 Velvet.

74 Bandora. Russian music and instruments would have infiltrated Kazakh society from the seventeenth century onwards through increasing contacts whether through trade with Central Asia, the building of the Yaik/Ural fortified line, captives or diplomatic contact.

75 The *kobyz*.

Pl.4

Castle and his two companions in a yurt with the Khan and his wives. The Khan sits under a folded canopy, his three wives are to the right under a lowered canopy. The Khan's principal wife, Bopai, is seated on the far right. Castle kneels before her, offering a present. Kazakhs approach the Khan and his wives with kumiss, served from a central vat. A man also approaches the vat for kumiss, while another possibly a sorcerer, kneels by the vat holding a burning lamp. Musicians play the *kobyz* beside the wives' canopy.

everyone to rejoice heartily, whereby it was remarkable how the mother evinced her extreme pleasure and the Sultaness herself gave me with her own hand a dish full of mares milk beneath the gauze, since the meal on that occasion was chopped horse and sheep's flesh. After this, I was pressed by the Sultaness to dance in the Russian manner, but I made my excuses, saying I did not know how to and that to dance in the German manner I needed to have a girl beside me, which was then the occasion for asking me how many wives and children I had? Whereupon I could do no less than tell the truth that I had until now no wife and fewer children, which was a cause of great astonishment to them, and they could scarcely believe it, because in their opinion no person could live without these. And since I argued the opposite very

1736
(June 24)

keenly, they regarded me as a poor man, and concluded that [27] European girls must be very rare and costly, and that consequently they enjoyed a slight advantage in this matter, and that among themselves, they, praise God! were able to purchase a fairly good girl for 20 to 30 mares, given the great value that mares' milk has in such negotiations, since they have no money at all and don't understand it.[76] I wondered greatly at the extent and strangeness of the payment for their daughters, and also wished to extol the speed with which their Kyrgyz people eat their food, since I had already noticed how they, in the manner of cassowary birds,[77] were able to swallow a handful of chopped horseflesh of 1 to 2 pounds in a single gulp. And since I was able to extol the Khan by claiming that a man's hardness can be established by the way he eats, the Khan answered that his people might be fast eaters but that they cannot endure long hours of work, whereas Russians may eat slowly, but are more enduring workers in consequence. Given that the Khan was now rather drunk on his nectar or

---

76 The bride price (*kalym*) was not fixed and was raised with each wife. Several wives were a sign of wealth. A moderate price for a marriageable girl (first wife) was fifty horses, a hundred sheep, a few camels or a slave with a cuirass or coat of mail (Georgi, *op. cit.* Vol.2, pp.294-95). The poor would pay up to 5-6 ewes; the rich up to 200 horses or 500-1000 ewes, as well as slaves (Levshin *op. cit.* pp.357-64).

77 A large flightless bird of the same family (*Casuaridae*) as the emu or ostrich.

mares' milk, and that I was ceaselessly prodding his tender spot by dwelling on his actual intentions and on the virtues of the Kyrgyz nation, although I had not observed any, which made the Khan so pleased that he asked me: as a person who had been far in the world, that I should honestly say, [28] what I thought of his country, and whether I had ever seen a better one than his? This question would have been almost too difficult for me to answer, since I had encountered a perfect antechamber to Hell there, given that the same was without timber, without water, without grass and wholly without bread, is furnished only with hills, and one must ride a great way before encountering one of these three most necessary things, though the last of these could never be found, in that they eat no bread at all.[78] However, I did not wish to deviate from my allegory and simulated flattery, so instead, I told the Khan that I reproached Heaven for not having allowed me to be born a Kyrgyz, since they have the best sheep, the most beautiful foals and the most delicate horses, added to which they can camp beneath the open sky at any time, and can change their quarters every day, for which an extensive territory has been provided. This charmed the Khan so much that he grasped his beard and said he regretted from his heart that I did not fully understand their tongue.

1736
(June 24)

Given that I was well aware on this occasion that something could be achieved here, I attempted to raise my credit with the Khan's eldest wife and at the same time win her favour; so I took out my paints, which I had prepared beforehand and had with me, along with a parchment that I had brought for the purpose, and painted the Khan in a short [29] time with my finger and freehand, with such a happy outcome that the Lady Khan was pleased to let these words fall; that no drop of water could be more similar to another than my finished portrait to her husband, as this current portrait demonstrated in several ways. A considerable time having passed at this collation, and a fair amount having been drunk, and many merry discourses having been conducted with great enjoyment, the Khan gave me leave to retire to my tent at midnight.

1736
(June 24)

---

78 See n.64.

On the 25th dito I travelled with the Khan's brother, Nyas Sultan, to the other horde, where we dined with the Khan and his elders, namely Tchack-Tschack, Buckumbey Batur[79] and Ackmaley Batur,[80] and they resolved there and then to punish those robbers and rebels who had stolen horses and camels from the Russians in Orenburg, on my reporting these facts, and also to deliver them to Russia upon request.

On the 26th we travelled 3 to 4 hours with the whole horde and finally dined at night-time.

On the 27th we travelled early in the morning and until midnight again. That day, an execution took place, since the Khan represented the Supreme Judge in his own person.[81] The

79 Bukenbay *batyr*, from the Shak-shak clan, Arghyn tribe of the Middle Horde.
80 Akmal *batyr*.
81 Kazakh law at the time was partly customary (*adat*) and partly Koranic (*shariat*) (Georgi *op. cit.* Vol. 2, p.260), and as yet unaffected by the early nineteenth-century Russian administrative and legal reforms (see Introduction) which criminalized certain customary traditions (Martin 2001, pp.46-47). The law was administered locally and orally by *biys* (judges and clan leaders, sought outside the clan or even horde, but see below for the Khan) (Valikhanov *op.cit.* pp.153-56; Zimanov has copious articles on the status and rulings of *biys*, e.g. 2004, 2008, 2010, 2011, 2012) and the Khan. Castle stresses the power of the Khan at this time in this horde, p.52, n.82, p.137. Sources on this law in the eighteenth century are miscellaneous and sporadic (cf. Tevkelev, *Diary* 1731-33, pp.105-06; Rychkov, *Dnevnik* 1769-70 in Asfendiarov and Kunte 1997, pp.233-34), but become considerably more frequent in the nineteenth century (e.g. Shangin 1816 date of writing, Levshin 1820, 1832, Samokvasov 1824, Bronevsky 1831; d'André 1846; Aitov 1846, Belov 1846; Valikhanov 1864). Some punishments, such as the death penalty for murder and theft, had been formalized under Khan Tauke (1680-1718, the *zheti zhargy* or seven charters), but could be mitigated depending on the circumstance, the status of the person, the location (an offence within one's own *aul* (extended family units from the same clan) was particularly frowned upon) and the ability to pay *kun* (blood money, compensation) (Fuchs ed. 1981, 2003; Martin 2001). 'Kirghiz' laws were first written down in the process of codification of the local laws of the Russian Empire by Speransky, the Governor General of Siberia, in the 1820s: Raeff 1969, p.279, sources: *PSZ* Vol. 38, no. 29, 128 (statute on the Siberian Kirghiz); Valikhanov, *op. cit* p.148; Martin 2001, pp.34, 39-40, 43-47). Rychkov writes that the only legal norms that existed for the Kazakhs were in respect of murder and theft and of the 'inviolable rule' *kun*, sometimes paid in cases of murder and

circumstances of this were as follows: There was a Kyrgyz man among the Khan's subjects [30] who had stolen 40 mares from the other horde; he had been caught and immediately brought before the Khan, whereupon no time was lost and a regular court[82] was held and his back was bloodied in a pitiful manner with sabres made of good iron and he was condemned to return the mares immediately.[83]

*1736
(June 27-28)*

On the 28th we dined at midnight for the very first time, and

---

mutilation, which also applied to Khans (*op. cit.* pp.233-35) Georgi has brief descriptions of penalties for murder, mutilation, assault and robbery, but does not give his sources (Rychkov?) or by which horde they were administered. Levshin gives further examples including the punishment for rape and adultery, the role of witnesses and elders, rulings regarding assemblies, weapons and *tamgas* (clan symbols) (*op. cit.* pp.399-401; see Russian edition 2009 for a fuller account). Valikhanov 1864 responds to Speranski's decree, writing that the court of *biys* was favoured by the majority of the Kazakh people (as opposed to the titled and rich) and should be kept for offences because it was public and understood by all. Exceptions to come under Russian law were murder, robbery and plunder, 'because Kirghiz judicial custom' only valued human life in livestock and other goods *op. cit.* pp.148-166. Fuchs [1948], in accordance with his times, stresses the importance of feudal hierarchy, the unlimited power of the head of the family, and the importance of ownership, which was directly linked to responsibility in crime or compensation (1981, pp.66-210).

82 A court of *biys* with the Khan, and according to Castle (p.137), a mullah reading from the Koran. Castle and Levshin emphasize the Khan's right to the final ruling: '...in the absence of the khan, the elders of the auls of the plaintiff and defendant and two mediators chosen by each party, investigate conflicts and pass judgement' Levshin *op. cit.* p.400. 'If a guilty person does not honour the court's verdict, or if the elder of the *aul* deliberately deviates from investigating the case and thereby... protects the criminal, the plaintiff carries out *baranta* (proportionate, justified revenge) with the elders' permission, that is, he and his relatives or closest neighbours can go to the defendant's *aul* and secretly drive away... the livestock... On returning home he (the plaintiff) must tell his chief about it because the quantity... must be proportionate to the claim and that is what the chief checks.' (Levshin, ed. 1996 p.370, as in the first part of the nineteenth century). In the case witnessed by Castle it seems the guilt was obvious or uncontested. It appears to have been a case of pure theft rather than *baranta* (Levshin, ed. 1996, p.370; Valikhanov *op. cit.* p.161).

83 The usual penalty for theft was the restitution (*aiban*) of up to 27 times the worth of what was stolen Levshin, *op. cit.* p.399; Valikhanov *op. cit.* p.161).

it was after this that some very strange events actually took place, one after the other, which actually did take place. It has already been described on 17ᵗʰ June above, how I cured the Guder Bey of his sore eyes, since when I had subsequently also removed the warts on the Khan's own hand, by applying a sulphur compound of my own preparation and had simply burnt them away and then dug out the roots with a needle, so a rumour of this had spread about me, to wit, that the Kyrgyz regarded me as a very skilled *medicus*, and placed remarkable confidence in me. It was under these circumstances that I managed to treat not only that sufferer, who on the previous day, had felt so ill that he desired with all his might to be freed of his pains, and I cured him by covering him with sheep dung, for lack of another means. But strangely enough, an abuys or learned man also came to me (who was held to be such because he could read and write), and [31] required a special cure of me. The good man had suffered a fatality, in that he had come rather too close to one of the Khan's wives,[84] which in itself would not have been too significant had not the Khan himself encountered him while so engaged. Thus the abuys was a man who was due to die. However, the Khan had reflected on the matter, and considered how the guilty man was a learned man, and he had changed the death sentence to a very honourable act of mercy, whereby he was deprived of that with which he had sinned, which I, as a renowned *medicus*, was then to restore the good man. This made me extremely fearful; but because I did not wish to lose all my credit completely, I called for burnt ashes of wild horse dung, which calmed his blood. This gained me still further fame, which the patient also found to be very appropriate, since his blood had been remarkably calmed by this means, for which he thanked God, who Himself had given such healing things to them in their own country! However, I learnt later on that the patient had died three days later, presumably because the

1736
(June 28-29)

---

84 Erofeeva assumes this is Bayana, the Khan's Kalmyk wife (2007, p.390). The punishment for a wife's adultery when caught in *flagrante* was, in theory, immediate death (Levshin, *op. cit.* p.399). Castle does not mention how the Khan's wife was punished, or whether she argued extenuating circumstances, such as rape (Levshin ed. 1996, p.368).

---

first operation had been performed far too unskilfully.[85]

On the 29th the envoys of Iambeck Batur paid me a compliment, and the names of the same were: [32]

Utebey Batur[86]
Tulecke Mursa
Mallaway Uttegisum
Schimekan Ruschelack

On this occasion they assured me unceasingly that they would adhere faithfully to the loyalty they had once offered to Your Imperial Majesty. After I had paid them my compliments in return, they withdrew in order to go to their tents, whereupon these envoys took their leave of me that evening and asked me to convey their best regards to the State Councillor.

On the 30th *huius*, the Khan sent for me, since the elders of Jambeck Batur had also arrived, in order to consult with them, and consequently I too was to listen to them. The first and most distinguished elder was called Bey Saubey and the other Buburack Batur,[87] the latter having spent the last 5 years in succession as Ambassador to the Kalmucks.[88] Both conveyed their greetings

---

85 This mutilation was considered a defilement of the body, rendering his death a shameful one (Fuchs 1981, pp.110-12).

86 Utebay *batyr*, Tulek *mirza*, Malibey Utegen? Shemiaka Rushelek?

87 Buburak *batyr*.

88 The Kalmyks were the traditional enemies of the Kazakhs, and despite moments of negotiated peace, mutual raids and skirmishes were frequent. This antagonism was exacerbated by conflict over roaming rights in the west, as the Russians gradually encroached on Kalmyk pastures of the middle Volga and its eastern banks and on the crossing the Yaik/Ural and movement along the Or for the Kazakhs. Tevkelev's *Diary* 1731-33 shows that the situation between the Kalmyks and Kazakhs was volatile, with envoys coming backwards and forwards (*op. cit.* pp.122, 124, 126-27, 132), including a peace offer from Cheren-Donduk when he became Kalmyk Khan in 1731 (*op. cit.* p.129). The Russians feared that alliances might be made between the two; such alliances were mooted (e.g. Tevkelev, *Diary* 1731-33, p.126; Donnelly *op. cit.* p.155) but never became a serious threat because of different factions and Russian resolve to promote hostilities between their frontier subjects. After the death of Ayuki Khan in 1724 (who had been a useful ally to the Russians, but also had power and autonomy) the Kalmyks faced increasing Russian control and their elites were in conflict, some pro-Russian, some against. In 1736, the Russians decided to appease the originally anti-

to the State Councillor along with an assurance of their loyalty, and that they would persist unvaryingly in the promise that they had once given. This said, I took my leave after half an hour had passed, and they subsequently brought me and my interpreter a piece of cold horsemeat, which I did not eat, since more than 50 people were staring at me, and, according to the manner and civility of that land, [33] I would have had to feed them this small amount with my own hand, which prevented me from having any appetite.

1736
(June 30 -
July 1)

On the 1st, the Khan ordered a great dinner on account of my arrival,[89] to which all the most distinguished members of three hordes[90] were invited. However, given that with them nothing of significance may be started or undertaken without the light of the new moon, I was asked earlier, as someone who in their opinion was capable of understanding everything, so I was asked by one of the Khan's elders as to which phase of the moon we now found ourselves in, and when we would have the light of the new moon? I had to laugh heartily about this to myself, since I observed that they did not understand even these things, which are after all visible and are so greatly esteemed by them, and yet they understand nothing at all, apart from the Northern Star and that the world is divided into 4 parts,[91] and indeed, with

Russian Donduk-Ombo, who became Kalmyk Khan (1735-41). By the 1740s the Kalmyks were increasingly impoverished and considered leaving the Volga for the Crimea and the Kuban. In 1771 they attempted a mass exodus to Jungaria. This resulted in the loss of 100,000 Kalmyks through cold, lack of provisions and Kazakh attacks (Khodarkovsky 1992, pp.220-235; Teissier 2011for the Kalmyks as seen by eighteenth-century European travellers).

89 This was the Khan's way of boosting his own importance with the Hordes.

90 The Junior (*Kshi*) Middle (*Orta*) and Major (*Uli*) Hordes or *zhuz*.

91 'They look to the stars like a European looks to his watch,' to paraphrase Levshin (*op. cit.* p.387). The stars, especially the Pole star, were used extremely skilfully by the Kazakhs for travel and to judge distances. Stars and constellations had names and properties (e.g. the Pleiades were considered to be a wild sheep (*Arkar* or *Urkar*) who comes down to earth to make grass grow for sheep and ewes; the Milky Way was called the Bird's Path, after migrating birds, Levshin *op. cit.* pp.386-87; Valikhanov *op. cit* pp.483-84). The sky, known as *kok tengri*, was also the highest spirit (God). It could punish you or reward you and was

the exception of their abuys or learned men, cannot even read or write.[92] Thereupon, at the start of this great feast, they called God to witness that they would remain loyal to your Imperial Majesty's intentions once and for all, and then they went to table, and 2 horses, 2 sheep and a great amount of kumis were consumed, of which no more than a small amount of finely chopped horsemeat was sent to my tent. During this solemnity, the Khan had laid out a robe [34] as a prize for whichever of the young people would win the riding competition that was expressly held for this purpose, and this prize was then borne away by a small boy aged 12 years. After the meal, the Khan sent a great following of people to summon me to him, and on arriving I found the guests and all those present rather drunk. Although I was of the opinion that they had had enough, they, however, did not cease emptying one bowl of mare's milk after another in honour of Yr Imperial. Majesty's most eminent well-being and that of Commander Teffkeleff. Although they intended to reduce me to the same condition as themselves, I simply begged to retire, though before so doing I wrote down, in the presence of the elders, the names of those who had taken the above-mentioned oath to remain loyal to Yr Imperial Majesty yet again, as they themselves told me to,

1736
(July 1)

---

filled with intermediary spirits/people, who wear belts around their necks, just as human do around the waist, and people in the underworld around their legs (Levshin *op. cit.* pp.386-87; Valikhanov *op. cit.* p.485). The world was divided into the sun, moon, stars and earth (Valikhanov, *op. cit.* p.479).

92 Kazakhs at this time were generally illiterate, except for scribes, some mullahs and interpreters. The letters of Khans, Sultans and *biys* were written by scribes and sealed by the official sender and sometimes by the translator (e.g. from Persian to Turki Chagatai), who is usually mentioned in the colophon. For the published letters of Abulkhayir see *K-R Otnoscheniia* no. 57 (a 1734 Russian translation of a letter to Empress Anne, sealed); no. 65 (a 1738 letter to the Empress, sealed, no translator mentioned; no. 69 (a 1740 letter to the Empress, with two seals including that of the translator Arslan Bekmetov; see also no. 74). See Erofeeva 2001 p.39 for an illustration of the Khan's teardrop-shaped seal impression with the legend (in Arabic) *Abu-l-khayir-bahadir-khan son of Khadji-sultan*, and a list of the Khan's official correspondence from 1738-1745. (Abulkhayir's chief translator was a Tatar named Yakub Guliaev. An edition of the Khans' and Sultans' Chaghatai correspondence is forthcoming: Erofeeva, personal communication).

which are as follows:

> Amuleck Bey
> Besch Bey
> Tochtara Bey
> Umre Bey
> Oral Bey
> Kokachul
> Tiloff Bey
> Koschara Bey

1736
(July 1)

> [35]
> Asan Batur and
> Jaick Bay.[93]

As I was proceeding from there to my tent, a Kalmuck envoy greeted me very politely and spoke to me in the Kalmuck tongue. Given that the Kyrgyz did not wish to interpret this, and perhaps they were not allowed to, this had to remain merely a greeting. Towards evening the sisters of the Eraly Sultan came to call, with their servants following on foot, and they brought a gift of sour sheep's milk. Their only request was this, to greet their brother in Orenburg for them, and to convey their best compliments to the State Councillor; the eldest of these young ladies was 7 years, but the youngest 3 or 4 years, and I gave them a few hundred needles and some other small items. When they had gone, I lay down to rest, but could not sleep from hunger, having asked the Khan that same evening for something to eat, but had received the reply that there was nothing left, since 500 persons from among their elders had been fed.

So, on the occasion of this great feast, which had been ordered in honour of my arrival, I had to go to sleep hungry.

On the 2nd *huius*, the Khan sent to me to inquire as to which way back I would take, or whether I would go straight to Orenburg or [36] Sackmara?[94] Whereupon I replied that I was considering taking the safest route to the State Councillor Iwan Kiriloff. As I

1736
(July 2)

---

93 Ammalik *biy*, Besh *biy*, Toktara *biy*, Umir/Umur *biy*, Urali *biy*, Koshkul, Tiule/Tiolesh *biy*, Koshara *biy*, Asan *batyr*, Aik/Aig *biy*.
94 Sakmarsk, a fort at the junction of the Ural and Sakmara rivers.

Prayer 3 Matt. Chap II

had now been summoned to the Khan himself, the latter began to complain earnestly about the way the Commandant of Orenburg had forbidden him from advancing further along the River Or,[95] and that he was at a loss as to what he should do, and given that he could not advise himself, was he to turn back again. However, since I was only too aware that these Kyrgyz had to follow the river for the sake of the fodder and timber along its banks, because the rest of the country was just wilderness, I did not attempt to engage conversation about these former and now superseded complaints and replied that Orenburg had been established on their behalf,[96] in order that they should trade with it and that the words of the Lieutenant-Colonel were indeed to be understood thus, that he had no other motive than that of providing fodder for his horses, and anyway, that they kept enough hay in Orenburg for three regiments which was why the Khan was asked to move on, and to refrain from grazing everywhere.[97] The Khan, who understood me very well, burst out laughing and spoke the following words to me: you are an honest man and speak the truth, like State Councillor Iwan Kiriloff, which some of his elders repeated, and thereupon [37] drank to my health and Mursa's. I would have gladly have done likewise, in that it would have relieved my hungry belly to some extent, since once again I had had nothing to eat all day, apart from a bowl of horse grease which had been brought to me in the night, which is one the greatest delicacies among the Kyrgyz people, and any one of them can eat between 3 and 4 pounds of it, since they have a great inclination for this, and it keeps them in constant good opening, given that horsemeat makes them constipated, which however, I was unable to enjoy,

1736
(July 2)

---

95 See Introduction.
96 The idea of placing a fort at the Or was not originally Abulkhayir's, but Tevkelev's (presumably with official sanction), and sold to Abulkhayir as a potential winter residence and court (Tevkelev, *IKRI* 3, pp.61-62; Bodger 1980, p.55 n.69). Abulkhayir rose to the bait, and subsequently requested the fort himself (*K-R Otnoscheniia* no. 42). Russian policy was to make him think the fort was his idea and for his benefit. Russian documents and historiography always present it as Abulkhayir's idea (e.g. Kirilov in *K-R Otnoscheniia* nos. 48, 50; Rychkov, *Topografiia*, p.148; Levshin, *op. cit.* p.175).
97 See Introduction.

and handed over to the Kyrgyz people who were awake near me as a special treat, which they ate with the greatest pleasure. An hour before daybreak a young Kyrgyz man who last winter had wished to go to Russia with the Kyrgyz envoy Bey Ian Bay,[98] and had been robbed and imprisoned by Bashkiri Tartars, and who I had greatly assisted upon my arrival with the Bashkirs in the month of May 1737,[99] having freed him from captivity, and who, along with his imprisoned comrades who had also been freed by me, had recommended me greatly to this Kyrgyz nation and made me loved, and had now, out of gratitude, brought me

1736
(July 2)

some dried [38] sheep's milk, which I willingly ate, and sought to restore some life back to my limbs, which were wholly wasted by hunger. He also gave me a case filled with drawing materials thinking that the circuls[100] in it were used by us for eating instead of forks, and because he said that having heard that we Europeans eat not with our fingers but with forks, he meant to bestow a splendid gift with this, and he then laughed heartily to himself, and admitted that compared with us they were far happier, in that they were not accustomed to these things and were able to eat with their fingers. I concurred with his opinion, and was curious to ask him where he had found these 'forks'? Whereupon he told me about one of his many heroic deeds, how a few years back they had unexpectedly fallen upon a very rich Russian caravan, which may have been led by Commander Gerber, and God had given him these forks! I accepted both gifts very gladly, and sought to revive myself with the dried milk, having already attempted to eat roots, but had been unable to enjoy them on account of their bitter taste. However, I noticed that there was not much of even this milk and it would not satisfy me. And how, being no little

1736
(July 2-3)

concerned about my stomach, since I could not purchase [39] anything nor would I have done so, given that this would have offended the Khan, *justement* at that time I was told the happy

---

98 Bayan *biy*
99 This is a typographical mistake. Castle means 1736, before his Kazakh expedition, presumably when he wrote his Bashkir diary, subsequently lost (see p.113.)
100 Compasses. My thanks to Sarah Tolley for this explanation.

news that on the following day I would be dismissed again, which was dearer to me than my hunger.

On the 3rd *huius*, the horde broke camp and moved to the River Or, and on that very day I dined with Bostaby, and during the following night slept in Teberd's tent. It was here that I was the object of a strange honour, in that when I went to sleep, a pair of very young girls, the first being a Kalmuck and the other a lovely Tartar girl, came to me in my tent, according to the custom of this country, and removed their clothes and washed themselves all over by the light of an oil lamp. I behaved as if this did not concern me and even went to sleep, which did not appear to please those dear children, who lay beside me without being invited to. My deep sleep had made me unresponsive, and I got a great surprise when I woke up the next day and found one lying in front of me and one behind me. And then, because I had made myself scarce in my fright, I had to endure being laughed at by Teberd my host, whereupon I made my excuses and said that my religion did not permit this sort of thing. [40]

On the 4th *huius*, the Teberd invited me to his yurt, and made excuses on behalf of the Khan, for having kept me for so long, so that I would not report this to the State Councillor, and also gave me 9 wolfpelts, and my interpreter 4 coriscken[101] or blue foxes and a fox pelt. At 9 o'clock in the morning, the Khan sent for me, and when I arrived I met him on horseback with his oldest son. He drew me on one side and said that I should convey to the State Councillor his fond desire to have his own dwelling in Orenburg, and his wish to dedicate his three sons to the service of Yr Imperial Maj, whereby he would not require to retain more people with him than would be permitted him, and that he wished this because he would thereby not only be better able to rein in his excessively wild people better and to some extent limit their all too great freedom, but also in order to make himself more capable of serving Yr Imperial Maj, and that he could also bring his neighbours, the Gewinser[102] and Bacharis,[103] to submit

1736
(July 4)

---

101 Corsik: a small fox-like mammal.
102 Khivans: from the Russian Khivintsy (Khorezmians).
103 Bukhara town and surroundings (Rychkov, *IKRI* 4, pp.71-72). In

1736
(July 4)

all the more rapidly to Yr Imperial Majesty, which the latter would be inclined to do anyway, and would be encouraged by his example to be even keener, once he had made a start, and people could see that he was thereby able to keep his people reined in more firmly:[104] [41] So he asked me to convey this, as soon as possible, indeed, to Commander Teffkeleff, who was already aware of all this, and who would be *à concert* with this, and would like to notify the State Councillor, and furthermore required me to furnish a portrait of Your Imperial Majesty since this would have a very good effect on his people, and in the meantime he desired a portrait of his wife, and wished to send me as an envoy to the Buchars, because he had placed special trust in me and knew for sure that I would be able to promote the interests of the Russian Empire and his own far better and more capably than anyone else, since I had fully passed the test that he had set me, and all his people were very pleased with me on that account. However, I made my excuses, together with a suitable expression of thanks, in that I was unable to ignore my Commander with regard to undertaking such a great design and would have to ride to meet him first. Whereupon, the Khan complained that he was

Russian sources the name Bukhara was also used generally to include Tashkent and Kashgar (Frank 2012, p.44).

104 These (the fort and a base in Orenburg, whence he could control his own people and the engineering of the submission of Khiva and Bukhara) were Abulkhayir's repeated arguments for promoting himself as an ideal subject of Russia (e.g. Tevkelev *Diary* 1731-33 p.91). Abulkhayir knew of the Russians' interest in the resources and trade of Bukhara, the need to pacify the Khivans for the sake of trade (in which the Kazakhs were intermediaries) and the use of the Aral Sea, and played upon this. However, Abulkhayir was in no position and too pragmatic to seriously influence or interfere for any length of time in Khivan affairs, despite the Horde's links with Khivan Khans and rulers of Aral through marriage and/or blood. The Russians, with a history of being repelled by Khiva, were aware of the volatile state of affairs in Khiva and of Abulkhayir's limited power. For example, Ilbars, the Khan of Khiva and related to Abulkhayir by marriage, predictably refused a request from Nurali (Abulkhair's son) to contemplate Russian subjection, and a subsequent threat of war with the Kazakhs came to nothing (Tevkelev, *Diary* 1731-33, pp.109, 127). Around the time of Nadir Shah's invasion of Khorezm in 1740-41 Abulkhayir and Nurali briefly occupied Khiva as Khans (Rychkov, *Topografiia*, pp.22/52-23/53; Erofeeva 2007, pp.332-34), but retreated in the face of Nadir Shah's military superiority.

not rich, in that he had to give all that was his simply to keep his discontented men in peace and quiet. After this conversation, the Khan took his leave and gave me a very good riding horse, about which, with regard to the previous 22nd June, it should be said that he had ridden it when hunting wild goats, [42] and which was subsequently stolen three times by Bashkirs, and that I got it back each time, but that the third time it died from the many wounds it had received. In addition, he gave me 30 corsicks and 6 fox pelts, and also presented my interpreter with a horse and 6 corsicks, and together with his elders accompanied me for 2 wersts. But his brother and eldest son stayed with us for 5 wersts, wherefore I fired my pistols on the way, which they enjoyed very much, in that they had never before seen a German flintlock being fired. My watch was at about 9 in the morning when I started on my return journey with the envoys from all three hordes, that I was taking with me, on a North – Northwest course to Russia and we travelled for 4 to 5 hours through nothing but yurts, the envoys bringing 14 people in their suite, and these are their names:

1736
(July 4)

Beybeck Batur
Schagerbey Batur
Sendiflet
Kurmandey
Ackmaley
Laca
Mammet
Altey
Kalebeck Gesaul of the Abul Geier Kahn
and
[43]
Leppis, envoy of the Jambeck Batur, and the others.[105]

1736
(July 4-5)

On the 5th *huius* I was invited very early to dine with Küttel Mahomersin Schuffel Jaghold,[106] who promised to treat me to

---

105 Beybek *batyr*, Shakir/Shagir *batyr*, Seit ip/blet ?, Kurman *biy*, Aka *mullah* ?, Lukei , Mamet (Muhammed), Altai, Kalbeck *esaul*, Leppis ? The order in which these delegates are listed most probably represents seniority or status.
106 Kutlu Mahommed *mursi/mirza* Schuschil Iagild/t ?

a Russian dish, which I was very *curieux* about tasting; when I arrived though, nothing appeared apart from their ordinary so-called Bishpermark,[107] or finely chopped horsemeat. It was merely strewn with some salt, and present at this entertainment was also Kurpe Narden,[108] who was considered a clever man, and who gave me an old fur, since all my coverings had gone and I could not sleep at night on account of the cold. I left at about 9 o'clock in the morning and marched through yurts, from which I could scarcely retain the Kyrgyz men that I had with me, since they were being handed something to eat from every yurt. However, Kalbeck our Adjutant, or Gesaul, had not yet been told about this form of civility on the part of the yurts, and demanded food for the journey in a very inept manner, and to give himself *authorité*, made threats with his whip while so doing, so the people in the yurts were affronted and chased him back to me with their whips back to me, where he sought protection, and his pursuers made their excuses very politely to me. However, Kalbeck was very honest in his behaviour towards me [44] and, with regard to his height, according to the former Prussian measurement, he was, in terms of his physical constitution, a perfect example of those difficult times, in that his whole body consisted of no more than skin and bones, and the former scarcely sufficed to cover the teeth in his mouth, and he was therefore a very fleet and nimble adjutant. As we had now passed through this place, we camped by a salt sea, where a great many families came to us in the greatest confusion, because they had seen people. That evening, a rumour was circulating, that the son of Altar, called

1736
(July 5)

---

107 *Bish-barmak* (five fingers).
108 Kurbey Narb/den ?

Miserr,[109] who had been sent from the rebel Kilmecks[110] with a party of 2000 Bashkiri, was not far from us on the steppe. I was no little alarmed by this and demanded that the Kyrgyz men with me should take me back to Abul Geier Khan. However, they decided that their Khan would not take the trouble to bring these people under control.[111] While we were still discussing the matter, 12 young Kyrgyz rode up on lame horses, showing very anxious and pale faces, and when I inquired as to the reason for their arrival, the answer I received was that they themselves did not know what they were about, since they could not tell whether they were beside the Jaick or the Or rivers, and knew even less about the people who had attacked them so fiercely! [45].

We assigned them the hide of a shot horse and some of its meat to encourage them to tell the truth, and, by drawing various accounts from them, we then obtained secure information that

1736
(July 5)

---

109 Misir Isiangeldin, the son of Aldar Isiangeldin Iskiev (c.1670-1740) who had been a Bashkir leader in the rebellion of 1711. He was co-opted by the Russians during the rebellion and was pardoned. Aldar had become close to Abulkhayir and proclaimed him Khan of the Bashkirs in 1709. He subsequently encouraged Abulkhayir in his petition for subjection to Russia. He was one of Abulkhayir's envoys to St. Petersburg and worked with Tevkelev on his 1730-31 mission to the Junior and Middle Hordes. He had a reputation for cunning and became a prominent, wealthy *tarkhan* (c.5-8000 horses), with this rank confirmed for his heirs. In the rebellion of 1735-40, while pleading for leniency for certain Bashkirs, he was accused of conspiracy, tortured and executed. (Rychkov, *Istoriia*, pp.5 6, 15, 45, 48; Erofeeva, *IKRI* 3, pp.403-404). A letter from Aldar to Tevkelev dated 1737 describes how he and his sons (including Misir) had been robbed by rebels and emphasizes his and his children's fidelity (Demidova 2002, no. 305, p.469). However Castle's mention of Aldar's son in the rebellion (unless it was a false rumour) shows that not all was straightforward, and must have been an added reason for suspicion to fall on Aldar. Misir is not mentioned as a rebel leader in Demidova 2002.
110 The number of Bashkir rebels given in Russian sources were not only estimates but highly variable, depending on the situation on the ground, time of year, type of attack, casualties etc. For example, the leader Yusuf Arikov is said to have mustered c.2000 in February and 8000 men in July 1736 (Demidova 2002, nos. 74, 128). Groups of rebels from different *volosts* (parishes) could amount from the low thousands to the low hundreds (Demidova e.g. nos. 72, 98, 107, 125, 188).
111 This passage shows the volatility of factional allegiances during the Bashkir rebellion.

---

88 men from the Jambeck's horde[112] and 80 men from the other horde[113] had departed, though they knew not whether they had gone to Orenburg, or to their Bashkirs. These new arrivals asked me for some tobacco and sewing needles, which I gave them, and I was then able to ascertain from the two previous occurrences that the attempted conjunction between Kilmeck and his Bashkirs could indeed have been effected with those Kyrgyz men, in that that I also heard afterwards that the 88 men from Iambeck Batur and the 80 men from the other horde had ridden against Orenburg, but had fortunately been driven back by the Russian Cossacks there. And I can without praising myself say at this point that I had travelled to the Khan in a very fortunate hour, because I had prevented the conjunction of all the hordes with those Bashkirs from taking place.

On the 6th *huius* we moved away from the salt sea[114] and headed north, since the Beybeck's envoy had told me in the course of the journey that the cause of the previous stand-off would have been the news about those above-mentioned people and their [46] quarrels, given that each was afraid of the other in this region. Around midday we shot a Bezvar goat, which I am able to name because I have seen the skeleton and bones of Bezvar goats in various cabinets of art and nature, both in England and Holland, and my travelling companions informed me that they sometimes find stones in these goats which they don't know how to use.[115]

1736
(July 6-7)

---

112 Janibek-tarkhan Koshtaruli of the Middle Horde (see nn.5, 31).

113 The Great Horde.

114 One of the larger salt lakes to the south-east of the River Or. Lake Aksakal (five days from Orsk) was large enough to be considered a sea, but was only partially salty and too far from the River Or and Orsk to be referred to here (Rychkov, *Topografiia*, pp.214/244. For the salt lakes used by the Kazakh Junior and Middle Horde and Yaik Cossacks, see Rychkov, *Topografiia*, pp.214/244-218/248).

115 Bezoar goat (*capra aegagrus*), a wild goat. Bezoar 'stones' are accretions found in the different organs of ruminants and other mammals, as well as birds and reptiles. They are attested in Europe as having magical and curative properties from the thirteenth century. In the sixteenth and seventeenth centuries demand for bezoars as part of collections in cabinets of curiosities greatly increased. In the seventeenth century they were also associated with the development of natural sciences. The oriental bezoar from a wild ruminant was the most favoured and

Due to the shortage of wood, the meat was roasted on horse dung and then, after a little swamp water had been found, was chopped up and put in a wooden bowl for lack of a pot; water was poured on top and it was cooked with glowing stones, and the ensuing meal was presented to me as a great delicacy.

On the 7th *huius* we rode on until sundown, and at 8 o'clock we camped by the source of the River Or,[116] where the envoy of Jambeck Batur, called Leppis, and two of Abul Geier's envoys took their leave and rode back, with the excuse that they were afraid that the State Councillor would wish to retain them for too long. At 10 o'clock in the morning, we camped in a region where there are many small lakes, called Kargalet and Yleck,[117] and among these I found many graves of their former heroes, and here one may also find a very great number [47] of wild horse and goats, which cover a few wersts of the country. I had one of the graves opened out of *curiosité*, and it was very deep, and on digging deeper I found human and horse bones, and also a pectoral of white Indian agate, with a pelican and two young carved on it, which was hanging on the dead body by a silver thread, and the remarkable thing was that the silver thread caused it to crumble when I picked up the pectoral.[118] Nevertheless, I

1736
(July 7)

the most expensive. This vogue created a large market in fakes, which contributed to its demise. Their efficacy had been regularly contested and they disappeared from Western pharmacies during the eighteenth century (Borschberg 2010; MacGregor 2007, pp.41, 45 Fig.34; and see also e.g. Monardes 1569; Slare 1646 or 1646-1727; G.L.L.Buffon, *Natural History* Vol. 1, 1792, pp.270-72).

116 The River Or is sourced from a confluence of rivers flowing from the western Mugodzhar Hills. Here Castle appears to mean the junction of the Or and the Jaik.

117 This is the Kargala area on the approach to the Ilek river, not the renowned Kargaly archaeological mining complexes to the north of Orenburg and Orsk. The kurgans (burial mounds) around the Ilek river date from the Early Bronze Age (c. second part of the fourth-third millennium BC) to the Sauromatian (eighth-fifth centuries BC) and Sarmatian (fourth century BC-fourth century AD) into the Medieval period (Koryakova & Epimakhov 2007; Davis-Kimball 1995). See p.71 n.125. Castagné *op. cit.* pp.20, 105-108).

118 The human and partial horse remains and the pelican pectoral suggest a Middle Sarmatian period kurgan (late second century BC-second century AD) on the basis of comparison with similar burials in the

kept the pectoral. At 2 o'clock in the afternoon we rode on, and my two interpreters now took their leave of me, and I sent them express to Orenburg, with a convoy of three men and a letter to the Commandants, and with my reports, which had simply been written in pencil on paper, for lack of pen and ink. I also sent my horses and the gifts I had received to Orenburg. For my part, though, I rode with my remaining 8 Kyrgyz in a north-westerly direction until midnight, and we could find no water on our way. Here, I could not avoid remarking that, because the Kyrgyz do not like to have to drink bad water during their journeys unless it is absolutely necessary, they take sheep's cheeses along with them,

1736
(July 7)
which are made precisely for this purpose and are about as [48] large as a Russian bean, but have been dried as hard as a bone. They place several lumps of this cheese in a flask prepared for this purpose, which is made expressly from the skin of the upper leg of a horse, and which they turn so the upper part forms the base of the bottle, which is also formed of horse pelt, and conversely, the narrow part from the knee area, must serve as the upper part of these bottles. They pour water over the cheese that has been placed inside, and each one hangs a bottle on his horse, so that in the course of their journey the cheese is given such a strong shaking that it turns to liquid and combines with the water that it is contained with to make a fairly thirst-quenching drink which also nourishes.[119] However, before they drink this a real butter will have formed on the top part, which is considered a very great delicacy, and to be given to the most respected person, wherefore they regaled me with this at any time during the journey, and each time placed it in my mouth with their hands, according to their custom, which made me feel very sick on account of the large

Pokrovka region, left bank of the Ilek, (Davis-Kimball 1995) and an imported metal vessel with two pelicans engraved on it from a grave in Sladkovskii (Moshkova 1995, p.143, fig.13c). The pelican with its young, notably feeding its young from its own blood, became a symbol of Christ's passion, but the early transmission of this iconography remains obscure. There is also confusion about whether birds with their young shown in early Christian iconography were indeed pelicans (Portier 1984, p.117; for Byzantium e.g. see Balkarek 2012).

119 Cf. Levshin *op. cit.* p.321 for this Kazakh method of sustenance during long journeys.

quantity of hair that was found therein, and also because, every time I received a smear, my eyes smarted, my mouth opened and the butter slipped down.

[49] On the 8th we travelled a great deal further before sunrise and came to the little River Kubeleck, which flows into the Jaick.

On the 8th *dito* we rode along for 4 hours through nothing but burnt steppes until the River Obeleck,[120] which we crossed with our horses, and which flows into the Jaick. Indeed, this river is so weak it is scarcely noticeable, with a little boscage of birch trees on either side of it. There are a terrible lot of flies everywhere here.

On the 10th day we travelled westward along the River Jaick, and saw 2 animals, at which we rejoiced heartily, with the notion of filling our hungry bellies with them, but as our first task was to catch them, and we took pains to do so, and we observed as we drew closer that they were 2 tame horses, which looked to be Russian. Notwithstanding this, they were just what we required as our own horses were quite exhausted. That day was so excessively hot that we could have collapsed and could scarcely sit on our horses.

On the 11th day I shot an animal that was unknown to me, which was somewhat similar to a marmot. While I was busy with this animal, I saw a party of people who [50] must also have been observing us, because they withdrew, apart from one single man, who came up to me, and who was a Bashkir, with a bow, arrows, sabre, tinder, knife and fishing rod on him, and, with regard to his own family, a Tangauer[121] man, who was known to me, since I had not only seen him during the previous winter with the Bashkirs, but also had noted his name, Beyhoscha, in my notebook, and I took him with me as a prisoner, after he had shot his 30 arrows at me, all on my own, since I had shot his horse in the eye with my

---

120 Neither of these rivers is shown on Rychkov's maps. Several unnamed rivers are shown as flowing into the Yaik (Ural) in the approximate region of Castle's travels, westwards between the Yaik and Ilek rivers, closer to the Yaik.

121 Tungaur was a *volost* (parish) in the Nohgay district of Bashkiria, below Ufa. It was involved, with many others, in the insurrection (Demidova 2002 e.g. no. 216).

musket and so contrived that he could not escape, whereupon he cast off his weapons and everything he had and when my Kyrgyz men came up, having kept themselves somewhat apart, he gave himself up to me as a prisoner. I also found a great many snakes here, one of which I killed, and it was 12 shoe-lengths long. Today the air was very cold and it also rained heavily.

On the 12th I could not sleep from hunger, rain and cold, and so continued my journey along the side of the River Jaick.

On the 13th the air was still continually very disagreeable, which incommoded me greatly on account of the poor state of my clothing.

1736
(July 13, 14)
[51] The people I had with me spied some Bashkirs and warned me to keep my gun primed. Nor did we forgo following these Bashkirs on foot as fast as was possible, but we could not catch up with them, whereupon our Bashkir prisoner tried to escape, but he was betrayed by his wounded horse which called very loudly to our horses. That day we came to a broad and fast-flowing river, which my Kyrgyz wished to cross. However, I consulted my chart which I was using as a guide and saw that we should have passed the river some distance away, and as I did not wish to approve their blind undertaking, so that night we stayed put. In the morning of the 14th *huius* I had to agree to following my people, and according to the opinion that they had formed among themselves, we travelled further up river, whereupon they grew reluctant because the region was not known to them.[122] So they fell back on their native superstitions and decided to resort to magic to discover the right action, with the result that they then wished to go back and return to the place they had started from, and which had already been pointed out to them by me. For their magic, they disposed themselves as follows: 2 Kyrgyz men knelt down facing each other with a fur blanket beneath them. In each hand, they held an arrow with their tips directed

1736
(July 14)
towards their bodies [52] and with the hinder part of the arrows, where the feathers sit, pointing towards each other, with the two ends touching as if they were a single arrow. Whereupon they

---

122 This shows how easy it was to get lost in this region despite a map or chart and guides.

3. Mat. Ch. II

Pl.5

Kazakhs, lost on the banks of the Yaik/Ural river perform a ritual. They point the arrow tips towards themselves murmuring an incantation while waiting for the arrows to point them in the right direction. Castle sits on the far right.

held these very firmly and began gradually to murmur Arabic[123] words, and to wait and see which way fortune would fall, since if the arrows turned to the right, we would have to travel towards the right, and if they turned to the left, we would have to go back. After this, they turned back, and, having no time to waste, made a structure of branches, which for lack of an axe they had to break off with their hands, in which we packed our equipage which consisted of no more than saddles and things, with the greatest care. My travelling companions tied me to the tail of a horse, since I had not learnt how to swim, and this horse was my only guiding star (Pl.6), by which means I was fortunately transported across. Having now traversed the River Jaick by this method, we found dense woodland before us, through which no path could be discerned, so we had to break a way through without an axe, as mentioned above, but using bodily strength, which task we were engaged in until midnight, when we encountered a lake and

1736
(July 15)

were obliged to make a stop, [53] which our exhausted bodies were grateful for and although we were tormented with dreadful hunger, we were so tired that we slept for a while. Then on the 15th *huius*, we travelled further and came quite unexpectedly on a settler's hut, and although the patron of this hut himself was not to be seen, we found a pot in it, a fishing net, an axe, and some smoked fish, the latter serving us particularly well. In that we were remarkably restored by this, and wished to thank our absent host, my people were resolved to extend their gratitude even further by removing everything that was to be found in the hut, which undertaking I dissuaded them from by placing 25 kopecks and a few sewing needles beneath the image of Mary that was in the hut in payment for what we had eaten, and thereby preventing my companions from carrying our their intentions by telling them this was the house of a dervish. On pursuing our journey, we found a lake before us, at which we stopped and had to make a structure of branches in order to cross it, wherein

---

123 There is no way of knowing whether Castle could distinguish between Arabic and the more probable Turki spoken here. It is always a possibility however that Arabic or a garbled form of it was used for incantations and magic (see p.35).

Pl.6
Horses and men crossing the Yaik. A man, possibly Castle, holds on to a horse's tail as he is carried across.

we transported our equipage as described above since both this article and myself were once again tied to a horse's tail with a hair rope and thus, more beneath than above, was I drawn through the water. [54] At this point, I was fairly close to drowning. For in my estimation the lake was a full quarter werst wide and very deep, so on this occasion and very much against my will I took in such a superfluous quantity of this green-grey, stinking water that I could scarcely breathe. However, my fear and my need taught me to use my hands and feet, whereby with God's help, we came across safely. As soon as we had landed, my Kyrgyz men went to great trouble to turn me upside-down by holding my legs up with my head hanging down, so that all the water that was in my body ran out, whereupon we got back on our horses and proceeded towards the North-East until midnight.

1736 (July 15, 16, 17)

On the 16th *dito* we passed through a very poor wilderness always North-East.

On the 17th we marched in a North-Easterly direction and that day I set my above-mentioned prisoner free, given that he was completely weakened by three days' starvation and so exhausted he could no longer ride, so my Kyrgyz exchanged all the clothes that he was wearing for their tattered clothes, and since he resisted this, he also [55] gained a good dose of blows. My men and I were also suffering terrible hunger since in this steppe there was absolutely nothing in the way of prey to hear or see, which the Kyrgyz rely on in any case, and for this reason take no supplies with them, but simply wait for what God sends them. So we resolved to kill the released man's horse, which we had been using for changing horses, in order to still our hunger, having eaten nothing in 2 days. My Kyrgyz were very displeased about this, and wished to go back at all costs, because they thought that the town of Sackmara must surely have disappeared. I tried to console them with all sorts of *persuasiones*, revealing to them, strangely enough, that I thought we had travelled too far, and indeed on my subsequent return to Orenburg, I established that we had travelled 200 wersts too far at the time. My Kyrgyz did not wish to hear this, and they absolutely insisted on turning back, and that I could either go with them or stay in the wilderness as

1736 (July 17)

I pleased. Whereupon I attempted every possible persuasion to convince them that it would be better to travel to Orenburg, which could not be far away, than to travel back along that terrible way. Even this prospect did not convince them, so I thought of another means [56] that might serve. Now, liberality was indeed the only way of retaining their good will, but I did not have anything with me, apart from money, which would anyway not have impressed them since they do not know how to use it, and I cast about for some good advice, and remembered how much they had admired my Persian silk shirt which I had kept on my body during the whole journey, except once, and I quickly resolved to remove it and give it to them, which gave them so much pleasure that they not only cut it up into pieces on the spot and divided it among themselves, but they also remained steadfast in the opinion that we would shortly be marching up to Orenburg and lived in the hope of better times, whereby they showed very little, indeed not the slightest concern that I had to ride without a shirt. So we continued our journey in a relatively steady manner to Orenburg and because our horses were so exhausted they could not carry us, we went on foot, whereby I noticed that my people were not capable of marching well in this manner, given that they are not accustomed to it, having ridden since childhood. Under these conditions, it seemed that Heaven was favouring us, since soon to our very great joy we soon saw Orenburg lying at no great distance.

1736
(July 17)

•   This town lies on [57] a pleasing eminence and is the furthest frontier defence against the Bashkir Tartars. It consists of a church and about 150 houses, which are inhabited by Russian Cossacks.[124] Close by the town the Yck flows into the River Sackmara, which gives the town its name and the region round about may truly be compared to the Elysian Fields because the ground is very suitable for many grasses and is filled with so many sweet-smelling plants

1736
(July 17)

---

124 This is confusing the site which was to become the third and final Orenburg (close to the junction of the Sakmarsk and the Yaik/Ural rivers) from 1743 onwards with the Orenburg of Castle's time, which was to the east at Orsk. This shows that the site already had a settlement there; the confusion over the naming must have occurred at the time the journal was edited.

that are a source of great pleasure to the living and to their souls. I do not mislead you when I compare this region with the Elysian Fields and indeed, many strange burial places established by the ancient Mungal and Nagay[125] Tartars are to be found here.

The stones on these are in the form of a pyramid for all that they are not cemented together, and they have been laid one upon the other in a very *curieux* and binding way, having stood there for several hundred years without being altered. The tombs themselves are in part extensive structures, and in part shaped like a sarcophagus, both sorts lying very deep in the ground.

Beside every dead body, which consists of nothing more than remnants of bones, one also finds the corpse of the horse they used in their lifetime, along with a full set of ornaments, often including the loveliest gold and silver [58] and everything that was necessary for the *dignité* of the person during their lifetime.[126]

1736
(July 17)

---

125 The Noghays were a confederation of Mongol and Turkic tribes, with the Mongol Manghits at their origin. They emerged as the Golden Horde weakened. In the fifteenth and sixteenth centuries they had pastures along the Yaik, Emba and Volga rivers (Frank 2009, p.245 for their early history). The advance of the Kalmyks contributed to their breakdown and migration to the North Caucasus and Azov (Khodarkovsky 2004, pp.9-11, and *passim*). One Kazakh tradition maintained that the Noghays were their ancestors (Levshin *op. cit.* p.131; the Junior Horde indeed appears to have had a Noghay component, see Introduction n.10). The tombs described by Castle are characteristic of an earlier period. Pallas also mentions kurgans in the region of Samara and Yaitsk as belonging to the Noghays (*op. cit.* Vol.1, pp.333, 339-343, 483). Rychkov mentions kurgans along the Iset river, but concentrates on describing settlement sites with remains of buildings, including the remains of a town on the Great Kobda river, south of Orenburg (*Topografiia* pp.107-114). For contemporary Kazakh burial practices described by Castle see p.139.

126 The Ilek and Orenburg areas in the southern Urals are extremely rich in kurgans of the pre-Sauromatian, Sauromatian and Sarmatian periods (see nn.117, 118). Some contained rich artefacts of the Sibero-Scythian or Saka culture and imports from e.g. Achaemenid Persia. (Yablonsky 2010). Burial pits (for single and multiple bodies) were of various shapes (oval, rectangular, chambered, with corridors) and used both timber and stone superstructures. Partial or part animal burials, including horse, became prevalent in the region from the Sintasha period (early second millennium) onwards and continued into the Sarmatian period. Whole horse burials were generally more common in the Altai to the east, notably exemplified by the fifth-third-century elite burials of Pazyryk and Berel (Yablonsky, *op. cit*; Samaschev 2012; for summaries of the

I now thought that all the need and misery I had experienced had completely ended; but instead, I found I was much mistaken, for when I arrived in Sackmara[127] and asked the Ottaman[128] named Weroffskin[129] who presided there very urgently to either provide me with a convoy to the State Councillor Iwan Kiriloff or at least to send a letter to him from me, he was unwilling to agree to either of these, and claimed that I needed to show him a written order for this. I explained at great length how it had arisen that I had come from the Kyrgyz, and that I had their envoys with me, and showed him, the better to attest for myself, the letter I had with me, which Abul Geier Khan had written to the State Councillor Iwan Kiriloff, all of which did nothing to help.

Now my Kyrgyz people insisted they could go no further without a convoy, since they were aware that enemies of the Bashkirs lay all around, and also that the State Councillor was still 200 wersts distant, so my Kyrgyz men wished very forcibly to return. I presented the matter to the Ottoman again, with the consideration that if these envoys from 3 hordes were to return without speaking with the State Councillor, [59] the Russian empire would suffer great harm and injury as a result. Whereupon the Ottaman asked me in an almost reproving way to be merciful since his people were Christians, and were thus obliged to be

1736
(July 17)

---

archaeology of the area see Koryakova, Epimakhov 2007; Dvornichenko, Barbarunova, Moshkova 1995; Epimakhov 2009; Yablonsky *op. cit*). A number of the kurgans seen by Castle would already have been looted by locals, Cossacks or passers by such as himself.

127 Sakmara, close to the junction of the Sakmara and Ural rivers, was established as a small fort or station (*stanitsa*) manned by Cossacks in 1725. It replaced Cossack settlement at the turn of the century which had been much closer to the mouth of the river. The aim of Sakmara was to control the Bashkirs and defend Orenburg. Despite being on fertile land and standing on copper ore, Kirilov found it poorly manned with unpaid troops in 1735. He recommended more Cossacks and salaries to come from the Yaik Cossacks. By 1740 the fort had grown, with c.200 Cossacks and a few infidels (*inovertsov*), making a living from the land, fishing and the transport of copper ore (Kirilov, *K-O Otnosheniia* no. 52, para 8; Rychkov, *Topografiia*, pp.83/443; Castle, Glossary; Donnelly, *op. cit.* p.55).

128 *Ataman*, a Cossack leader or military commander.

129 Verofskin. The *ataman* in 1725 had been Fomoi Sibiriaki (Rychkov, *Topografiia*, p.187, Indices).

cautious, because all those who he could provide as a convoy or could send with a letter, would surely get lost.

However, he did have a Tartar Cossack whom he wished to give to me. Although I replied that I was also a Christian and furthermore a foreigner, notwithstanding which I did not spare my life in Your Imperial Majesty's service, the Ottaman did not alter his opinion and told me I had leave to do as I wished.

The previous day, a Captain from the Orenburg regiment of dragoons called Ragusin had arrived with provisions from the town of Jaick[130] and I sent an under-officer to him, and went myself to report on my situation and to seek his advice. As soon as I arrived, his first question was, what was my rank? Being determined to gain his good opinion, I resorted to the pretext that I was an envoy from the Khan to the State Councillor, and, because I did not speak the Russian language very well, and did not know the manners of this country, I was [60] asking if he would be so kind as to advise me as to what I should do, in order not to waste any more time. Whereupon his reply was almost the same as the Ottaman's. I also applied in writing to a Jaick Ottaman who was there with 50 men, to assist me with only 8 men! However, he replied by means of a verbal message that he took his orders from Iwan Kiriloff. Since there was nothing to achieve with this person either, I turned to my Kyrgyz, those poor people who had endured wish and misery with me, and spoke from my heart, and comforted them, saying that a fort lay 50 wersts from Sackmara where a Captain could be found, who was a good friend of mine, and who would immediately provide us with a convoy, and I then assured them that they were very dear and precious to Iwan Kiriloff and that he would show them every favour when they arrived, and that they should not turn back on account of these people here, since the State Councillor was not aware of the poor manner of their reception. This made these poor Kyrgyz more confident about undertaking this journey, and every day I bought them a sheep, and beer, brandy and mead, as much as they wished, with my money, and, because I was never even lent

1736
(July 17)

---

130 See p. 98, n.156.

anything, I also had to buy them a cooking pot, and gave them knives, axes, boots, [61] tinder, tobacco and I distributed powder and lead among them for the journey, so that in the event of being attacked while on our way, we would be able to defend ourselves. For my part, I put on Tartar clothes as a precaution, and had my head shaved in the Tartar manner.

1736
(July 17, 20,
21, 22, 23)

On the 20th I continued my journey, since given the circumstance that I did not wish to stay there any longer, I had to resolve to go on foot, since my horse was completely done in and my money bag was empty, so that I could not buy another one, but I had done everything for my Kyrgyz men that was necessary to reach the newly built fortress.

On the 21st I fortunately arrived on foot with my Kyrgyz people and came to Captain Sowrin of the Pensich Regiment, at the mouth of the River Yck,[131] and the above-mentioned Captain showed me and my Kyrgyz men all possible honour and kindness, all due praise being due to the same.

On the 22nd I sent two loyal Bashkirs to advise the State Councillor Iwan Kiriloff of my arrival.

On the 23rd I sent a letter to State Councillor Iwan Kiriloff, but this involved the greatest trouble in the world, because he was surrounded by enemies. [62]

1736
(July 23,
August 3, 4)

Given that the people I had sent to deliver this letter were repulsed, I was now resolved to travel on my own to the State Councillor, and so after a great deal of pleading I finally secured 2 Cossacks, who also set off with this letter, and advised the State Councillor for the second time of my arrival.

On the 3rd August, my Kyrgyz came to me with very cheerful faces and reported that they had made magic and had learned thereby that we would soon very certainly receive good news.

On the 4th a letter from the State Councillor Iwan Kiriloff came to me in the evening, followed by a convoy for me and my Kyrgyz. Here below are the contents of the letter:

Esteemed Herr Castle!

---

131 Where the Sakmarsk flows into the Yaik.

Your letter of 22nd July was received by me on the 27th, informing me that you have 14 persons as envoys from the Abul Geier Khan with you; you are therefore summoned, to convey yourselves here as soon as possible with the same envoys, wherefore, to accompany you and show the way, I herby send loyal Bashkirs from Pushmas Jsiugun [63] Kipzoiskoy of the Useinmunascheff, Domzey, Kolumbeteff et Confratres[132]

1736
(August 5)

> *I remain,*
>
> *Your obedient servant,*
> *Iwan Kiriloff*

The 3rd August
1736[133]

On the 5th at midnight, I took my leave of the Captain of the fort, who had been so good to me, as mentioned above, and of the other officers, and set out very early, whereupon I met up with Captain Astankoff,[134] who was marching with his commando to Orenburg; I was *justement* with my people on the mountain when I espied the afore-mentioned Major with his commando of about 700 men in the valley, so I immediately sent one of my Tartars to this commando, but the Major did not trust me and formed a battalion square, taking up position on a small patch of wooded ground, with growth on all sides, which was to his advantage, and which I was cut off by. I walked confidently up to the commando, and after I

---

132 Husein Munashev, D/Tomzai, Kulumbet and companions of the Pushmas-Chinkin-Kipchatskaia volost (for the latter, in the Noghay district, see Demidova 2002, e.g. nos. 37, 367). Russian messages regarding Bashkirs during the rebellion characteristically put the name of the district before that of the people.

133 See Editorial Note in the Introduction.

134 Major Boris Lukish Ostankov (?-1742). Commanding a detachment of Yaik Cossacks he dealt brutally with Bashkirs in 1736. He was ordered to replace Lieutenant Chemodurov in Orenburg in 1736, and on the way built a fort garrisoned by Cossacks on the Ural, later known as Verkhneozernaya. He eventually became a colonel, commanding Orsk and the Yaik region up to the border (Demidova 2002 e.g. nos. 33, 96, 107; Rychkov, *Istoriia*, pp.24-26; 42, 47, 62, 66, 67; Donnelly, *op. cit.* p.86). He is not to be confused with his brother, Grigory Lukish Ostankov, who also served in the campaign (see Demidova, 2002, Index).

had been obliged to stop by the wooded ground and the Major had
sent his Cossacks to me, I crossed the wooded ground along with
the Cossacks and the people with me, since even my best friends
would not have recognized me in my Tartar clothes, [64] but as I *1736*
(August 5)
did not announce my presence and went on letting them seek me,
I was initially only recognized by my pistol and dagger. This then
gave rise to a happy circumstance. There was in this commando a
German stonemason called Jacob Reiner,[135] who had been born in
St Gall in Switzerland, and I asked him for a shirt, given that I had
not had one on my body since the 17th July. That day, after covering
106 wersts on horses borrowed from the Bashkirs who had been
sent to me, I was glad to arrive with my Kyrgyz in the evening
and reach the State Councillor Iwan Kiriloff, as was recorded in my
journal that was submitted to the Orenburg Chancellery, which I
had in fact concluded with a reference to my arrival, it having been
satisfactorily shown that the same, together with the present *piece*,
to which I have added no more than improvements to its *stylum* to
make it easier to understand, and have explained a few other things
more fully, does indeed correspond completely with the contents of
the principal matter. However, I intend to do no wrong in relating
what subsequently happened to me in the course of this expedition,
in its various circumstances, such as the customs, usages and other
curiosa, which I observed among the Kyrgyz people and other
neighbouring peoples, and thereby provide a fuller description than
is provided in the same journal that is to be found in Orenburg,
which [65] includes fully *obiter* simply my journey and expedition *1736*
(August 5)
among the Kyrgyz; thus I also mention the continuation of the
events that occurred to me elsewhere as follows.

My arrival with the State Councillor Iwan Kiriloff occurred
when he was still in the encampment and 150 wersts from Ufa,
whereupon I delivered over my journal, written in pencil, and

---

135 This Swiss craftsman had been asked by the authorities to teach
lapidary skills to workers at the future Ekaterinburg (1723) and Isetsk
works (1735). He apparently only knew hand working techniques,
which proved to be insufficient to satisfy the demands of the capital.
This led to the establishment at the future Ekaterinburg of a factory
using water to industrialize cutting (1747). (Chistyakova 2007, p.98; see
also pp.106-7, n.171).

gave him a full report of the same, how I

1st considering that the Commander in Orenburg did not wish to send any of the envoys that the Kyrgyz were demanding, while at the same time, Eraly Sultan and the envoys of the Kyrgyz had revealed in confidence to me the looming danger of namely 40000 Kyrgyz who, if the Russian envoys failed to arrive, would combine with the Bashkir Kilmeck rebels against Russia, attack the much-mentioned State Councillor, and engage in all kinds of dangerous assaults, accordingly, I resolved to prevent all this and to go on a journey to the Khan, and to sacrifice myself in my loyalty to Russia. So I took my leave, and everyone thought it was the last time they would see me, and commenced this journey on 14th June, having previously received only [66] a verbal instruction from the Commander, in the course of which I was obliged to observe that the same was firmly convinced that I would definitely be lost, and for that reason did not wish to give me anything in writing. And, in this way, I had

1736
(August 5)

2nd after undertaking this journey, found that that which Eraly Sultan and the Kyrgyz envoys had revealed to me in confidence was actually true, and that if only I had been able to visit Guder Bey on the 18th June, he would have been very glad to see me and would have found consolation in knowing that the Kilmecks would then have abandoned all hope of joining the conjunction that the Kyrgyz were planning, instead of which it has been truly shown how *sub die* 5th *Iulii* the Kilmecks were already willing to begin this conjunction and that Alkar's son Miseer[136] and 200 Bashkirs, since 88 men from Jambeck Batur, and 80 men from the others' hordes were already gathering. Furthermore, I did not fail to inform the State Councillor,

3rd fully about the circumstances that gave me the opportunity on 20th *Iunii* to insinuate myself with the Khan's sons during his absence, so that I had real hopes [67] of achieving good results, and I further reported what

1736
(August 5)

4th during my first audience on 21st *Iunii* with the Khan was to the advantage of Russia, which occurred on account of my arrival

---

136 Aldar's son Miser, see n.109.

---

there, and how he on that occasion had spoken openly, saying that he would now be able to forbid his people from forming the conjunction with the Kilmecks, whereupon I did not fail to

5th inform the State Councillor about the region that the Khan showed me on 23rd June, where it would in his words be very advantageous, should Your Imperial Majest. so desire it, to place a fortress on that same mountain, given that he could thereby confront all his enemies and it would present him with the opportunity of offering Your Imperial Majest. the fruits of his loyalty; and how then the Khan, while making such honest utterances, had also shown me a situation in the South East which would also be very advantageous for building a fort, given that in this region there is a great wealth of gold and gemstones to be found. I also told the State Councillor that during this journey Beymarat Beyla Batur had promised to send 1000 sheep to Orenburg at his request, to which the Khan had added that he knew someone who could send 2000 sheep. Also how the Khan on this occasion had also [68] subsequently called me aside and thanked me very much for having come, in that a great danger had thereby been averted, and that I would not believe how carefully he had to handle his people. Besides this, I reported to the State Councillor how I

1736
(August 5)

6th on 24th June had given the Khan gifts, which I had procured at my own expense. I also reported

7th how following my representations, it was decided by the Khan and his elders on 25th *Iunii* that those Kyrgyz robbers who had already started the rebellion, and had in this guise robbed Russian horses and camels near Orenburg, would either be punished for this, and on request even delivered over to Russia. I further reported how

8th the envoys of Jambeck Batur on 29th June had earnestly assured me they would keep faith with the loyalty they had once offered to Your Imperial Majest, which then

9th the elders of the above-mentioned Jambeck Batur had likewise on 30th June repeated once again. I also provided an extensive account of

10th the very great dinner on 1st July that the Khan provided, to
Verse 5 Math Ch. II

1736
(August 5)
which the elders and leaders of all three hordes were invited, who came from all over [69] and, calling God to witness, had vowed yet again to remain loyal to Your Imperial Majest. Whereupon they also toasted your Imperial Majesty's eminent health in my presence and told me their names, which I immediately wrote down. Further, I reported in the Khan's name,

11th how he requested State Councillor on 14th *Iulii* to erect a dwelling for himself in Orenburg, and also what had moved him so to do, and how he could serve Russia by so doing; he also asked to dedicate his three sons to Your Imperial Majest, and also did not wish to have more people with him in Orenburg than would be permitted, and that he would be desirous, in the interests of your Imperial Majest and his own, to send me as an envoy to the Buchars, since he, in his own words, could not trust anyone apart from me in this matter. Nor did I omit

12th to report, that the Khan had complained to me on 2nd *Iulii* about the Commandant in Orenburg's prohibition from moving further along the River Or and how I had answered this and had explained this order in such a way that the Khan and all his elders were very satisfied with it.

After I had reported this to the State Councillor, along with all the other things that befell me, including those which I had undergone [70] during the previous winter with the Bashkirs, on several occasions, and had presented the Kyrgyz envoys to him, he appeared to be quite beside himself for joy, kissed me, and thanked me in the name of Your Imperial Majesty, and promised emphatically that he wished to submit my very great efforts to the Court, and would send me together with the things I had found and brought back with me to your Imperial Majesty, given that he was not rich and could not reward me sufficiently for my loyalty, and simply had to leave this matter for Your Imperial Majesty's gracious favour. In that we were now engaged in a variety of discourses, the State Councillor also informed me that the Commandant from Orenburg had written to him about me to wit, that I had indeed told him that I wished to go to Abul Geier Khan, but he was much more inclined to believe that I had devised this simply in order to get away from Orenburg. Whereas I had

1736
(August 5)

now given the State Councillor a very different *idée*, and was able to show that the Commandant believed me already lost among the Kyrgyz and was consequently anxious about having granted permission for this, on account of the enquiry, so although my proceedings were honourable, I was made to suffer on account of [71] this Commandant's fearfulness which caused me to be inscribed as a deserter for the second time in the Orenburg records.[137]

1736 (August 5, 12, 14)

On the 12th *huius*, the State Councillor himself brought me a packet of letters for Orenburg with the *ordre* to convey the Kyrgyz men I had brought with me, along with others from this nation, who wished to travel home again, to the River Jaick, for which purpose 12 Cossacks were given to me, and I arranged with Major Astanckoff, who was on the way to Orenburg, to bring my most necessary affairs back with him, and leave the rest in Orenburg, since after that he was to accompany Lieutenant-Colonel Tschemaduroff along the River Jaick to the town of Jaick, and then to Sinbirky[138] via Samaria.[139] So I took my leave of the State Councillor, who gave me a fur for my journey, which I had very great need of, given that in those countries, which are excessively hot, it grows so cold at night time that one encounters frost and even ice in the morning.

On the 14th *huius* I met up with the above-mentioned Major

---

137 For Castle's fractious relations with the Russian authorities see Introduction.

138 Simbirsk: a fort established in 1648 north-east of Samara on the Volga by the boyar and armourer Bogdan Matveitch Khitrov. It developed as part of the Simbirsk line. Kirilov temporarily moved his headquarters there during 1736 (Rychkov, *Topografiia*, pp.106/466; Donnelly *op. cit.* p. 83.

139 Samara: founded in 1586, on the left side of the Volga, at the junction of the Samara and Volga rivers. Its situation made it a pleasant and profitable trading place, even though at danger of Kalmyk and Bashkir raids. The town had churches, monasteries and fortifications. Kirilov temporarily moved his headquarters there after Simbirsk, in 1736. In Rychkov's time it had c. 2000 households, and a mixed population of landowners, serving people, foreigners and Cossacks (Rychkov, *Topografiia*, pp.103-4/263-4; Donnelly *op. cit.* p.83). For impressions of Samara in the eighteenth century see Teissier 2011, pp.23-25. See Pl.8.

Astackoff at the mouth of the Yck[140] and came in the course of our march to the fortress of Osorka,[141] 120 wersts this side of Orenburg, whereupon I had to walk again, since the horse that the State Councillor had given me had gone lame [72] and I had to leave it in the wilderness, although Major Astanckoff, under the pretext that he had his orders, did not provide another horse.

1736 (August 5, 12, 14)

On the 31st I hired a horse, and early in the morning went with 2 Kalmuck Cossacks in advance to Orenburg, but I became so ill on the way that I fell off my horse and had to be carried into the town, since I had ridden 95 wersts that day, as well as suffering the *fatalité* that Major Astanckoff had provided little in the way of victuals during the journey, to wit a small piece of ham, which I had stored in a silken cloth from around my neck and tied to my dagger hilt, but had then lost on the way, on account of the excessive heat and the innumerable flies. So I resolved to eat with my Cossacks, who had made camp by a well, and share their food, which consisted of dried meat which I had previously taken to be crumbled biscuit and which I subsequently realized, having swallowed it and been so revolted, had contributed substantially to my above-mentioned indisposition. After arriving in Orenburg, I asked the presiding Commandant on 3rd Sept. to give me a troop of 50 Cossacks for protection and a few instruments, with a view to reaching a certain mountain that lay not too far from Orenburg [73] near the River Tan Atlack,[142] since I had found the trace of a valuable lapis on my previous journey back from the Bashkirs in the month of May in this year, and had recently presented the State Councillor with a stone of extraordinary beauty, and

1736 (September 3, 4, 5)

---

140 By this Castle does not mean the actual mouth of the river (i.e. Guriev on the Caspian Sea), but most probably the junction of the Sakmara and Yaik/Ural rivers.

141 This fortress, not mentioned in Rychkov, would have been situated approximately half way between the third Orenburg (just below Sakmarsk) and Orsk (Castle's Orenburg), a total distance of 236 versts. (Donnelly 1968, Appendix 2, for a chart of distances between fortresses; Rychkov, *Topografiia*, Indices pp.181-82).

142 This river, or one sounding like it, is not mentioned in Rychkov. The name may relate to the Tanalik district of Orenburg, where a fortress called Tanalisk was built in 1743 (Rychkov, *Topografiia*, pp.224/254, and *idem* Indices p.195.

how, on that very mountain, which I had not dared approach openly on account of the hostile Bashkirs who lie far too close, I had found a stone while wandering about at night time that was green and shot with red, for it had been spoiled by lying outside in the air, and so I wished to visit the mountain, for the sake of greater certainty, given that I had noted the region very well and would soon be able to find the mountain; the Commandant's only response was the excuse that on the one hand, the horses were lame and on the other, he had no orders about this, so this very useful undertaking remained fruitless.[143]

On the 4th Major Astanckoff arrived in Orenburg.

On the 5th the Beybeck came with another 3 persons from Jambeck Batur to Orenburg again in order to learn from the Commandant whether the State Councillor had arrived, and they also wished to be kept informed by Eraly Sultan, as to whether the Declaration proclaimed by Your Imp. Majest. had been cancelled.[144] Now the worst thing [74] was that these people were not given any provisions, given that such things could not be purchased in Orenburg for money, and, if there had been some to purchase, the Kyrgyz had no money, so these people all came to me and upbraided me, wishing to consider me a fine man who was not keeping back that which Your Imperial Majesty had promised them, since they had not yet received their two-thirds money.[145] I was not to blame for this state of affairs, yet wishing to act in the interests of the Empire, I could do none other than console them and apply every care in the world to soothing their bitter feelings once again, wherefore I observed that the Commander, if to

*1736
(September
5, 6)*

---

143 See Introduction.

144 It is not clear which imperial 'declaration' this refers to. It may refer to Erali's position as a hostage in Orenburg; to the fear (mistaken) that the Russians might withdraw privileges from the Junior Horde on account of a Russian caravan having been ransacked by a party of Junior Horde Kazakhs (*K-R Otnoscheniia* no. 60) and withdraw favourable trading rights for the Kazakhs in Orenburg (*K-R Otnoscheniia* nos. 61, 62, 68) or to Kazakh action against the Bashkirs (*K-R Otnoscheniia* no. 62).

145 Any Imperial dealings with subject Kazakhs were based on reward and payment, whether in kind or coin (cf. Tevkelev, Diary 1731-33, 1748 *passim*; Dobromyslov 1900, pp.90-91). The amount varied according to circumstance. It seems that middle men took advantage of this.

blame for this, would certainly get his reward for it because I had asked the State Councillor about the payment and the guilty ones, who had been ordered to make the payment, would definitely be punished for this; I also promised them that I would not fail to report all this to the State Councillor as soon as I had come unto him and he had given me audience. Whereupon they were somewhat pacified and afterwards they went to the Commandant and told him the truth.

On the 6th *huius* the Beybeck and Mummet brought the clothes that the Khan had sent me including a bonnet with velvet *1736* culottes, together with a pair of leggings [75] of white cotton, a *(September* pair of boots of black chagrille shagreen, and a sable, and also a *6, 7)* fire-arms three and half arsines[146] long, and a pouch with knife, tinder, bullets and powder, with a horn inside. For my part, I presented the gift-bringers with 4 Iusten purses ?, 8 mirrors, 8 knives, 4000 sewing needles and an old piece of cloth of gold, and that evening I also treated all the Kyrgyz envoys present, including the son of the Khan, and the Taskent envoys, which came to 40 persons in all, who were truly gratified, because I provided music as well, and the feast was held under Commander Teffkeleff's own tent, to which I had also invited the Commander and all the officers present as well, though they did not actually attend it, but my other guests were fairly drunk with delight, because I had supplied them with proper Kyrgyz food and drink, which they had prepared themselves according to their taste.

On the 7th *huius* I was keen to make another drawing of the town of Orenburg, but the terrible number of flies prevented me from so doing and consequently I could not wait any longer for the order to travel. In spite of this, I thought it useful to provide some information about Orenburg, since it is not well known that *1736* it lies in the 51st degree *latitudinis*, and that this town, which [76] *(September* takes its name from the River Or, was established in *Ao.* 1735 on *7)* the 12th of August[147] close by the River Jaick, which arises 2 short

---

146 See n.70.

147 According to Rychkov, the first Orenburg (renamed Orsk in 1740, Rychkov, *Topografiia*, Indices pp.181-82) was established on 15 August (*Istoriia* p.16). Castle's description tallies with that of Rychkov

Pl.7.

A view of a fortified Orenburg (Orsk) between the Or and Yaik/Ural rivers with houses, a church and a watchtower on top of a hill above the fortress. A flat bridge is shown across the Or, with the Ural mountains behind. Orenburg's coat of arms is in the sky.

days' ride into Siberia, close to Catharinenburg, where the River Or flows into it at a distance of 2 wersts from the town, whose own source lies a few hundred wersts south of Orenburg. Its region is surrounded by wilderness and steppe, and it lies 960 wersts from Catharinenburg, 632 from the town of Jaick by land, 485 from Ufa, 240 from Sackmara, though 621 wersts from Samara on the

(which mentions a fortress with four towers and a small citadel on the Preobrazhenski hill, and a subsequent fort with nine bastions—this was delayed until 1736) but is more fulsome. Instructions given by Empress Anna in June 1734 (Rychkov, *Istoriia* p.9) for the foundation of Orenburg specified that *teptiars* (Bashkir farmers who paid rent to landholders, Donnelly *op. cit.* p.33) and *bobilei* (Bashkir farmers without rights, Donnelly *op. cit.* p.33) were to be used in building works; that half a regiment from Ufa and one or two from Kazan were to be used for the defence of the town, but that recruits would eventually complement the garrison; landowners, Cossacks and young (noble) men from Ufa and Menzelinsk were to be brought to the town, as well as Yaik and Sakmara/Sakmarsk Cossacks; that *tarkhans* (tribal or clan leaders exempt from taxes in return for military service) and *meshcheriaks* (Tatars, some originally from the Kazan region, used at this time in campaigns against the Bashkirs, living on land confiscated from the Bashkirs, eventually obtaining title deeds (and thus a particular source of resentment among the Bashkirs, Rychkov, *Topografiia* pp.100/130-103/133, for a detailed discussion; Donnelly *op. cit.* pp.91, 108) were to be brought in as needed; that guns, mortars, falconets and instruments were to be prepared in Ekaterinburg and powder and lead to come from Ufa and Kazan. The edict continues with other matters e.g. that the tax revenue from Ufa should be used for the (Orenburg) expedition (Rychkov, *Istoriia*, p. 9; *Topografiia* pp.6/36). This edict, and one of 7 July 1734, which mentions the prospective non-Russian merchant (e.g. Kazakhs, Siberian Bukharans, Khivans, Tashkentians, Persians, Indians, Persians, Europeans) and workers to be settled in Orenburg, shows the Russian Empire's practice of creating forts and centres with immediately mixed populations and functions at its frontiers (cf. Rychkov, *Topografiia*, pp.189/219-190-220). These then created their own fluid socio-economic orbits (Barrett 1999, Introduction). This ambitious scheme did not go to plan in Orsk because of the rebellion in the first instance. Things were slow in the third Orenburg as well; besides trading Tatars only a small number of Asians settled there at first: eight Khivans, one Bukharan, three Kashgaris and one from Balkh. Besides these who settled out of their own free will there were up to 212 fugitives (runaways from the Kazakhs; Persians, Arabians, Afghans, Uzbeks etc.), some of whom were baptized. (Rychkov, *Topografiia*, pp.189-192/219-222). For a sketch of the Orsk fortress see Rychkov 1999 ed., p.13. For the relocation of Orenburg and a description of the third Orenburg, see Rychkov *Topografiia*, pp.13-21.

Volga,[148] and the town itself, which has a circumference of 1½ wersts, is provided with an earth wall and a ditch.

Close by the town is a hill in which a kind of agate lies buried, with a wooden watch tower on top, in the castell, the latter being also supplied with a earth wall and a ditch, with Spanish reuter carriage guns? all around the wall. The ground here has not yet been cultivated, so it is like all the Kyrgyz lands, in that it very seldom rains there, and so the gardens all have to be irrigated by running water through them. For nourishment, there is plenty of fish and cut hay, and there is some timber but very little bread or meat, since it's not possible to pasture cattle here or keep them safe from robbers.

[77] The commerce here, which is why this place was actually built, could in future be very profitable and extensive with the Buchars, Taskents and other Asian peoples, given that, in my opinion, the next road after this town leads to India, if one wished to take the Aral Sea from the Russian side for this purpose, given that the Rivers Sir and Anu[149] are both very strong-flowing rivers full of shipping and they extend through the whole of Bucharia right up to the aforesaid Aral Sea, and in my estimation, the latter could be effected within only 14 days' journey from Orenburg, and the mastery of the Aral Sea should not be difficult, since on the one hand, the Buchars and neighbouring lands know nothing of shipping or canons, and on the other hand, there is enough timber to be found along the Aral Sea, which could possibly be used for building and repairing the ships, that these depths might be traversed and other countries along with their treasures thereby brought into subjection, by which means Orenburg's potential for use might one day be fully developed.[150]

1736 (September 7)

---

148 The giving of distances to and from Orenburg was standard practice in reports of the time dealing with this region (cf. Rychkov, *Topografiia*, pp.12/372).

149 Sïr Darya, Amu Darya.

150 Castle is reiterating Russian ambitions for developing trade with the east, which at the time included building a wharf and putting a merchant fleet on the Aral sea (Kirilov *K-R Otnoscheniia* no. 50, para 10). For the English Captain and engineer John Elton who was involved in the building of the first Orenburg and of the Aral Sea wharf, see p.104 n.162.

However, just as my original sketching project was undone by the flies, I have overreached my mark in this description of the town and must now attend to the order to march to Sinbirsky,

and, since this involved travelling along the River Jaick, [78] I applied to the Commandant for a barge for my equipage, which was duly granted me.[151] While I was employed in placing my things and my carriage in it, a voice rose up from far off: who is responsible for taking this barge! I was initially alarmed, but when they drew closer I saw that it was the Adjutant, who then told me that he wished the barge for himself, and that I should immediately unload, or he would throw all my things into the water. So I replied in all modesty that the Lieutenant-Colonel, he being the actual Commandant of this barge, had ordered that it to be assigned to me. However, since the Adjutant did not turn away and started to lay hands on my things, I had to remind him again, and he responded with such effrontery that he complained about me to the Commandant, as if I had wished to shoot him, whereupon the said Commandant summoned me immediately and reproached me for being, as he very well knew, a desperate man, whereas the complainant was an officer! As I was now only too well aware, the Commandant set about preaching a sermon to me about my endeavours, these being directed in the first place, at the Bashkirs, and then the Kyrgyz, and primarily at securing the preservation of the town of Orenburg, in the course of which I

[79] had spared neither my life nor my own wealth in the interest of the Empire, and had feared no danger, all of which constituted an accusation of desperation. I simply replied that nowhere else would a stranger have been given such a disagreeable reception as the one that the Orenburg officers had given me in this place! And although I was well aware that the complainant was an officer, I was serving Your Imperial Majesty and they had no right to throw my equipage in the water.

On the 8th *huius*, 24 soldiers were ordered onto my barge, and they cast most of their equipage on top of my baggage and lay down on it. It was unfortunate that the baggage did not collapse

---

151 For eighteenth-century voyages down the Volga described by British merchants and others, see Teissier 2011.

and injure them. The Sergeant who was also on the barge, was not only displeased with the soldiers' behaviour but he absolutely insisted that the things I had loaded should be cast into the water. I realized they were simply harassing me in order to do a deal with me, and as I did not wish to get involved in an argument, I complained about this to the Lieutenant-Colonel, informing him thereby that if he was unable to protect me, I would be obliged to remain in Orenburg during the oncoming winter. Thereupon he finally and very angrily ordered that no one should importune me in the slightest manner. At this time, the Beybeck's [80] envoy took his leave of me, because he was desirous to go to the Khan. He recommended the Kyrgyz to me and promised to meet me again in the town of Jaick, and then to go with me to the State Councillor.

1736
(September
9, 10, 11)

On the 9th *dito* I rode out at 5 o'clock in the evening, in the company of the Major and other officers, and of a German *chirurgi* and the above-mentioned stonemason from St Gall, who accompanied us part of the way, to the river bank, when we all toasted each other and made our farewells. Then we boarded our conveyances and floated downriver for 2 hours, and that night we slept on land.

On the 10th *huius* our barges were tied together, so as to make 3 out of 6, in such as way that the Lieutenant-Colonel's was combined with a Captain's, mine with a Lieutenant's and the Adjutant's was filled full of Kyrgyz and Cossacks, so that we were 120 man strong, though there were many barges with Cossacks as well.

On the 11th we sailed between many high mountains and crags and found a terrible quantity of pike here, which were caught with hooks by 3 Cossacks in nearby barges, and I was able to buy four pike, each one arsine long, for a pipe of tobacco, so that 120 men were fed on pike for a *bagatelle* and otherwise nothing.

[81] The pike were pale-coloured, and the Cossacks used a particular instrument for catching them. They had an oval iron plate in the shape of a leaf from a tree, about 6 thumbs long and tin-plated. On one end of this was a hook, and on the other a hole, though which a 10 arsine-long thread was tied, and the

1736
(September
12, 13, 14,
15)

Cossacks would hold the other end in their mouths, with their teeth. They throw the plate into the water, while rowing their boats and keeping quiet nearly all the time, and on catching a pike by this means with their mouth, they have to pull it out, because it goes so fiercely after the plate.

On the 12th *huius*, we hit a sandbank. At this point, a Cossack of the Kalmuck nation ran away, taking a fur and a loaf with him, he having been a prisoner. At night time, we slept every time on the Kyrgyz side.

On the 13th we came to a region where some woodland could be seen.

On the 14th, we spent all day, from morning till evening, sailing round two mountains, so that by evening we arrived at the place that we had set out from in the morning, and the weather was rainy.

*1736
(September
16, 17, 18)*

On the 15th *dito* in the morning we saw the newly established little town of Osernoy,[152] [82] which is halfway to Sackmara. A little wooden house on a high mountain was flying Your Imper. Majest.'s flag, and since Cossacks were on guard in the house, we addressed them, and they then told us that they had only a month's provisions left, and they also informed us that our Orenburg horses had passed through that little town with the Cossacks 2 days ago.

On the 16th we left this place 3 hours before daybreak, and encountered low-lying country and nothing but wilderness. Our Cossacks were given boats and they shot a wild pig, which was, however, swept away by the River Jaick. On the 17th we left land again 3 hours before dawn and by 7 o'clock we became aware of 2 stocks or stacks of hay on the right side of Sackmara, and then we also saw a watch or guardhouse on this side at about 10 o'clock.

The river was clean, with no trees, and very deep. That afternoon, we once again observed many structures and haystacks, and could also spy a little wooden house on the bank.

---

152 This fort, with a palisade, ditch and bank, was established by Kirilov in 1736, and manned by Yaik Cossack gunners. Its name was taken from the many lakes around it (*ozero*=lake in Russian). (Rychkov, *Topografiia*, pp.136/496, ed. 2010 Map X).

On the 18th we found a low bank and that afternoon we found a fish weir. All around here many Roskolshicks[153] are to be found on the right side of Samara. That afternoon, at 4 o'clock, we sent 3 Cossacks to Sackmara, with instructions to enquire after the 3 officers who had been posted by land with horses from Orenburg [83] to the town of Jaick, and also to discover whether the sick soldiers had already left the afore-mentioned town?

On the 19th *dito* at around 10 o'clock in the morning we came to the mouth of River Sackmara, and waited for the return of the Cossacks who had been sent off. Here, right by the river mouth, lies the old town of Sackmara, which was destroyed by the Bashkirs more than 30 years ago, and which is 30 wersts from the new town of Sackmara. That afternoon, at 4 o'clock, the 3 Cossacks who had been sent off returned and reported that Lieutenant Lekin had left with his horses and Cossacks and had gone by land to the town of Jaick. As for Lieutenant Karamsin, though, they had no idea where he was staying. Having completely ruined his uniform, his horse and likewise my horse in the course of the journey through his drunkenness, he appears to have left the town, and consequently they thought he must have lost his way in the steppe or wilderness. However, with regard to Ensign Schokoloff, the latter had also left on the 15th *huius* with the unfortunate ill soldiers in 3 chaloupes. Here, I showed the Lieutenant-Colonel a place that was about 2 wersts in diameter, and a peninsula, formed with the assistance of the River Jaick, and which [84] was amazingly suitable for a fort. At 6 o'clock we set out again, and since we had now had only 4 oars on our tied-together barges, we cooked on land that night, and ate, and rowed by day and night, though we did get some sleep, after

153 The Raskolniki were schismatics, dissidents from the established Church in Russia. Sometimes known as Old Believers, they wanted to keep Slavonic customary rituals and texts in the face of the 1654 reforms of Nikon, Patriarch of Moscow, and of Peter the Great. Initially persecuted, many became fugitives or settled abroad. The group split into a branch with a priesthood, and one without, then into sects (e.g. *stranniki*, wanderers, or *molchalniki*, mutes) and included non-conformists and fugitives from various social classes (online Catholic Encyclopaedia; Hughes 2002, p.7 and *passim*). The group Castle comes across (see further) seem to be of this latter type.
Prayer 5, Matt. Ch II.

which two more oars were added, so we cooked on land and ate at noon, rowing by day and night, whereby we frequently came to rest on sand.

On the 20th we encountered low land and oak woods. A Roskolschik man followed us in a barge; these Roskolschiks are Russian serfs who have run away and live in the wilderness, and are deemed to be settlers, and they cultivate little cabbage and beet plots on their settlements, while feeding themselves by catching fish, which are found in far greater numbers in the Jaick, than anywhere else in the world. On the Sackmara side, we passed 2 little rivulets, and we frequently encountered sandbanks and were much impeded by old trees.

On the 21st we met the 3 chaloupes with the ill soldiers and came into land, in order to cook our food. The under-officer with these ill soldiers told us how they had seen a fellow on horseback on the 19th, who had called out to them for 2 hours, telling them to put in to land, because his people wished to converse with them.

1736
(September
21)
[85] So, our people had got a Kalmuck interpreter to enquire as to what sort of people they were? Whereupon they had replied that they were Mayti[154] people, indeed Kyrgyz, who wished to engage in commerce with them, since they could see that the Russians had so much red cloth. When our people replied that these were the soldiers' coats, and were not for trading, the Kyrgyz present on the land were not satisfied with this, and made further demands, saying that since our people did not wish to come to them, they would simply indicate a place where they could come to our people, and that they supposed the Russians had abandoned Orenburg, and consequently wished to be informed as to whether the Lieutenant Colonel was already ahead, or whether he would come after. Now, since our officer and soldiers had grown irritated by these frequent demands, they replied that they were soldiers, and nothing other than blows were to be had from them, whereupon these Kyrgyz robbers started firing with their long firearms, and inflicted four wounds on two Russian soldiers. Now, our fellows were not asleep and

---

154 Possibly a (bandit?) clan name (cf. Matai?, Zimanov 2008, pp.108-09).

would have dearly liked to fire back, but instead were obliged, in view of the fact that the Kyrgyz were on a high bank while our soldiers [86] were floating on the water and did not have a clear line of fire, to make for the opposite shore and land. Under these circumstances, the robbers called out that they were expecting a further 400 men of their company, whereupon our chaps replied that it would be a pleasure. Although they called to them, saying through our interpreter, that they were subjects of Your Imperial Majesty, and that consequently, it was not necessary to engage in such hostilities, the Kyrgyz robbers merely replied mockingly that they had udders for guns, whereupon our side fired a fierce round at them. On the Russian side, Ensign Schokoloff and a soldier had stayed behind, but a grenadier who had lain behind a stone on land, and fired steadily at them, had his legs shot to bits. Now, after these robbers had spent 4 hours disturbing the Russians, and had finally quitted our people, we were left with 2 dead and 3 wounded.

1736 (September 21)

For our part, we could not know how many of the robbers had been wounded or killed by shooting, because they had appeared to be only 10 men. The under officer reported how the robbers had shot very accurately, because they had lain on the ground while firing, and that [87] their guns, for all that they had no flint-locks, were 2 to 3 arsines long and could fire a very long way. In this area, we subsequently passed many sandbanks and encountered many trees that were floating in the water.

1736 (September 21, 22, 23)

On the 22nd, we saw many fishermen coming up with wooden poles, who reported that they were 6 to 7 days into their journey from Sackmara and intended to reach the town of Jaick. In this area live many Roskolshiks, and red beets were brought to me from all over, which were amazingly large and yet yellow and firm inside. That night we passed many vessels, which were going to Orenburg, and at midnight we passed the confluence of the River Yleck on the Kyrgyz side. Three days' journey up this river is where the mineral salt is extracted, which is exceedingly good, and has the virtue that every time a piece is broken off, it increases by so much again.[155] Women and children gather sloes and berries up to this point. Otherwise, this land is wilderness and uninhabited, since if people were to go there, they would encounter these horrid Kyrgyz and Bashkir robbers.

On the 23rd *dito*, we passed along a peaceful bank, which sported a yellow clay, and the weather was rainy today. We also met many people from the town of Jaick, who were travelling from Sackmara to Orenburg with brandy [88] and salt fish, and otherwise, there is not much timber in this region.

*1736
(September
23, 24, 25)*

On the 24th we hailed the advance guards of the town of Jaick at a very early hour, and then passed by many chalky mountains on the Kyrgyz side, and by midnight we had covered a good distance along the River Jaick and when we were 10 wersts from the town the soldiers put on clean clothing; there were many strange plants to be found along the river Jaick. On the 25th we arrived in the town of Jaick[156] at 8 o'clock, and here I had to

---

155 The rock salt quarry of Iletsk was one of the richest and purest salt producing centres developed in the region during the eighteenth century. In the 1770s it replaced that of Lake Elton in output and quality. Other salt-producing centres were the Caspian, Perm province, the White Sea region, western and eastern Siberia. Edicts of 1753 and 1754 proclaimed that salt from Iletsk, which had previously been free for the inhabitants and workers of the local fortresses, should be bought from the Treasury at the state price of 35 kopecks a *pud* (c. 16.38 kg), and that the salt, which was stored in magazines in Orenburg and locally under guard, was to supply the area. Extracting and bringing in the salt to Orenburg drove the price up to 60 kopecks a *pud*. The salt industry, state-owned and private, was plagued by transportation costs, shortage of labour and fuel and the necessity of storage. State prices per *pud* varied accordingly, and in the eighteenth century ranged from 3-60 plus kopecks per *pud* (less for fisheries) rising to 1 rouble by the early nineteenth century (Rychkov, *Topografiia*, pp.264/294-97); Smith and Christian 1984, pp.181-88 and Kahan 1985, Table 3.20, p.9, are still valid sources.

156 Yaik township (Uralsk from 1775) was the administrative centre of the Yaik Cossack host. It was founded in the late sixteenth century (according to their own traditions, recorded by Rychkov) by Don Cossacks raiding the Caspian, joined by Volga Cossacks, Tatars, fugitives and other local peoples. By the early seventeenth century, they were autonomous. Their own tradition also asserts that they were granted possession of parts of the Yaik river by Tsar Michael (1613-45) in return for frontier duties and taking part in campaigns. This assertion is not proven. Cossack society was religious and conservative, believing in autonomy

unload my things myself, because the soldiers were forbidden to assist me in return for a tip. The officers passed the time smoking tobacco, and took pleasure in watching me at my work. That day, everyone in our suite was very pleased and content after their unpleasant experience. On account of the excessive movement and rapid flow of the River Jaick, I thought that we had put back 1200 wersts on it, and I complained that I would not be able to put this river down on paper, because my compass had been spoiled, many of my books were entirely wet, and many other things had been ruined or lost. For its part, the town lies on a peninsula in the River Jaick and is surrounded by wooden bulwarks and fitted with Spanish reuter (carriage guns?), and also has a fair number of iron canon. Its inhabitants consist [89] of 3500 men, who had previously been Danube Cossacks, but are now called Jaick

*1736
(September
25)*

with regards to fighting, electing their own leaders and settling disputes. The Yaik Cossacks began to be severely regulated and mobilized by Peter the Great, and were placed directly under the command of the College of Foreign Affairs and later the War Office. Their rights to select their own atamans and elders were taken away from them. This, as well as a dislike of new settlers, resulted in a tense and ambivalent relationship with the government and some of their leaders, leading to lack of communication and/or deliberate obstruction or disobedience (cf. Tevkelev, *Diary* 1731-33, p.124), and eventually culminating in the Pugachev rebellion of 1771. The Cossacks' interaction with the local population was also volatile: there were reciprocal raids by and on Kazakhs, Bashkirs and Kalmyks, disputes over fishing rights, but also local trading (Tevkelev, *Diary* 1731-33, pp.123, 155; Demidova 2002 e.g. no. 79). Yaik was nevertheless crucial during the Bashkir rebellion as a centre of troops, communication and provisions (Demidova 2002, e.g. no. 181). Numbers needed to quell the rebellion meant that runaway serfs, exiles and converts from various races were recruited and registered as Cossacks. A census of 1723 gives a number of serving Cossacks as between 3200 and 3600. By 1748, the Cossacks were divided into seven regiments, with a total of 3572, including atamans and other ranks. Castle's figure tallies with this number. Rychkov describes the town as having four churches, a cathedral under construction, narrow roads and well defended with a double fence and ditch. An old town had been built along an old branch of the Yaik. The Cossacks' main livelihood was fishing, with some local trade (Rychkov, *Topografiia* pp. 60/420-81/441; Pallas, *op. cit.* Vol. 1 see below; Donnelly, *op. cit.* pp.31-32 and *passim*; Sokol 1987; Barrett 1999; Malikov 2011, and review by Penati 2012, the last two for other Cossack hosts, but with related problems).

Cossacks, although they have retained their Danube Cossack law, which is not written down, but consists remarkably enough of various prerogatives, according to which they can instantly form a circle in the market place, and thereby immediately condemn a wrongdoer without any lengthy hearings, and oblige him to pay a penalty. Otherwise, these inhabitants live entirely in the wilderness without the slightest agriculture, because they are surrounded by bands of Bashkirs, Kyrgyz and Kalmuck robbers; however, since the River Jaick has an abundance of the most delicious fish in the world, the inhabitants live from fishing, isinglass and caviar, or iskray.[157] With regard to this matter I cannot refrain from providing a more precise account of the last two, which are the objects of so a great commerce in the world, and about how they are prepared. Accordingly, with regard to the isinglass, it may be observed that they are found in fish, namely beluja, and also sewruja and assetrina, which are fairly similar to sturgeon, since like these, when their innards are removed, these fish, as is also the case with the smallest herrings, have a white skin located right by the spine, which, when removed, and halfway dried [90] and the very thin skin that lies on it is subsequently rubbed off and removed by hand, and is then, depending on the nature of the fish, it is rolled up just like the isinglass that is sold in Germany and other places, but with this difference, that the isinglass that is taken from assetrinas is much better than that belujas or sewrujas. With regard to caviar, or ikray, it is taken from all three of these fishes, but the very best comes from assetrinas, and this is how they proceed: the roe is rubbed through a spacious sieve, without crushing the little eggs, which removes the fatty skin that they rest on, after which, once a sufficient quantity has been obtained, they are covered with salt, by which means the caviar is ready in four hours time. However, since it does not keep for long, and can only be exported in the wintertime in Russia, and is eaten chilled, the inhabitants make pressed caviar, which is far more salty, and pack it into barrels or into the stomachs of these fish, and then

1736
(September 25)

---

157 *Ikra* (Russian for caviar, roe). See Pallas, *op. cit.* Vol.1 pp. 448-58 for the Yaik Cossacks' extremely efficient and well regulated fishing practices, types of fish caught in the Yaik and resulting trade.

frequently export them to Italy, Germany and other places. The fish are caught in late autumn for this purpose, and indeed in such quantities that they can frequently be pulled out of the water with boat hooks, whereby each Cossack who [91] takes part in the catch receives an equal portion, so that no one receives a greater share than another, on pain of death. They obtain the salt for this iskray or caviar from a lake which lies in the wilderness, at 12 days' journey from Jaick, and where the salt can be found floating like ice.

On the 28th all the members of our suite were ill and sleepy on account of all the exertions they had undergone, so we did not undertake anything in particular. Today, a canon was fired to warn those in the fields that they had spied people, and this signal was given every time people were spied in the distance. That evening a Kalmuck girl and boy aged 13 years came to us, having both run away from the Kyrgyz, and they brought news that the Kyrgyz were not far away.

On the 29th *huius*, a canon was fired yet again, the Beybeck having arrived with the Kyrgyz that he still had with him, and bringing a Bashkir man called Rubeck with him, he being the first of those whom Colonel Teffkeleff had sent during the previous Spring from Siberia to the Kontaisch[158] of the Kalmucks, and subsequently to Abul Geier Khan, and who had been ordered to proceed from there to the State Councillor Iwan Kiriloff. Here, I underwent a strange turn of events, since the State Councillor

---

158 *Kontaisha* was a title given by the Russians to the ruler of the Jungars (an Oirat tribe), Galdan-Tseren (1671-1745/6) (Perdue 2005, p.210, and *passim*).The title was derived from that of Mongolian crown princes (Hong taiji, Khong Tayiji). It was also the name of the Emperor Abachai (1592-1643) of the Qing Dynasty. In the first half of the eighteenth century Jungar territory stretched approximately east from Lakes Balkhash and Issiqul to the Qing Empire. Their 'empire' was profitable due to the transit trade between Russia and China, and the tribute of conquered lands. They were responsible for raids which deprived the Kazakhs of Tashkent, Turkestan and Sayram from the late seventeenth century onwards and precipitated the Kazakh hordes to move south and west in the 1720s, and in part to seek cooperation with the Russians (see Introduction). Animosity, mutual raids and parleys continued between the Kazakhs and the Jungars until the Qing conquest of Jungaria in 1755-57.

[92] had given me a sealed order to take to Orenburg, whose contents stated that I should be provided with as many horses as I required, and I had given this order to the Commandant on arriving in Orenburg, but, when I asked quite unsuspectingly when would I get my horses? the Lieutenant-Colonel's answer was that he had no orders to that effect! Whereupon I was once again tacitly obliged to hire five horses with my own money.

On the 2nd Karamsin, the other, supposedly lost, Lieutenant, turned up on a barge, which he was rowing himself, dressed in a linen smock, quite alone; he claimed that he had stayed behind a bit because his horse had fallen and he had been obliged to follow after with this barge.

On the 3rd Lieutenant-Colonel Tschmaduroff arrived in the afternoon with a commando of 140 men and I requested permission to remain another day, which he also granted.

On the 4th I left the town of Jaick, and caught up with the Lieutenant-Colonel by the River Tschagan,[159] since this river flows into the Jaick near the town of Jaick. The way to this place

from the town of Jaick runs through empty wilderness, and [93] there is no timber, and not a single house or village where people might live, to be found there.

On the 6th we encountered 200 Cossacks who had been billeted onto their homeland. It was a very merry journey, since our people had plenty to drink. I observed the following little rivulets during this journey 1) the Bresnuscha, or dirty one, which flows into the Sollona, 2) the Sollona, which flows into the Tschagan, and 3) the Tschagan, which aforesaid river flows into the Jaick. On the way, I was beset about by almost all the Kyrgyz, because the Lieutenant-Colonel was accusing them of being the very ones who, according to the under-officer's report of the 21st *dito*, had attacked those ill soldiers of ours who had been sent to Orenburg on 3 vessels, and he would not give them any food. However, given that this was a groundless accusation, and that the Beybeck, who had conducted me to Orenburg and back again, had assured me of the opposite on his arrival in the town of Jaick

---

159 River Chagan.

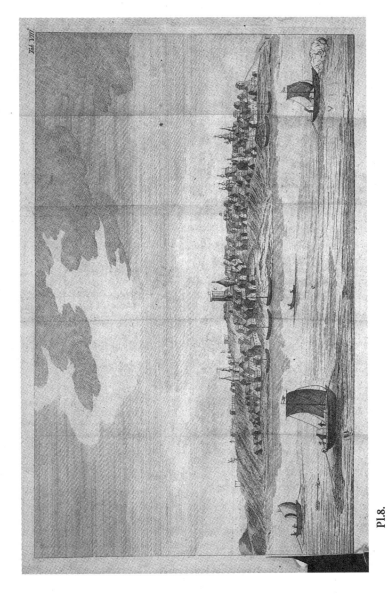

Pl.8.
A view of Samara on the *Volga*.

on 29th September, and that these people had placed their trust in me, and were seeking refuge with me, I had to give them brandy, meat and bread.

On the 9th we passed the Otschensirt mountain,[160] which has a smooth plain alongside it, in front of the mountain, where the above-mentioned rivers flow into the Jaick, but on the other side

1736 [94] of the mountain, the rivers Irdisch, Karuluck and Motscha[161]
(October 9, flow into the Volga, and thus these rivers all have their origins in
13, 14, 16) the above-mentioned mountain.

On the 13th we crossed the River Samara, which flows into the Volga near the town of Samara, and the distance between the towns of Jaick and Samara is 260 wersts, and on arriving in Samara I had to seek some quarters. I made enquiries as to whether any of my countrymen were to be found, and met with a Captain of the Navy called Elton,[162] who was an Englishman and a member of our expedition, along with an English merchant called Hogg.[163]

---

160 This name is a compilation of the Russian *ochen* (many) and Turkic *sirt* (ridge), i.e. the Many Ridged mountain, possibly the same as the Siny Syrt (or Blue Ridge), the source of the Mocha river.

161 Rivers Irghiz, Kutluk ?, and Mocha (see Hanway Vol.1, Map 1, p.14 for the latter).

162 John Elton, sea captain and merchant (d.1751). Elton is chiefly known as one of the chief promoters of British trade with Persia via Central Asia and for having worked for Nadir Shah, the Persian Shah. He was first enrolled as a captain and surveyor in the Orenburg expedition. This involved the potential exploration and mapping of the Aral Sea (which could not be accomplished because of the Bashkir rebellion), helping construct Orenburg, and mapping the Yaik, Kama, Belya and parts of the Volga rivers (cf. Lake Elton, the salt lake named after him). In the course of this work he realized the potential of trading with Persia via Central Asia, and, leaving Russian service, he attempted to visit Khiva and Bokhara with the Scot Mungo Graeme in 1739 (Hanway, Vol.1 1753, pp.14-16; Spilman 1742; Rychkov, *Istoriia*, pp.28, 35, 41; Demidova 2002, no. 53, p.107; RGADA f.248 kn.1164 l. 525 para. 12; kn. 1164 l. 556, courtesy of TsGARKaz; Teissier 2011; Searight DNB). Elton accepted an offer from the Persian Nadir Shah to become his chief ship builder on the Caspian in 1741. This engagement was greatly disapproved of by both the British and the Russians, and led to a suspension of British trade on the Caspian. Elton settled in Resht, and following Nadir Shah's death in 1747, was murdered there in 1751(Hanway 1753 is a major source for Elton and the story of British attempts to trade with Persia via Russia; Searight 2004; Teissier 2011).

163 Hogg traded in Russia in the 1730s and 1740s, where he seems to have

---

They were both extremely pleased to meet me, and I was able to restore my limbs, which were entirely worn out as a result of my sufferings, chagrin, and discontent.

On the 14th Captain Elton had a very disagreeable encounter with a Lieutenant from Orenburg called Paltoff, whereby the latter attempted in a drunken manner to drive the former out of his own house that he had built.

On the 16th I was invited by a Russian Knias, who was married to the daughter of General Tschernischoff and was called Beloselsky,[164] as his guest, and was entertained very well by him. On this occasion he asked me about Orenburg and my travels. [95] This cavalier treated me with greater honour than I had hitherto experienced from various people in the course of my travels, and so I am very grateful to him on this account.

On the 21st I took my leave of Lieutenant-Colonel Tschmaduroff, whereby Captain Elton, and the merchant Hogg, and a German *chirurgus* called Wachtler accompanied me for 6 wersts, and I arrived in Krasnojar[165] at the next midday, which lies at 43 wersts distance from Samara, and where is found the main barracks of the Sakamsky[166] line against the Bashkirs, which

1736 (October 16, 21, 23, 24, 25)

been part of George Napier's circle of merchants in St. Petersburg. He travelled on an exploratory trading mission to Khiva and Bukhara with George Thompson in 1740 (Hanway, Vol.1 1753, pp.345-57; *K-R Otnoscheniia* no. 88 (their 1742 report in Russian; also RGADA fonds 1183; 1191, courtesy of TsGARKaz). He appears to have had a scheme in c. 1738-39 to make camel hair (obtained very cheaply in Orenburg) a British trade import (LMA, Ms. 11741/6, Russia Company Minute Book 1734-56, pp.129, 150).

164 Naval-Lieutenant Prince Beloselskii. He became one of the commanders of the Bashkir and Orenburg Commissions after Tatischev left this post in 1739 (Rychkov, *Istoriia*, pp.37, 42; Donnelly *op. cit.* p.119).

165 Krasni Yar, a fort on the second Trans-Kama line, on the Sok, to the north-east of Samara (Hanway, Vol.1, 1753, Pl.1, and see below).

166 The second major Zakamsk or Trans-Kama line built to control the Bashkirs. The first properly fortified line ran from the Volga, west of Samara, along the Cheremsan north-east to Menzelinsk and was built in the mid-seventeenth century (Donnelly *op. cit.* p.21). The second, just east of Samara, running north-east and joining the old line at the Kichui river in the Kazan district, was built in the 1730s. It became part of the Orenburg fortified line in the mid-eighteenth century (*IKRI* 3, p.155). See Donnelly *op. cit.* Appendix for a list of the main forts along the Orenburg line compiled in the mid-eighteenth century (from Rychkov,

is 400 wersts long and has a fort every 15 wersts. On this journey, I also passed a bridge over the River Sock, near Krasnojar, which is of medium size.

On the 23rd *huius* I crossed a little river called Musoia.

On the 24th I passed the village of Kesan across the River Birla, which is also of medium size. That afternoon, we crossed over the River Scheremtzscham,[167] which is large and fast, by means of a ferry.

On the 25th I crossed the little River Beriskla near the town of Beriklinskey,[168] which flows into the River Tscheremtzschan, and this town is inhabited solely by retired country militia. [96]

On the 26th I arrived in the Schuwasisch[169] village of Kamajur, and also crossed the little River Kamajur.

On the 27th I set across the Volga in a *struse*,[170] and fortunately met with the State Councillor, Iwan Kiriloff, who was located in Sinbirsky, 180 wersts from Samara.

My arrival pleased him exceedingly, once I had shown him all the samples of stones, ores and other *curiosis* that I had found. It is worth taking the trouble to provide a short description of only those stones[171] that I had brought from my Kyrgyz and Bashkiri

1736
(October 26, 27)

IKRI 4, pp.220-21). For contemporary map see Hanway, Vol.1,1753 Pl.1).

167 River Cheremsan.

168 Biliarsk, a fort on the Trans-Kama line.

169 The Chuvash, an ethnic group of probably Turkic origin (specifically from the Volga Bulgars, according to some Chuvash traditions, Frank 1998, pp.6-7, 165, 185-86, my thanks to Alexander Morrison for pointing this out), centred in the Nizhny Novgorod and Kazan areas. They originally paid tribute to the Khanate of Kazan and came under Russian control from the mid-sixteenth century onwards, when they were subjected to forced conversion to Christianity from their native animism. In the eighteenth century they were partly relocated to Bashkiria, where they worked as *teptiars* (farmers paying rent) (Kappeler 2001, pp.25, 40). For the Chuvash in the Kazan and Volga areas as seen by eighteenth-century British travellers, see Teissier 2011, pp.20, 49-51.

170 A river craft (Sarah Tolley).

171 In returning to one of his primary objections regarding his treatment by Kirilov, Castle draws attention to the different types of stones he collected on his travels. This variety is corroborated by Rychkov who lists the great number of stones and minerals found in the Urals (Rychkov, *Topografiia*, pp.248/278-252/282). Stones for expensive buildings and the luxury decorative market were marble, alabaster, jasper and agates of

travels and which Iwan Kiriloff gradually took from me.

1) A noble white translucent stone weighing 62 pounds, which is supposed to be sent to Your Imperial Majesty from Samara.

2) A yellow translucent stone, as large as a walnut, which Your Imperial Majesty should also be presented by the State Councillor himself.

3) A green translucent stone, darker than an emerald, and not too hard.

4) A piece of agate of extraordinary beauty, to which Iwan Kiriloff had given a *façon* like a heart, and which Your Imperial Majesty has also received. [97]

5) A green lapis which has no equal, and which Iwan Kiriloff also demanded of me.

Now, without extolling my own part, the work of finding these noble and very beautiful stones did involve considerable pains, and indeed, pleasure, pain and experience were required on my part in order to seek them in the appropriate places; no wonder then, that the State Councillor took pleasure in them, as he did in all the other benefits that I secured from the Kyrgyz people, and I do not know why he subsequently failed to fulfil his promise to send me to St Petersburg together with the account of my report. In the meantime, on my aforesaid arrival there, I met with a significant setback, in that the State Councillor presented me with a letter, addressed to him by my late father. I could scarcely wait to view its contents, and to my regret was obliged to read that my father, and indeed my whole acquaintance, had been grieving for me for half a year, having to their very great sorrow received the news that I had had been cut down by hostile

---

various colours. Luxury market stones were assessed by experts from St. Petersburg, and polished and worked on at the Peterhof cutting factory established in 1721. Local workshops were also established: at the site of the future Ekaterinburg (1723), at Isetsk (1730s), at Orsk in the 1730s. In 1751 a hard stone cutting factory (jasper and agate) was established in 1751. By 1752 there were three factories at the Ekaterinburg works (including one for faceting and polishing) and one nearby at Siversky. The true industrial development of the Ural stone cutting industry however occurred after Catherine IInd's 1765 edict on the prospection of stones (Chistyakova 2007, pp.97-98).

1736
(October 27)

Bashkirs in the Oral Mountains[172] in the month of March, and that consequently my possessions and outstanding wages had been committed to the then assessor and present Councillor Heintzelmann, and he had expressly requested authorization [98] to have them extradited. Now, since the State Councillor was able to observe the contrary in my own living person, he pointed out to me in jest, that this might well be indicative of a long life. Whereupon his then stepfather, called Peter Stepanitz Bachmetoff,[173] who was present, could not sufficiently express his amazement at my previous undertaking, and asked me: what I was thinking of in undertaking such dangerous and desperate journeys, and furthermore of my own free will and at my own expense? Whereupon I simply replied that I owed God only one death, and could desire no more glorious one than in the service of Your Imperial Majesty, and that the circumstance whereby I did not fear death, and was not unduly attached to money, had supplied the requisite courage. Some time after my arrival, I reminded State Councillor Iwan Kiriloff of his promise to me, namely to send me with my reports and found objects to Your Imperial Majesty in St Petersburg. But he did not pay much attention to my reminder, and simply urged me to be patient and promised to take care of me. However, by then I felt that this care was being stretched pretty thin, and that the said State Councillor

1736
(October 27,
December
27)

was seeking [99] to retain me, on the pretext of having no money, and permitting my outstanding wages to be paid out gradually in small amounts, and only in sufficient quantity to allow me to live from hand to mouth, whereby I grew annoyed, because I clearly saw that all his other servants were receiving their wages in full; for instance, under these circumstances, the said State Councillor was allowing the apothecary, the surgeon and other

---

172 Ural mountains.
173 Peter Bakhmetev, Kirilov's father-in-law, and among the first to leave with the Orenburg expedition. He was responsible for building Krasnosamarsk and Krasnoborsk forts along the Samara river and was in charge of the Orenburg project (between Kirilov and Tatischev) in 1737. He was promoted from Naval Lieutenant to Lieutenant-Colonel and involved in the relocation of Orenburg to Krasnaia Gora in 1737 (Rychkov, *Istoriia*, pp.14, 25, 26, 29; Donnelly *op. cit.* p.202).

necessary persons to go to Moscow almost daily, but when I asked for permission to go there and see my old father again, the State Councillor would not hear of it, and merely advised me once again to be patient. Since it was now clear to me that he would neither send me to St Petersburg, nor allow me to visit my father in Moscow, and wished to keep me within bounds by the little stratagem of allowing me out of his extraordinary graciousness to be paid my outstanding wages every now and then, I summoned my brother from Moscow, who arrived on 27th December and was very well received by the State Councillor, who praised my achievements in particular to him. After my said brother had stayed with me a few days, I sent him on my behalf [100] on the 3rd Jan. to St Petersburg, where he reported to the High Cabinet as already stated. After my brother had ridden off, I requested on the 14th *dito* my outstanding wages and my decommission, which the State Councillor was, however, very angry about. He started to express his anger more strongly when he was informed that I had sent my brother to St Petersburg on my affairs, about which he asked me to tell him the truth, and as I could not deny this nor wished to, so I fell wholly into disfavour with him and matters proceeded as follows, in that he not only threatened to send me elsewhere as soon as possible but, without heeding my request in the slightest, he also departed from Sinbirsky and indeed went to Samara, leaving me behind on my own, since I had in the meantime prepared my departure and, scarcely had I finished this task, when on the 13th March I received a letter from the State Councillor, in which he ordered me to proceed to Samara, because he had now received his orders from the Cabinet. I lost no time in obeying his order, and set off, after leaving my people and my superfluous baggage in my Sinbirsky quarters, and travelled to [101] Samara that every evening at my own expense, and when I was 10 wersts from Sinbirsky, I suffered a misfortune, in that my Iswoschick,[174] who was a little boy, conducted me into the river Volga which was iced over, and as a result I lost almost everything I had with me, and though I was able to save my life in my hour of

(January 3, 14, March 13) Anno 1737

1736 (March 13, 16, 17, 22)

---

174 *Ivozchik*: a driver, carrier.
Verse 3, Matt. Ch. II.

---

need, I lacked for every necessity.

On the 16th *dito* I arrived in Samara, and presented myself to the State Councillor.

On the 17th I presented my finished work to the State Councillor, which I had packed in a wooden case for journey and had fortunately succeeded in saving by swimming, and thereby demanded my outstanding wages and my decommission, which I was once again assured of, but did not receive either of these.

On the 22nd Iwan Kiriloff sent Peter Iwanewitz Ritzkoff,[175] his former bookkeeper and acting secretary, to me, to persuade me to travel as an envoy to India[176] with an Indian merchant called Manwari, whereby I was promised 800 roubles for the year, and

---

175 Peter Ivan Rychkov (1712-77) served in various capacities in the Orenburg region (e.g. secretary of the Orenburg Commission, provincial chancellor, director of the Salt Office) but is chiefly known for his geographical, historical and ethnological writings, such as the *Istoriia Orenburgskaia* (1759; 2nd edition 1816) and *Topografiia Orenburgskaia* (1762) and see *IKRI* 4, pp.195-265, his writings on the Kazakhs. These are fundamental sources for the region and history of this period. (Ovchinnikov, *MERSH* 1983, pp.238-39; *IKRI* 3, 4 *passim*).

176 Embassies from Moscow to Persia with a view to the Indian trade antedate Ivan IV and the conquest of Kazan (1552) (cf. the merchant Afanasi Nikitin's diary 1466-72; Major 1857, translation). Investing in trade with India was promoted under Peter the Great who encouraged merchants to trade within Russia (Dale 2002, and review Subrahmayan 1995; for Indian traders in eighteenth-century Astrakhan see Teissier 2011 pp.72-77) and sent investigative missions (e.g. Tevkelev's 1716, aborted). An account by the Indian merchant Maravi Baraev (Russianized surname) from 1735 summarizes the advantages and problems of Indian trade with Russia. He lists the four possible trade routes from Delhi: from Kandahar to Gilan via the Caspian to Astrakhan; from Delhi to Kabul through Bukhara and Khiva to Astrakhan, by land or via the Caspian; via the coast to Persia, then inland to Gilan; or inland via Qalat, Kirman, on to Isfahan and Gilan. Baraev complains of the duties the merchants have to pay, which have severely impeded this trade. He advocates free trade via Bukhara as the best option. He then praises the Indian climate and its richness, and finally lists the articles of trade. From India: diamonds, rubies, *lal* stone (see note 23 n.50); spices (e.g. cardamon, cloves, nutmeg, cinnamon, pepper, ginger, mace; materials such as silk, linens, muslins, belts). The trade from Russia included seeds, canvas, mirrors, needles and clocks (Dobromyslov 1900, pp.47-49). Peter the Great's vision of copious Indian trade ended in failure due to several factors: competition from the Armenians, political events and restrictions within Russia (Dale 2002; Teissier 2011, *passim*).

---

that 500 roubles for the expenses I had accumulated with the Kyrgyz would be paid immediately. This offer would have been very acceptable to me, given my current shortage of money, but because I saw that this summa did not accord with [102] my *sans vanité* deserts, and that Iwan Kiriloff's promised commitments did not add up, I made my politest excuses.

1736 (March 22, 23, April 17)

On the 23rd the State Councillor summoned me and showed me the petition that my brother had been ordered to submit to the High Cabinet on behalf of my person, but said that I had not needed to do this, in that I should simply have been patient, but that he was not angry with me on this account, and, because I loved travelling, I really should go on the India tour, but I excused myself, citing my many previous difficulties, and asked yet again for my outstanding wages and my decommission. Now, since the State Councillor was continuously ill after this, and finally died on 17 April,[177] I then handed Commander Teffkeleff and Lieutenant-Colonel Bachmetoff various *donoschenies*,[178] with regard to my outstanding wages and decommission, given that I was living in the greatest poverty and even had to beg linen of my good friends, on account of having left my baggage behind in Sinbirski; but they did not wish to grant me these two *desideria*, under the pretext that if they were to give me money, I would immediately leave for St Petersburg. And when I assured them that I [103] had no desire to quit without my decommission, they did not trust me, but insisted that if only I had enough money to travel, I would not ask for decommission so much and would get my money in St Petersburg. The result of all this was that I was obliged to live in the greatest misery, and had to submit many petitions on account of my small reward for suffering so much trouble and need, so they finally tried to get rid of me, and on 12th June I received a note of credit for 345 roubles 15 kopecks from Colonel Teffkeleff and Lieutenant-Colonel Bachmetoff on the Ensign Kusnitzoff, who was coming from Catharinenburg[179] with

1736 (April 17, June 12, 14, 17)

177 14th of April, according to Rychkov, *Topografiia*, p.28.
178 Russian *donesenie*: reports.
179 Ekaterinburg was founded by Tatischev with the assistance of Gmelin in 1723 as a fortress and iron-works. It was the headquarters of Tatischev

money and was supposed to pass through Sinbirsky. It was clear to me that I now had to ride back to Sinbirsky in order to raise the money there, and would be able to take advantage of the baggage I had left there and this note of credit, so I simply gave thanks to God, that I would be able to find my own linen in Sinbirsky, and so rode off, in hunger, care and need.

On the 14th *Iunii*, with no further misadventure, I travelled to Sinbirsky, and on the 17th *dito* arrived there safely during the night.

Scarcely had I spent one night there in peaceful sleep, when
1736 very early in the morning, [104] 1736 (June 18) on the 18th I
(June 18) was obliged to undergo a new disturbance, *justement* when I had opened my coffer in my old assigned quarters, and had unpacked my best things and was examining them, I was attacked by a Sergeant with 16 men on the orders of the local Chief of Police Iwan Iwowitz Schukoff,[180] and, along with my people, with my head uncovered and clothed in a shirt, having been given a vigorous drubbing, I was conducted to the police station in a bloodied state with a torn shirt, through the whole town, where more than 1000 people saw me. I had to stand there in front of the police station as a public spectacle for more than 2 hours until the order came from the Chief of Police about what to do with me, whereupon my people were allowed into the police station. Finally, I was brought to the Chief of Police himself, who was sitting at table with 2 or 3 others, and he asked me laughing whether my people and I had passports? I reacted by saying that he knew me, and had shown me my quarters, including the fact that I had a note of credit to receive money here. Given that while I was under guard, my quarters had in the meantime been left with doors and widows wide open, he was *gracieux* enough to offer to set a guard over my quarters, so that nothing should be stolen from me. Since he was now about to dismiss me in this
1736 manner, [105] and send me home, I pointed out clearly that I had
(June 18) no intention of prostituting myself any longer and would not go home in my current state of dress. Finally, he allowed me to send

---

when he managed the Urals (1734-37, see n.186).
180 Ivan Ivanovich Shukov.

a boy to fetch my clothes but nothing else, which the guard who had been sent there would find. As soon as I came away from the Chief of Police I went straight to the same locality where so many thousand people had seen me, to the secretary of the Orenburg expedition André Iwanoff,[181] who was there at the time, and who was *justement* about to set off from there by water to Samara; he was already on the *struse*, about to cast off, when I appeared in that state, bloody and beaten up as I was, in the presence of the Sackmara Ottaman[182] called Castiloff, together with the Mayor of Sinbirsky Wasiley Casleschnikoff,[183] and also the tax-man Petrowitz Cascheloff,[184] and many others besides, who had conducted the Secretary there, and he immediately drafted a report in German for the Orenburg Expedition Chancery, and gave it together with the following letter, of which I still have the original, to the above-mentioned Chief of Police Iwan Iwowitz Schukoff. When I got home, I found that a large part of my best things, [106] jewels and ores, including some of my written notes, the Bashkir journal and the drawings that went with it, had been stolen along with some other things. Although I now sought to secure the appropriate protection from the Orenburg Chancery, I did not receive any reply from the said Chancery, let alone any kind of satisfaction. And though I now attempted to resort to the presiding Woyvode[185] in *loco* whose name was Iwan Iwanewitz Nemkoff, and submitted 6 Schelebitten or petitions to him within 44 days, asking him to investigate the causes of these terrible and more than Tartar-like proceedings, with a view to recovering my property, I was unable to secure any helpful measures from him either and what's more, was evicted from my previous quarters, to which I was contractually entitled by order of Your Imperial Majesty, four times with the greatest *solennité* by order of this Woyvode. When this happened, I had to wait for Councillor Tatischoff[186] who would be passing by Sinbirsky on his way down

*1736
(June 18,
August 3)*

181 Andrei Ivanov.
182 Ataman Kastilov.
183 Vasili Kaleshnikov.
184 Peter Petrovich Kashelov.
185 *Voevoda* : the title of a military governor.
186 Vassili Nikitich Tatischev (1686-1750) administrator and governor,

the Volga, and to my good fortune, he landed on the 3rd August, and I complained about my need to him, but the advice he gave me was to suffer the Chief of Police and his [107] subalterns, and wait for Ensign Kusnitzoff to arrive, for whom I was keeping my note of credit, since I would then be able to ride with him to Samara where I would obtain my money and my decommission.

1736
(August 3, 4, 6, 13)

On the 4th *huius* the said Ensign came by water from Catharinenburg but paid me no money, whereupon on the 6th *huius* I travelled with him by water to Samara and as soon I arrived on the 13th I reported to Privy Councillor Tatischoff, and urgently requested payment of my outstanding money and my decommission. It was clear to me from the start that I must seem horribly sinister to the latter, so I made sure that I was frequently seen by the Councillor, whereby I was fortunate in that he became better acquainted with me and possibly found me to be someone

---

chiefly remembered for his historical scholarship and ethnography. His career took off under Peter the Great who put him in charge of developing the Urals mining industry (1720-22). In 1724-26 he was sent on a mission to Sweden to learn about mining and other industries, and to bring back ideas and skilled workmen. In 1730 he administered the Mint. From 1734-37 he administered the Urals, and from 1737-39 he was head of the Orenburg expedition. In 1739-1741 he was head of the Kalmyk Commission, and Governor of Astrakhan from 1741-1745. He was a controversial figure, accused of embezzling funds and bribe taking. He was impeached in 1745 and exiled to Boldino, his country estate. He was pardoned on the eve of his death. He was a serious scholar: the first to compare documentary sources with traditional legends, and to develop instructions and questionnaires for his information gathering in the Urals and Siberia. His great work, *Istoriia Rossiiskaia*, started in the 1720s, was controversial because of his reworkings of material and claims to have used chronicles that were subsequently lost (to show the antiquity of the Slavs and to justify autocratic monarchy). He also published on law and historical geography, and compiled the first Russian encyclopaedic dictionary. Parts of the *Istoriia* were published in 1768 and 1774 by Müller; Part 4 in 1768, Part 5 in the nineteenth century. For complete series see *Istoriia Rossiiskaia*, 7 Vols. Leningrad 1962-68. (Hellie 1984, pp.191-96; Thadeu 1984, pp.196-200; Black 1986, pp.38-39; Semionov 1999, pp.27-35; Toropitsyn 2006 pp.1-3). He was considered difficult but also admired for his learning by British travellers of the eighteenth century (cf. Hanway 1753, Vol.1 pp.117-119; by Cook who worked under him as a doctor when he was Governor of Astrakhan and visited him just before he died (1774, Vol. 2 pp.46-47, 93-94, 146-148, 427-430 and *passim*).

---

quite different to the reports about my person. His kindness to me increased from day to day, and I did not miss any opportunity to establish myself more firmly in his good graces, given that I was all the more fortunate in really benefitting from his mental and other qualities, which included a sufficient and developed knowledge of the *historie, naturalibus* and other *curiosis*, which was all the easier for me, in that he could perfectly understand German and other languages, and knew how to [108] express *1736* himself, which he was then kind enough to do, as well as take me into his house, and show me all honour and kindness. In short, he was my patron, who knew how to draw me to him so that I was truly devoted to him, and allowed myself to be persuaded by him to renew my contract of service, whereby, prior to completing this contract, the full amount of my outstanding wages was paid, and the new contract was made out with an final end date of 1737, and signed. And so, with due regard for this sensible comportment, I lived satisfactorily enough until this contractual year had passed, whereupon, finally, when the year was up, I received an honourable discharge from the said Councillor Tatischoff *sub die* 28th *Iunii* 1739. At this point, I could be reproached with having strayed too far from my Kyrgyz journey by recounting these events, and with having included things that did not pertain to it! As these events have shown only too clearly, how the reward that the State Councillor had so often assigned to me, which had been promised on account of the expenses arising from this journey, which I had actually incurred, and how my property was in part requisitioned and taken, and in part stolen from me during wholly undeserved assaults on me, so I hope [109] that you will pardon all my errors and allow me some discretion, in that what I here present in the spirit of submissive loyalty is only for Your Highness' eyes, who alone need know this matter, in order to graciously examine such things as were contrary to Your Highness' command and prior knowledge on many occasions, which can cause alarm in the most honest and upright minds, and in my case, when, in my enthusiasm to serve the empire loyally, I undertook very dangerous and yet successful enterprises, for which I should have been rewarded, and was instead most extraordinarily beaten and reduced to nothing, and so all this constitutes an essential part of my account, and belongs within this journal, since I was thereby forced to demand my decommission. At the same time, I am extremely desirous of not providing occasion for the opinion that I thereby intend to make a complaint and recognizance about matters which occurred a few years ago, on the contrary, I humbly assert that my intention is simply directed at reporting these things, more out of duty than from private passion, and thereby to provide a greater insight and honestly to serve the Empire in submissive loyalty. However, as I now close this journal, so I hope to do no wrong in adding the following for the sake of greater knowledge of foreign lands, and also to demonstrate my zeal and the keen observations recorded in this journal, [110]

1mo how the Kyrgyz country is shaped, and such further opportunities to benefit from nature's bounty in its waters and other elements as are to be found here.

2do how the inhabitants are formed, their mentality and constitution, also what customs, religious observance and laws they have among themselves and in what manner they are accustomed to extract nature's bounty, and further on their customs with regard to illness, death and burial.

3tio however, by whom and how the nation is ruled or governed in peace and wartime, and what further intentions they have.[187]

First Section

The Kyrgyz-Khazak land borders the Kantaisch[188] Kalmuck land to the east and the Buchars to the South, and to the west the Caspian and the Aral Seas and China, with Siberia and the Bashkir people to the north. And although the climate is generally rather warm, with a generally very mild winter, when one considers that country itself lies too far from the ocean and that there are too

---

187 For the nature and context of this type of categorized observation, added with particular care when Castle was editing his journal in St. Petersburg in the early 1740s, see the Introduction.
188 Kontaisha.

---

few rivers and that a little cold or warm rain falls only every 3 or 4 months, it is not at all fruitful, and consists mainly of wave-like hills [111] which resemble nothing so much as the open sea, in which the waves are still riding after the storm has passed, and the grass in this wilderness grows so sharp that it is capable of slicing such shoes as one may be wearing to walk over it in the course of one day, though it grows no higher than a finger's length, and, along with the many thistles, serves for nothing but feeding the wild horses, goats and camels as best it may, and this is why the inhabitants are constantly obliged to seek good grass for their tame flocks along the rivers and streams. Given that the countryside has a very high yield on account of the snowfall in winter and the rain in spring, so too the precious grass grows in these places, and they permit their cattle to graze there, because they do not stay in one place for longer than the grazing allows, and certainly have no notion about making hay. So, just as the rivers and long gulleys keep flowing, so too the inhabitants keep on the march with their flocks from springtime through summer, always in the direction of Russia as far as Orenburg; then, with the onset of autumn and winter with its wild geese, they turn back towards the Aral Sea. They have no timber, apart from a little woodland that is to be found very occasionally here and there along those rivers. Among the herbs and roots here are *rhapontica*, wild garlic, [112] *serpillum, trifolium,* and a terrible quantity of burnet and Nieswurz, or *helleborum.* There are other herbs to found found in greater quantities, though compiling this *botanica* would require a special person, as my other great endeavours have affected my recollection, which would only corrupt it, and my lack of certainty about their names might harm it, and, given that I found it all too difficult, I have left this task to the successors of the famous Tournefort.[189] Of fruits, nothing is to be found apart from *persico* or bitter almonds and wild cherries, which grow to about 2 to 3

---

189 Joseph Pitton de Tournefort (1656-1708), a French botanist. Castle may not have been aware of Linnaeus's seminal *Systema Naturae,* which came out in 1735 and had a major impact on the field of botany in Russia (cf. e.g. Rowell 1980, pp.15-26). See Shaw 2010 on the utility of the environment in eighteenth-century Russia as reported by S.P. Krasheninnikov and P.I. Rychkov.

hands in height, and are generally burnt every year, along with the grass. There is no cultivation here, and consequently the inhabitants have no knowledge of bread, and they have no tame fowls, since they would not be able to take them with them during their frequent travels. On the other hand, the country is filled with quantities of widespread game, wolves, foxes, wild horses and goats, so that sometimes a whole terrain is covered with them, as mentioned above. There are also occasionally tiger-cats and a great many marmots and badgers. And, as mentioned above *sub die* 6th *Juli* 1736, these wild goats must be Bezoar goats,[190] given that some of these are distinguished [113] from the Bezoar ibex here, as in India, but they are seldom encountered and very small, which I consider this to be due to the fact that the fodder in this country which nourishes the ibex is not like that found in India, and that consequently, with regard to the current instance, we should recall that it is found only in summertime in this country, and that in winter they return to India and Persia, and as a result, grow to a size almost equivalent to that of young deer, only that these have heads that are not dissimilar to those of a horse, though with goats' horns, the latter being very neatly adorned with rings. They have very soft snouts and their cry is like that of ordinary goats. Once they have galloped a little while, they leap into the air, and then resume their course. They also have this peculiarity of sleeping unnaturally deeply during the great heat at midday, which means that they are very often caught alive. Their flesh is extremely delicious to eat, almost like veal, so it is a pity that it is not prepared in the European fashion, with salt and herbs. The coat is similar to that of a deer, and has the same colour, but the hair is rougher. Their eyes are large, round and beautiful, and the upper jaw overhangs the lower one, which is much shorter and hardly visible.

Their hooves are split, as with other goats, [114] and this animal is truly beautiful in its natural state. Now that I have now made sufficient observations about these Bezoar goats, I find that I have equal *curiosité* about the wild horses,[191] and would like to

190 Bezoar goats, see n.115.
191 Judging from Rychkov's and Levshin's descriptions there appear to

Tab. IX

Pl.9.
Wild ibex.

mention that each stallion, depending on his age, will lead 8 to 10 mares, and appoint himself guardian of these mares and their foals, so that if anyone approaches them the mares will remain on the mountain and the stallion will rush down to attack by biting and kicking, and anyone not watching out could easily be hurt by this. Now, if he is knocked down or shot at, he will immediately return to his mares, who, however, will be fully on the alert, and upon his return will retire further into the mountain with him and their foals. However, careful as these creatures are, they are easily duped and caught by the Kyrgyz. For, as soon they encounter a herd of these wild horses while on their travels, the whole company will lower their heads onto their horses, and so dupe the wild horses into thinking that the tame horses are the same type as them. In this way, they surround the wild horses in a devious manner, by throwing themselves from their tame horses, and when they have tied them with their reins to each other, they creep very low along the ground on their hands and feet, [115] behind the hills, on the ground, drawing them behind them and thereby making the wild horses more secure until they are surrounded, and they shoot them with their guns, whereby they often shoot the foals from where they are lying on the ground, and then stand up and shoot the fleeing wild horses, which often produces a considerable bag. As soon as they have killed a foal, it takes only 10 minutes to remove its hide, which

have been different types of 'wild horse' and the degree to which they were domesticated by Kazakhs. Levshin mentions two types, a larger type, the *tarpan* (*equus ferus*) and the smaller *kulan*. They were not so different from the fully domesticated horse except for their heads and a bluish tinge to their coat. He notes that (non semi-domesticated) wild horses were used only for food, portage and medicinally, their hide used to wrap the sick in (*op. cit.* p.73). Rychkov only differentiates the horses by degrees of domestication and notes that they were extremely hardy, handsome and light. They were brought in thousands to the trade fairs of Orenburg and Troisk, and when trained used by the Russian cavalry because they were speedy and unafraid of gun-fire. They could fetch 15-18 roubles each. (Rychkov, *Topografiia*, p.293). Pallas refers to them as semi-domesticated, deliberately bred by stud (op. cit. Vol.1, p.625). Georgi only mentions 'fine horses' ornamented 'almost as their own person' (*op. cit.* Vol.2, p.280). Castle's description points to differences in breed.

they require partly for thongs and partly for clothes, while the horses are looking on. The flesh is immediately cut up into pieces and a portion is given to each man to carry, who hangs it from his horse and often carries it along for 3 or 4 days through very great heat, during which time it will not start to stink. Otherwise, these horses are so fashioned that they have small heads, very lovely eyes and incomparably white teeth, elegant feet and hard hooves, and altogether their size is a sure sign that they must belong to another race. Nevertheless, among these there are others, that are quite heavy-boned and very robust. However, both sorts are extraordinarily nimble and so excessively wild they cannot be tamed in any way, and would rather starve to death. They are variously coloured, being brown [116] black, chequered and other colours too. Otherwise there are also very many wild boar here, which feed on the sweet tree roots or *laquiritia*, and on *persico* or bitter almonds, along the lakes and grow amazingly fat on these, so that they weigh 20 to 30lb, but are not relished by the inhabitants on account of their Mohammedan religion. Here too, there is a terrible quantity of tortoises, which are a great delicacy but are not eaten by the inhabitants either. Of feathered game, little or none is to be found here on account of the lack of woods, apart from partridges and quails among the grasses along the rivers, and many ducks on the lakes, of various sorts, including wild geese, swans, cranes and bustards, who retire here from the cold countries, along with a great many herons of various types and hues. With regard to raptors, one finds the same eagle itself and the bird called pickurt,[192] which, as mentioned above *sub die 22nd Junii 1736*, is twice as strong as an eagle and is used to hunt wild horses and goats, as well as various sorts of hawks, which live off the common hamsters and field mice. However, the Kyrgyz do not shoot or make use of many of these wild creatures, and the tame animals that these inhabitants have, camels, dromedaries, horse and the most valuable sort of sheep, [117] which have crooked noses and long hanging ears like dogs, and instead of a tail have a curtuck, or a very broad lump of fat, which weighs

---

192 See pp.43-4, n.58.

Prayer. 5. Matt. Ch. II

---

more than 20 to 30 pound, and is a great delicacy to eat, as is their flesh, so that English sheep's flesh cannot compare with it. Their tame horses are of a lovely Persian race,[193] and are therefore very speedy and *extraordinair commode* to ride, given that they are trained for this from youth onwards in a skilful way in accordance with the art of equitation, whereby they are lunged using a rope of horse or camel hair and made to run in a circle until they have been trained. When the Kyrgyz wish to go raiding they give their horses little to eat for 2 to 3 days, to make them all the lighter, and when they have grown heated, they give them nothing to drink until they have completely cooled down. Of muscles, snails, *cornu ammonis*, fish, bones and other *curiosis*, which have been turned from wood into stone all over these mountains, one finds an indescribable quantity. The whole country is full of the finest saltpetre, because there are a huge quantity of lakes on which the clear salt lies, but which the inhabitants do not use for food and in any way at all. What nature has concealed in the earth here, I cannot state with certainty because, apart from my [118] fingers and dagger, I had no tools with me for visiting it in depth, and on the other hand, the inhabitants are not at all disposed to inquire into their natural wealth and had no notion of how to inform others about it. All the same, I found iron, copper, and presumably gold and silver and other ores, and since I was not able to analyse them, have given them all to the State Councillor.

Lapis, porphyry and agate, along with other gemstones and minerals, but especially an incomparable sort of veined marble, which is far more valuable than the Florentine kind, are to be found in fair *quantité*, and asbestos or Flachstein, which the ancient Romans, in accordance with their traditions, used for burning the bodies of their dead, occurs frequently here. Apart from this, I have been assured that there should be good quality lead in the Suwundu mountains[194] near Turkestan, of which a few

---

193 These may have been Turcoman horses, possibly from Atrak and Gurgan. They were known for their beauty and strength and traded via Khiva (Muraviev tr.1824, p.147).

194 Presumably part of the Kara-tau range of mountains. For Rychkov on stones, metals and minerals see *Topografiia*, 248/278-252/282; 263/293-278/308.

balls of lead were given to me, which allows me to assume that there must be a great deal of *mercurium*, since the whole nation with its constant to-ing and fro-ing seems very mercurial to me.

Otherwise there is supposed to be a mountain in this region near the Anny Daria[195] river, which contains a great deal of gold, and also near Badachan,[196] where the lapis lazuli was found, [119] vitriol, alum and other things, especially a strange kind of bitumen, which occurs with black amber, and similarly sulphur is found in large quantities. As I now believe, all these things which the country bears have been attested to with a fair degree of accuracy, and all that is left to observe is that I must furnish the appropriate indications to all the lakes and rivers that are to be found there, along with their peculiarities. With regard to these, it has already been mentioned that there are various salt lakes and that I have heard strange reports about the Aral Sea, in that 2 months are required to ride around it, and that it is also very deep and horribly salty. It has no outflow, but is traditionally supposed to have flown into the Caspian Sea,[197] and that this outlet was blocked in an earlier age and that it now resembles a pot from which no water can flow, a fact which is consequently all the more amazing, in that various powerful rivers pour into this lake, about which I consider the following report to be necessary, since it belongs to my description of the Kyrgyz country, where it is to be found.

1mo the River Sir,[198] which rises in the mountains above the town of Taskent, and flows on the one side through Bucharia and the Kyrgyz-Kaysack lands, [120] and thus falls into the Aral Sea.

2do the Anny Daria or river, which is a powerful river, and rises above Badachsan and also flows on one side through Bucharia and the Kyrgyz-Kaysack lands into the Aral Sea.

3tio the River Kowa, which also pours into the said Sea.

4to the River Gomuth, on which lies the town of Chiwa, and

---

195 Amu Darya, see further.
196 Badakhshan, see p.40, n.50.
197 The presumed old link between the Aral and the Caspian is shown on a map of 1755 (Rychkov, *Topografiia* ed. 2010, Map. XI).
198 Sïr Darya.

which also flows into the Aral Sea.[199]

There are further rivers, which flow through the Kyrgyz-Kaysack lands into the said Aral Sea, but these are not yet known to me, so I have not been able to list them.[200]

Of these, the Sir contains a great deal of gold-bearing sand as does the Tschiltzschu,[201] a river in Bucharia, and both rivers are carefully worked at their sources. In this regard, the Kyrgyz have not been engaged in gathering it, and this has been practised far more by the Buchars, but to describe the manner of its collection and to include it in my account and describe it more fully might be considered very extravagant, for I am currently writing about the Kyrgyz and not reporting on the Buchars, however, [121] I wish to give satisfaction to *curiosité* by mentioning at the end of this report that the Buchars have to pay an annual tribute to

---

199 A tributary of the Amu Darya (see Bregel 2009, p.67 for its numerous tributaries in Khorezm).

200 Much of the Aral Sea was still unsurveyed in the 1730s, despite the efforts of Peter the Great, Tevkelev and members of the Orenburg expedition. Captain Elton (see p.104, n.162) had been involved (although this is not shown on the maps published in Hanway 1753). In 1741 Lieutenant D. Gladyshev and surveyor I. Muravin produced a map, which informed the *Atlas Russicus*, St. Petersburg of 1745. (Zonn, Glantz, Kostianoy, Kosarev 2009, pp.152-153; Rychkov, *Topografiia*, p.206). The 1755 maps (nos. I, IX, XI) in Rychkov's *Topografiia* ed. 2010 show the two main rivers (the Amu and Sïr) with a tributary of the Sïr Darya, the Kuban Darya, flowing into the Aral Sea. The Aral could be shown schematically or of different sizes (particularly in European maps and into the next century e.g. Moll 1732; Drury and Sayer 1761; Laurie and Whittle 1806). The names given by Castle are not found on any of these maps or in Rychkov's text, but it is perfectly possible that these names were once valid, having been given to Castle by local people and surveyors, or taken from documents in St. Petersburg. Ebulgazi Bahadir Khan 1929-30, Vol.2, p.451 mentions the many rivers (tributaries of the two main rivers) falling into the Aral Sea, and makes a point of the fast changing tributaries of the sea and their canals. For Rychkov on the Aral Sea, sometimes called the Blue Sea or the Aral 'Dungis' (Deniz), by the locals see *Topografiia*, 211/241-213/242).

201 This may be a corrupted form of Kizilsu, but may refer to or be another name for the Zeravshan or the 'sprayer of gold', a river flowing from Tajikistan to Uzbekistan, past Samarkand and Bukhara, known for gold in its upper reaches (Burnes 1973 ed., pp.334-35). The actual Kizilsu has its source in modern Kyrgystan and is not associated with gold.

---

the Kyrgyz[202] and that one can learn from this how a nation may feel subject to the other, though it may nevertheless be superior to the other in industry and assiduousness, and this also relates particularly to the Buchars' gold gathering. Thus, the latter only work the water during the springtime in places where it emerges from its sources, where it is thick with sand, and they pan it in cloths with holes or slits, which are then dipped in the stream and shaken until the gold nuggets settle on account of their weight in the holes in the cloth and the superfluous sand is washed off. At the same, it should be observed that the gold-sand from the Tchiltzschu is of much better quality than that from the Sir and Ami rivers.[203]

SECOND SECTION

The inhabitants are of medium stature and are well built with the same colouring as Europeans.[204] Otherwise, the men have uniformly black hair, and it is shaved off their heads, though some will retain a braid at the back. Their ears do not lie flat against the skull, as with us Europeans, but are larger and project, [122] and they leave them the way nature has formed them. The result is that they can hear far further in the distance than we Europeans, and if anyone calls them from afar, it is immediately apprehended by their projecting ears and conducted to their ear canal and tympanum, whereby I am firmly of the opinion that we Europeans destroy our hearing, because, although our children are all born with projecting ears, they are induced to lie close

---

202 Who levied tribute on whom varied according to whoever had the upper hand at the time. The Kazakhs had recovered some of the upper hand after the Jungar invasion or made settlements with them, but the area was still subject to Jungar raids and in need of protection. Parts of wider Bukhara paid tribute to the Jungars (see nn.210, 212).

203 Rychkov mentions gold in these regions but does not address the issue, intending to in a third (unfinished?) part of his *Topografiia* (Rychkov, pp.273/303). Verifying the many anecdotal stories regarding gold in this region was very hazardous at the time.

204 See the Introduction for the nature of these ethnographic comments. For eighteenth-century ethnographic and historical observations on the Kazakhs see e.g. Pallas *op. cit.* pp.608-09; Bardanes 1774, *IKRI* 4, pp.93-194; Georgi *op. cit.* pp.242-304.

---

to the head by means of felt caps, thereby interfering with the course of nature to our disadvantage. Their eyes are extremely sharp-sighted and are able to perceive something sooner than we Europeans with the help of perspective glasses, and I consider this to be due to the fact that from youth onwards they practise observing a wild animal or any other useful prey, from far off. However, it is worth noting with regard to their eyes, that so long as they marry wives from their own nation, these tend to be quite large from one generation to the next; however, should they take Kalmuck girls captive and take them as their wives to do the housework, so that they are not obliged to pay as many mares for them, their children will have small Kalmuck eyes, wide faces and crooked legs. Their teeth generally resemble the finest ivory, and they use them for nothing [123] other than to talk through, given that the inhabitants have nothing to chew, since they have no bread, and their meat is chopped very fine, so that they put it in their mouths and swallow it down without chewing it. As for beards, they only have a few hairs on their chins and they remove all the rest, on their bodies too, with tweezers made for this purpose.

Their bodily constitution is strong and rustic, but when stirred up, once they have grown warm they are accustomed to refrain from drink, just as when they experience great heat, they make sure their chests are kept constantly warm.

The Kyrgyz mentality is very crafty, uncouth and suspicious, as well as rapacious and they do not trust anyone easily, unless they have been encountered in a special manner. However, I have in fact found that if one is able to insinuate among them and show them that one is upright, they too will be trustworthy and are not nearly as terrible as they have been described.

With regard to the sciences, they know nothing but what they have observed, the sun by day, and by night the moon and northern star, along with the four parts of the world, although this produces the unfortunate effect that once their young captives have secretly learnt this from them, they are generally able to escape with 2 or 3 of their best horses and [124] return to their homelands, because they know how to get there. The most distinguished men wear clothes of linen and cotton, but common men wear horse and sheepskins, and felt made of camel hair. Their coats and caps are of felt, and they wear pelts or fleeces as coverings, though they are not able to walk far, given that they are accustomed to riding from childhood onwards. Their women wear boots, trousers and costumes which almost resemble the men's, which is why they are scarcely to be distinguished from them, were they not distinguished by their headdresses with hanging veils, which they cover themselves with in order not to be seen. Their unmarried girls wear a fairly tall Schiffs Mütze[205] with a side-flap projecting on either side, and the face in-between; the turn-up is usually made of beaver, while the head covering is of Buchar velvet. However, they have a variety of bonnets, which are decorated with silver ornaments and strange feathers, and they hang various kinds of pendants from their ears, and I have seen many captive girls from the Nagaish Tartar nation, sporting a ring through their noses. Otherwise, Kyrgyz girls who are not yet married plait their hair on top of their heads like Russian girls and, especially [125] with the Buchar girls, their clothes are made of velvet and silk, and taffeta, as well as striped and flowery cotton, and, with both men and women, their boots in particular are in different colours, yellow, black, green, blue and red, though with the veritably finest chagrille shagreen.[206]

When Kyrgyz people meet and greet each other, they grasp both hands and shake them twice back and forwards in a sawing motion, then they let go of the hands and lay them crosswise on their breasts, whereupon the one says 'Effalo maleckum!'[207] and the other replies: 'Aleekum salam!' The same courtesy is shown by women to their men and closest relatives, whereby they fall onto their left knee before them and lay they their hands folded together on the right knee, while saying the above words. They can have up to 3, 4 or 5 wives, depending on how much they can

---

205 Sailor's cap, sa'wkele? (Sarah Tolley).
206 For descriptions of male and female Kazakh dress see e.g. Pallas op. cit Vol.1, pp.279-81; Georgi op. cit. Vol.2, pp.279-81.
207 This is a garbled version of the greeting: as-salam 'alaykum (peace be upon you) and its response alaykum wa'salam (upon you be peace). See Pl. 10.

Pl.10.
Kazakhs with short beards and moustaches, wearing their traditional felt hats with long, pointed, split brims, greet each other. A woman kneels in greeting to the right. Yurts are in the background.

Tab. X.

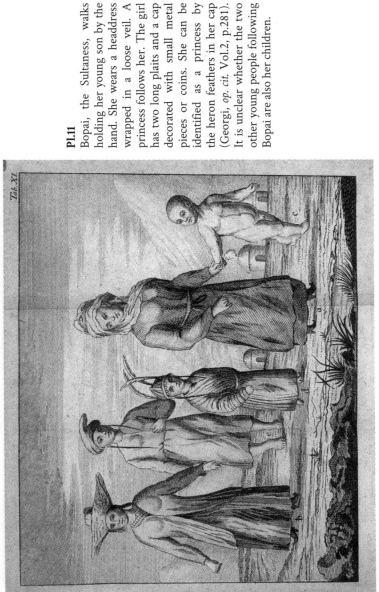

Tab. XI

Pl.11

Bopai, the Sultaness, walks holding her young son by the hand. She wears a headdress wrapped in a loose veil. A princess follows her. The girl has two long plaits and a cap decorated with small metal pieces or coins. She can be identified as a princess by the heron feathers in her cap (Georgi, *op. cit.* Vol.2, p.281). It is unclear whether the two other young people following Bopai are also her children.

Pl.12

Kazakhs on the move with a flock. Camels carry women, children, yurts and goods. A basket of babies is attached to one of the camels. The far procession is headed by the 'fairest daughter' of a family riding a horse. She wears a plumed, pointed bonnet. The Khan (?) rides on the lower left, with Bopai and a baby, followed by a young son, riding before him. Armed men on horses bring up the rear, while others patrol the hills.

Tab XII.

pay, and they purchase them, in view of the fact that they know nothing of coinage, for mares, wolf pelts, fox pelts and *corsisken* or Siberian fox pelts, since their value is not set by the 20-30 mares price that the Khan established, see above *sub die 24 Iunii 1736*, but according to their beauty at 50 and 60 or more mares, and a wife may be purchased for the equivalent value in pelts. As soon as the deal [126] has been completed, they immediately hand over all that they have and pay the rest with whatever they secure on their raids, but the wife is not given up until the man has delivered everything, since his bride must work in her parents' house until the sum has been paid in full. However, once the deal had been concluded, it so happens that he is at liberty to spend every third night with her and to sleep with her in a curious fashion. The matter is done thus; a carpet is laid down in one corner of the yurt, with one part inside and the other outside the yurt, both parts being divided by a wooden frame wall. The bride lies within, the bridegroom without. Now, although the new pair is very kept firmly separate, the parents are frequently unable to prevent the bride and bridegroom from secretly slipping together and joining as one. Once the first night has passed thus, the bridegroom sends his new wife 2 shirts, a pair of trousers, and a cloth to wrap round her head, whereby the deal between them both is duly observed. So long, as stated above, she has not yet fully been paid for, he will not secure her, and is not allowed to be seen by her parents and relatives while this is still lacking. This is why, on meeting one of these people, they immediately turn their faces away, and the others immediately do [127]

likewise until they have passed by each other. But, once the bridegroom has made full payment, he will fetch her, and the best foal will be slaughtered and a marriage meal will be offered, sometimes not before 3 years have passed. Among their women, the one that has the advantage of bringing the first son into the world is the one who takes charge of the household. However, all the wives are treated very slavishly, they may never eat with their husbands in public, and have to do all the work, even saddling their husband's horses, lifting him off his horse on his return, and unsaddling the latter, watering, feeding and bedding it down, so that the husband has no more to do than go raiding and hunting, and when not engaged in these pursuits, in sleeping, whereby he retains his full commando at home, even obliging the girls that have been captured to attend him, and when he causes one of these captives to bear a child, the latter enjoys the same rights as children from a proper marriage and is as honourable as them. At this point, I cannot but mention that most of the girls run around naked until their 5th year, and the boys likewise until their 6th year, and that the latter's heads are shaved with a knife, leaving [128] a tuft of hair on their napes. When their parents are travelling, the children are placed by the dozen in baskets and loaded onto a camel in such a way as to balance both sides, and nets are pulled over the baskets to prevent the children from leaping out and, to provide for greater security, a girl of 10 to 12 years old is sat on the camel[208] to keep an eye on the packed children, and to hand them some sheep's milk and meat from time to time, thereby keeping them quiet. It is *curieux* to observe the manner in which an entire caravan moves, and the circumstances of this should not be left untouched on. Each family has its own particular caravan, whereby their fairest daughter rides ahead on their best horse and leads the troop in this manner. She is dressed in a very costly dress, wearing a distinctive, pointed bonnet with silver ornaments on her head, set with a special kind of red goose-feather, with a little bell hanging from it. After her follows a camel that she leads, whereby this one is always tied to the next, on which the carpets and other household goods are loaded. After this camel follows another with the children, then come the camels with the yurt and other things, and, finally, the horses and sheep bring up the rear, [129] whereby the sheep are driven by boys, one of whom is on horseback and the others on foot, in such a way that the ones on foot have long poles tied to their backs, with which they direct the sheep in the direction they must go, and the one on horseback must keep the sheep together, which those on foot cannot achieve with their poles. Alongside the procession ride the father of the household and his

---

208 See Pl. 12.

frequently pregnant wives, who have often packed 2 or 3 children onto their horses, in front and behind, some of them still at the breast, and others that cannot yet stand or walk, while some slightly older and bigger children are even tied to a chair on a foal, and the whole effect is most amusing, when one sees an entire caravan, composed of so many families, moving from one place to another, whereby they are truly enjoying themselves, singing and playing flutes, with the young men riding about alongside the caravans, watching out for the enemy, to prevent them from attacking the caravan. As soon as they come to a place where they think they will find enough fodder, everything is unpacked, the yurts are raised, everything is done as if one had constantly been living there, although they cannot remain in one place for longer than 2, 3 or 4 days on account of the fodder. Their yurts are made of wooden slats, [130] in such a fashion that they slot in and out of each other, and are so disposed that when one is raised, it resembles a perfect hayrick, round and joining at the top, where a hole takes the place of a chimney. This framework is pegged down all round at the base, and it is covered with the loveliest felt. The Kyrgyz people are obliged to offer a constant welcome, to the extent that if one hungry person or more of that kind sees but a wisp of smoke coming from another's yurt, they will all descend on it like a swarm of bees, and will greet them by getting down on their knees, with their legs stretched out behind, and their whole body resting back on their heels, like a camel, expecting whatever God will provide from their host, without having been invited, and even if he has only 1 pound of meat, he may not refuse to share it with his guests and gives each of them something, even if its is only the size of a flea, whereby many an honourable gulper will go away hungry, and his host will be left with nothing to eat. So they know how to take the greatest care in preparing their food, so that no smoke is made, before a horse or a sheep is slaughtered.

I have often mentioned, how, when one of the sheep or horses is to be slaughtered, [131] it is first led out and shown alive, that it can be approved.

After this solemnity is over, and thanks have been given to

God, calling on Him to pour a thousand blessings on the giver, many of the young men will already be standing ready, constituting a quintessence of miscreants gathered together from all kinds of nations, and who live from nothing but raiding, hunting and scrounging, whereby the Kyrgyz are obliged to feed these good-for-nothings, because they serve as their guards, and receive nothing for this apart from their food and drink, standing ready to slaughter with their little sharp knives, and as soon as they have been shown the creature that is to be slaughtered, and it has been brought back, they descend on it like a flock of ravens on some carrion and throw it down, cut its throat, and know how to remove its hide so briskly that one cannot cease from marvelling. In the *osteologie*, or division of the bones, they are such consummate *maitres* that the best *anatomicus* could not set about it more accurately. As soon as the meat has cooled somewhat, they place it straightaway on the fire, in an iron or a brass pot, and while it is cooking, the guests are treated to kumis or mares' milk, and sheep's curds, whereby some of them engage in true discourses on matters of state about [132] their quarrels and raids, and in the course of which *raisonnement*, some of the others who are listening will pluck each other's superfluous hairs from their beards, as a loving service, while others will open their shirts and seek whatever tame cattle nature has provided, with which they are well supplied, though they do not kill them but, however many they catch, throw them to the ground alive, thereby supposedly earning their gratitude for this kindness, while commenting that there are no fleas at all on them. In the meantime, once the meat has cooked, it will be handed to the expectant young men to cut up, and they know how to separate it from the bones in a very skilful and brisk manner. As soon as the meat has been set down and chopped up very small, those bones that are not quite clean of flesh are thrown to the elders and most distinguished men, who suck them and clean them up so well that the keenest trail-dog would be unable to find any meat or fat on them at all. Now, once hands have been washed and thanks been given to God, the chopped, unsalted, and barely cooked meat is set in a great dish in front of the most distinguished man in that company, who must feed the other distinguished men sitting on their knees in front of him, by putting his hand to their mouths, [133] and to other lesser men than him, he will give their *quanti* in due proportion, in a small wooden dish, whereby they too will do each other the honour of feeding each other by hand. They do not spend a long time eating, but in under 4 minutes, they will have swallowed the meat from one horse. As soon as they have eaten, their boots serve as napkins, and they start by wiping their hands on them, then they renew them fully on their heads and beards, and wash their hands with water, and dry them on their leggings. Then the zchurpa[209] or soup is poured into wooden dishes for drinking. After the meal, at a distinguished and grand dinner, flutes will be played, and a great deal of kumis or mare's milk will be drunk, whereby they become extremely intoxicated. Their flutes are made of pipes of white and black Nieswurz, called hellebore, which everyone knows how to make and which produce very wonderful tones, whereby they place them against their teeth and hum into them, using each one only once, so that there is a huge quantity of flutes to be found here. The songs that they play on these recount the deeds of their ancient heroes, and the chivalric tale of how they raided, and warred and surrendered their souls, though the melodies are mostly melancholy. With regard to their kumis, or drink, it is made [134] from mare's milk in this fashion. The mare is milked a good 5 to 6 times a day, because she produces only a little milk at a time. This milk is placed in a leather sack made of horsehide, along with the sour sheep's cheese that I have already described at length *sub die 7 Iul. 1736*, and some fresh water is added to the milk, to make it foment. It foments so rapidly that the presiding housewife will take a big stick which is thick below and pointed at the top, with grooves below, and will stir the fomented milk energetically, pour it into a dish, and offer it to the guests. It tastes rather better than sour milk with us Europeans, but it is as strong as wine, and has the virtue of not inflicting a spogmelie or a sore head the next day, since kumis is an excellent remedy for hunger and makes one very fat, as can be observed

---

209 *Çorba*: soup in Turki.

---

among the Kyrgyz people, who grow very thin in the winter, when they do not have enough kumis, but are on the other hand, are very fat in the summertime, with the result that it can be difficult to recognize a Kyrgyz man whom one has seen in his fullness in summertime, on account of his thinness during the winter. They also make a brandy from this kumis, or mares' milk, which they call arack, whereby they set two iron pots one on top of the other, and macerate them strongly, set a pipe in them, and [135] thus distil brandy, though is only produced as a *medicia* for great lords. Alongside this kumis they have another drink made of sour sheep's cheese, which I have also reported on *sub die 7 Iul. 1736*, which I refer to, and which they call ayran, and which they employ both on their journeys and at home, because they are not accustomed to drinking water except in the greatest need. At their feasts they also smoke tobacco, which they procure from Bucharia. For this they use a *compendiculum* manner of pipe that they obtain from the riverbanks, which are usually clay, whereby they straightaway take some earth, roll it into a ball, make a hole in it with a finger, and insert a strong blade of grass inside it, whereupon the pipe is ready. They strew a little tobacco in the upper hole, holding it in place with two fingers, and setting fire to it, and sucking 3 or 4 draughts of the tobacco smoke. No sooner have they done this, then they fall unconscious to the ground, turn their eyes up and resemble nothing so much as people with epilepsy, until clear steam comes out of their throats and they sit up and expel the slime from their throats, whereupon their pleasure comes to an end. Otherwise, all their eating utensils are made of wood, but they store kumis and fetch water in utensils made of leather, which [136] are fashioned by the Kalmuck and other captive girls. Their religion or faith, in brief, consists of resting on their knees, with their heads covered, and praying and washing five times a day, whereby they also circumcise their children in the Mohammedan manner, and venerate Almighty God, while also being very superstitious and amazingly given to sorcery, and I have already provided two remarkable examples of this *sub die 19 junii* and *14 Iulii 1736*. They have very few priests, who have anyway learnt nothing, and have little reading and writing, and their writing is done with a reed dipped in Indian ink, and written from the right to the left. The laws that are customary with them do not constitute regular written rules or laws, only those that are taken from the Koran, which their Agun, or the most distinguished priest, reads to the elders, who adjudicate according the nature of the matter and leave the final decision to the Khan, who immediately has it executed in full, and among themselves they have a rapid and martial law, whereby they employ no extravagant procedures, and they are not easily induced to usher someone from life to death, but their judgements generally come out in favour of a drubbing, which they administer [137] with sabres. To engage in war, they have breastplate-shirts, arrows and bows and the above-mentioned firearms, which are bored like canon, and also fire a very long way and accurately. And though they are very unorganized in war, they employ this stratagem when attacking just the way a cat catches a mouse, whereby they surround the enemy at a distance of about 2 to 3 wersts, and creep on their hands and feet on the ground between the grass and the hills just as they do when catching wild horses, until they believe they have surrounded their enemy, then they lie on the ground with their firearms and fire their guns and almost every shot hits a man. They understand nothing about manufacturing, apart from the fact that their wives and daughters make all kinds of felt, such as felt caps, and they tan the various sorts of fur on the wild pelts that their men bring back from hunting, and they make thread from the sinews of horses, and finally, even the men, during periods of excessive idleness when they cannot sleep, can fabricate their saddles and equipment, including gunpowder they have such great need of from the saltpetre that is to be found in the countryside, along with their *pfiltz* pipes, and this powder is peculiarly good. Furthermore, they have no knowledge of gold, silver or jewels, and with regard to all other sciences they are as stupid as their cattle, [138] which is why they obtain all they require for clothing, such as sheets, cotton, velvet and silk cloth, including the chagrille shagreen on their boots, iron and copper utensils, horse bits, knives and other necessities, from the Buchars, who are very industrious and skilled people, but who, as mentioned above, are placed below the Kyrgyz people as tribute payers, in exchange for sheep, horses and furs. And, as I have reported above with regard to their physical constitution, they are a healthy, strong and enduring people, and I can say that I have never met any cripples among them, but, with regard to their illnesses, death and burial, I must add the following, how they, with their sharp-sightedness suffer mainly from eye-disease, and are otherwise much travailed by colic, and must frequently chew the grass on that account, whereby their mullah, who is a priest, or the old wives, are unable to help them, and employ the following cure; they place a little salt in a small bowl of water, breathe 40 times on the water while murmuring a few words in Arabic, whereupon the patient must drink a little of the water and be led on camels while engaged in his cure, because they have no carts and would not be able to use them on account of the rivers. But when someone becomes so ill that he can no longer sit on his horse, and really sees death before him, he will immediately be abandoned by his own people, [139] in this way: they will give him no further medicine, of which they have none apart from the above cure, and will probably place him in a small yurt that has been set apart, on account of the aversion they have for ill people, and leave him to the mercy of God, setting food at some distance away for as long as he lives, and when he dies, the dead man will be washed by his family and wrapped according to the Turkish manner in 9 napkins and conducted up to the mountains near to the earlier heathen graves, and buried in an orderly manner, setting stones on the grave, and decorating it with branches to indicate that he was a Muslim, while the mullah and the dead man's entire family sing songs for the dead, slaughter a horse and distribute it as alms for the poor, that they may pray for his soul, because they believe in a *purgatorium*. As a memorial to the dead man, the hide of the slaughtered horse is cut into strips near to the grave, and each of the attendants and others present is given one of these. And it should be understood that this manner of dying and burial only applies as long as they are with the horde and their family, whereas those, on the other hand, to whom the same befalls while engaged in a raid or warfare, and are incapable of sitting on their horse, are left behind in God's almighty power, under the open sky, without any human succour, leaving them [140] but a piece of meat, some water and cheese, and (it cannot be otherwise then that they must die in the wilderness) they hang a Koran on the dead man's chest so that the first people to find him will immediately recognize him as a true Muslim and will bury him in accordance with the custom of their people and their means.

[141] 1737

THIRD SECTION

Since the Kyrgyz-Khazaks are divided into 3 hordes, they also have 3 Khans, of whom the most distinguished is he who possesses the town of Taskent[210] along with the district that pertains to him, who is called Scholbars[211] Khan. The Khan of the other horde is also powerful, and possesses alongside his district

---

210 Tashkent, between Marawara'al-nahr and Turkestan, was on one of the major trade routes from Central Asia to Orenburg. In the 1730s it was under Khan Cholbars of the Great Horde, who shared power there with a Kazakh *biy* called Tiul. Both received tribute. After Cholbars' death, Tiul *biy* was eventually supplanted by Kusiak *biy*, subject to the Jungar leader Galdan Tseren, and Tashkent came under the Jungars (Levshin *op. cit.* pp.155-59). An account of Tashkent from the late 1730s describes it as being 4 *wersts* in length and breadth (1*w/v*=1.066 km), surrounded by mud-brick walls of 2 sagens high (1 *sagen*=3 *arshin*=72cm) with 8 gates, and long narrow streets. It was watered by canals from the Sïr Darya ? Chirchik It had c. 6000 houses and c. 150 mosques, and some very handsome buildings (medreses and mausolea), now neglected. The great bazaar (the *registan*) was in the centre, by a large pond and surrounded by smaller bazaars and many shops. It had much agricultural (wheat, barley, millet, cotton paper) and garden produce (apples, pears, apricots, berries, vines, peaches.) It produced silk, but had no factories. Its main imports from Russia were: '*karmazin*' cloth (from the Arabic *qirmizi* or crimson), dyes, 'foreign' furs and cochineal. (Rychkov, *Istoriia*, pp.39-40; *Topografiia* pp.31-434).
211 Cholbars, Jolbars, Zholbars, Khan of the Great Horde c.1690-1739, became Khan in c. 1720 (Erofeeva 2007, pp.443-44).

---

the town of Turkestan,[212] and his name is Schmiaki.[213] The third Khan of the smallest horde is this Abul Geier Khan, with whom I stayed. However, since none of these 3 Khans can give orders to the other, each one rules on his own behalf and they simply maintain good relations with each other.

So I remain with that particular Khan about whom I am able to report something special, given that I have no great knowledge about the other ones, who I did not stay with, and will therefore report on Abul Geier Khan, how he is a ruler of large and distinguished stature, white and ruddy of face, with something very amiable about it, as well as being very strong and forceful, in that no one in his entire nation can match him in stringing a bow.

His name Abul Geier could almost be regarded as a title, since Abul means good and Geier means father. However, [142] it cannot be clearly stated whether he was given this name as *nomen proprium* in his youth, or whether it has been attributed to him since then.

Before he was made Khan, he was only a Sultan, which all his children are still characterized as. However, during the war against

---

212 The town of Turkestan, on the Tashkent-Orenburg trade route. It became very prosperous during the Timurid period partly because of the shrine (built by Timur) and cult of the Sufi Sheikh Ahmad Yasawi (1093-1166). It became an important religious centre on various levels: it was a focus for pilgrimage and royal and holy burials, as a centre for the Yasawi Sufi order and its rituals, and was the linchpin in a network of shrines associated with Yasawi in the region. Influence was exercised through the patronage of the site (de Weese 2012, Chapter X, pp.353-54). The town was disputed between the Uzbeks and the Kazakhs; the latter eventually controlled it until driven out by the Jungars in 1723. It was then disputed between the Kazakhs and the Jungars (Poujol 2000, pp. 680-81). An account of the late 1730s mentions mosques and the mausoleum of 'a great honoured' saint. It was poorer than Tashkent, with apparently no bazaar there at the time, and local commerce concentrated instead in Tashkent. It had an irregular fortress, winding streets and c. 1000 houses. Millet, barley and cotton paper was grown. They had a Khan, but he was controlled by Jungar overlords (cf. Tashkent). It had been Abulkhayir's base until the Jungar invasion of 1723. (Rychkov, *Istoriia*, p.39; *Topografiia*, pp.20-21). See Introduction.

The town remains an important pilgrimage site (Privatsky 2001, pp.53-57 and *passim*).

213 Shemiaka, Semeke, Khan of the Middle Horde from 1723/4-1737/8, the son of Khan Tauke, d. 1737/38.

Tab. XIII

Pl.13.
Khan Abulkhayir.

the Zungurisch Kalmucks he captured their leader Contaischa[214] with his own hand, and subsequently distinguished himself greatly in the last war[215] against the Bashkiri Adaar,[216] so he was made Khan of this little horde, and now has his residence by the Aral Sea, since the Kyrgyz derive his family from Timerleck, which is the same as Tamerlane.[217] He may command 40.000 warriors,[218] but he does not enjoy any kind of sovereign rule, since his rule is subject to the approval of his elders, and his orders ensure that which the elders have approved is carried out. His prerogative consists of this, that he may be highest person in the court of law, but he does not hold more than two votes, hence all public matters that arise, as well as his judgements, must also be approved.[219]

He must deal very carefully with his subjects, because he lives [143] in mortal danger among them, given that no sooner have they grown displeased with him, they will immediately cut him down, for which reason, whenever the Khan wished to speak secretly with me, he had to draw me aside every time.[220] He

214 See n.158.
215 The Bashkir uprising of 1705-11.
216 Aldar, see n.9, p.64, n.109.
217 Timur (Lang, the Lame, c. 1336-1405). Castle is probably confusing Timur (who was not a Chingisid, but married a Chingisid, and thereafter referred to himself as *Kurugan*, Mongolian for son-in-law, to draw attention to this. My thanks to Alexander Morrison for this comment) with Chingis Khan or believed, with Abulkhayir (?), that Timur was from the line of Chingis. Timur was also the name of a number of other Golden Horde Khans. After the death of Chingis Khan (d. 1227) his empire was divided into appanages (*ulus*) amongst his sons. Jochi's *ulus*, which went to his son Batu, included the westernmost part of the Mongol Empire, encompassing lands which remained to be conquered. Batu became Great Khan whereas Orda, Jochi's eldest son, became the first head of the left or eastern wing of Jochi's *ulus* (sometimes known as the Blue Horde) (Bregel 2003, p.38). Rulers of the Junior Horde claimed descent from Osek, the youngest son of Janïbek, great grandson of Urus, allegedly descended from Orda, a grandson of Chingis Khan. See Introduction n.000
218 In *K-R Otnoscheniia* nos. 38, 50 the numbers given are 30,000; in Rychkov, *Topografiia* p.141/171: 20,000 families. By the nineteenth century these numbers had dwindled considerably: from c. 150.000 families at the beginning of the century to 12-13,000 at the turn of the nineteenth and twentieth centuries (Erofeeva 2011, p.81).
219 See p.52, n.81.
220 This secrecy echoes Tevkelev's negotiations with the Khan, *Diary*

receives very few revenues indeed, since they give him no more than he needs merely to live, and he has to give what is his to the discontented in order to maintain them in good humour, and for this reason he is also bound to dine with his subjects, and thereby retain their good will.[221]

Apart from the Khan, the elders who are constantly around the Khan and are commanded by him also give orders. These elders are generally of good family, they are murses[222] or dukes, beys[223] or nobles, as well as baturs[224] or heroes, and most of them are far richer in cattle than the Khan himself. War and peace are, so to speak, all one with them, because in the event of a victory they envisage no more than looting the enemy's wives and children, likewise their cattle and baggage, but they are not in the slightest bit concerned about land. In wartime, however, those elders who the young men or militia consider to be the cleverest take the command. However, these same are subject to the Khan's order in all matters, and in spite of all this confusion, the militia must be directed by the napkins or little flags that are fixed to their sticks or lances.

[144] With regard to proofs of graciousness, the Khan, as was mentioned above *sub die 21 Iunii 1736*, is accustomed to grant a special honour to a stranger and his subjects, by touching their right shoulder with his right hand. Apart from these regalia and prerogatives, the Khan has nothing more than the right to eat wherever he wishes to. About coinage and other things that could be very advantageous to him, he knows nothing, and though he might well wish to introduce one or the other, he may not venture this without considerable support and other safeguards, because his generally suspicious and wild subjects would otherwise soon make an end of him.

1731-33 e.g. pp.67, 70 and *passim*.
221 For the position of the Khan see the Introduction.
222 *Mirza*: a title given to noblemen and others of good birth (*E.I.* Index 2009, p.399).
223 *Biy*, see n.5.
224 *Batyr*, see n.9.

GLOSSARY

Page numbers refer to those in the original German text (found in square brackets in this edition).

Ankunft [arrival] – of the author at the Kyrgyz (camp), whereby the latter made magic to discover whether he was bringing them good fortune, page 13; prevented the conjunction of all three Kyrgyz hordes with all the Kyrgyz and the Bashkirs against Russia from taking place, page 8; with State Councillor Iwan Kiriloff.

Ankunft [arrival] – in Orenburg, 72; in Sinbirsky, 96; in Samara, 101

Ami-Daria, or River [Amu Darya], in which there is said to be a mountain that contains much gold, 118

Arabische Sprache [Arabic tongue] is used for Kyrgyz sorcery, 12

Arack, a brandy, which the Kyrgyz distil from mares' milk in two vessels that are balanced one upon the other, 134

Aral See [Sea], with regard to its nature and circumference, the former has no outflow at all; is supposed to have previously flowed into the Caspian Sea, 119

Asan Abuys, an envoy of Jambeck Batur, 7; takes leave of the author and asks him to come unto his principal, whereupon the author makes his excuses because he has no gifts to present, 7

Asbest or *flachstein* [asbestos] is frequently to be found among the Kyrgyz, 118

Assetrina, a fish, from which the best bladders and the best caviar or *ikray* are made, 89, 90   Assignation [note of credit], obtained by the author to present to Ensign Kusnitzoff for the payment of 345 roubles 15 cop.

Astankoff, Major in a Russian unit, who the author met while travelling, who did not trust the Tartars that the author sent to him, and formed a battalion square, 63; the author met this man several times on his return journey to Orenburg, because he sought to obtain horses for his journey from him, but the Major did not give him any.

Audience – the author's audience with the Khan's sons, 15

Augen – the Kyrgyz peoples' [eyes] are extremely sharp-sighted which allows them to see somewhat further than we Europeans with our perspective glasses, but when they take Kalmuck women to wife, their children acquire smaller eyes, 122

Auctor [author] of this work, how he has sacrificed himself for Russia, and how he thought to make himself worthy of his service in Orenburg, and why he settled in Orenburg, 2; how the same with no advice or help from anyone furthered the interests of the Russian Emperor, 2; served Eraly Sultan, a son of the Kyrgyz Khan with a variety of friendly actions, 3; his disquiet about the Kyrgyz on receiving their news, which moved him to undertake his Kyrgyz journey, 4, 5; starts his journey on 14th June 1736, 6; the Kyrgyz take him for a Russian envoy, and receive him as such, 8; on arriving at the Khan's yurt, a Buchar tent of white cotton is erected for him, in which he receives countless visitors, 9; the Kyrgyz hold him to be a skilled *medicus*, 8; is consoled, and told the Khan will soon arrive, 11; is obliged to ride with the three sons of the Khan onto a mountain, in order to gain audience with them, whereby, though, a ridiculous ceremonial was observed, which gave him the opportunity to ingratiate himself, 14, 15; fortunately, is recognised in his Tartar clothes by his German dagger and pistols, after which he rode 106 wersts on his hired horse in one day, reaching the State Councillor that very evening, 64; purchases from his hostess a rather large but unpolished *palle* ruby for a little clasp knife, 17; is summoned to the Khan and on his arrival a white Buchar tent made of cotton is set up for him, 16, 17; how he was conducted to an audience with the Khan and what occurred at it, 18; his dismissal by the Khan and what kind of proofs of his favour the author was dismissed with, 20; how he was presented with food from the Lady Khan's kitchen, and what the dishes consisted of, 23; how he gained an audience with the Khan's three wives, and presented them with gifts that he had brought and purchased with his own money, 24, 25; is asked, how many wives and children he has, 26; praises the hasty manner in which

Kyrgyz eat, 27; tells the Khan of his esteem for his country, in that he possesses the best sheep, the best foals, and the most delicate mares' milk, 28; paints the Khan in a very short time with no brushes, using his fingers, 28, 29; is summoned by the Khan to hear what the elders of Jambeck Batur are about to advise him, 32; writes down the names of those Kyrgyz elders who had approved remaining loyal to your Imperial Majesty, 34; is asked, which route I intend to travel by, and wish to join the State Councillor, 35; gives the Khan an answer to his complaint which pleased him and caused him to call the author an honest man, 36, 69; is very hungry, attempts to eat roots, but is unable to enjoy them on account of their bitter taste, 38; is presented with gifts by Teberde, a Kyrgyz, 40; makes his excuses to the Khan with regard to going to Bucharia as his envoy 41; takes his leave, and is accompanied by the Khan, 42; travels towards the North-West on his return journey with the Kyrgyz envoys, 42; desires on account of fighting among the Bashkirs to be conducted back to Abul Geier by the Kyrgyz envoys, and thereby obtains secure information that 88 men from the other Kyrgyz horde, 8 men from Jambeck Batur, have left, without knowing whether they are proceeding to Orenburg or to the Bashkirs, 45; is convinced of the projected conjunction of Bashkirs and Kyrgyz, and consequently his visit to the Khan was most timely, 45; could not sleep for hunger, rain and cold, 52, 53; informs State Councillor Iwan Kiriloff of his arrival through 2 loyal Bashkirs and resolves to ride wholly on his own to the latter, 61; sends a further 2 Cossacks with a letter to the State Councillor and the Kyrgyz inform him with cheerful faces that they have made magic and thereby learnt that good news would come from the State Councillor, following which on the 4th Aug he also receives good letters and a convoy of 24 men, 62; presents an account of his report to State Councillor Iwan Kiriloff, 65; presents the Kyrgyz envoys to the State Councillor, 70; is able to convey to the State Councillor quite a different idea of himself compared with the Orenburg commander's opinion that was conveyed to him in writing, and acquired merit thereby, 70; receives from the State Councillor the order to convey the Kyrgyz envoys he had brought with him back to the River Jaick and transport their most necessary things from Orenburg, and so return with Lieutenant-Colonel Tchmaduroff to the town of Jaick along the River Jaick and thus reach Simbirsky via Samara, wherefore the author takes his leave of the State Councillor, who gives him a fur and a horse, 71; is obliged to eat the food that his convoy of 22 Kalmuks is eating which consists of dried meat but which he takes to be spicy biscuits, and it renders him unwell, 72; Asked the Orenburg Commandant for a unit of 10 Cossacks and a few instruments, since he had encountered the trace of a precious Jaspis at no great distance from Orenburg on a mountain by the River Tan Atlack, and was consequently eager to pay this mountain a visit, which, however, the Commandant dissuaded him from, 72, 73; is rebuked by the Beybeck and blamed for failing to obtain provisions in Orenburg, wherefore he was obliged to mollify them, 74; gives various presents to the Beybeck and to Mamet, who had conveyed the Khan's gifts to him, and entertains the Kyrgyz in Commandant Teffkeleff's tent, 75; is assigned a barge by the Commandant for his journey on the River Jaick, which the Adjutant then wishes to remove from him, whereupon negotiations take place on account of which complaint about him is made to the Commandant, 78; is considered quite unwarrantedly by the Commandant to be a desperate person, and the author explains the reason for this, 78-79; a unit of 24 soldiers is ordered onto this boat, and they attempt to break his conveyance into two, but were not able to effect this, much to the chagrin of a Sergeant, who in consequence was absolutely determined to throw the author's things into the river, which obliged the author to address his complaint this time to the Lieutenant-Colonel, 79; began the journey by water to Sinbirsky with Lieutenant-Colonel Tchemaduroff, they were 120 men strong, 80; shows the Lieutenant-Colonel a place at the mouth of River Sackmara that would be vastly suited to a fortification, 83, 84; receives no horses from the Lieutenant-Colonel, in spite of a sealed order to that effect from the State Councillor, and is obliged to hire these with his own money, 92; travels away from the town of Jaick and catches up with the aforementioned Lieutenant-Colonel that evening, 92; while travelling was obliged to give the Kyrgyz men brandy, meat and bread at his own expense, 93; receives great honour from Knias Beloselsky 94, 95; arrives in Sinbirsky and shows State Councillor Iwan Kiriloff the stone and ore samples and other curiosities which he had gradually amassed 96; wherefore he has been mourned by his friends for half a year on account of the rumour that the Bashkirs had slain him in the Ural Mountains, 97; is asked, what indeed he thought to gain from such a desperate journey, and replies that he could have incurred no more glorious a death than in the service of His Imperial Majesty, 98; is vexed because the State Councillor does not keep the promise he made him, and is even less ready to send him to St Petersburg with his account, and only pays him his wages little by little, for which reason he asks for his decommission and his wages, 97, 98; seeks permission to visit his father but cannot obtain this, 99; writes to his brother in Moscow and sends him on his behalf to the Cabinet in St Petersburg, 100; receives from the State Councillor the order to proceed from Simbirsti to Samara, and on the way he nearly drowned in the Volga and lost all his things apart from a wooden case in which his journal was kept, 100, 101; following the death of the State Councillor, conveys various reports to Colonel Teffkeleff and First Lieutenant Bachmetoff for his overdue wages and concerning his decommission, but he was accused of wishing to depart immediately for St Petersburg, and they neither could nor would give it to him, 102, 103; travels again to Simbirsti with a note of credit for 345 roubles 15 kopeks to Ensign Russnitzoff, but on the way has to endure hunger and distress, 103. In Simbirsti he was attacked with his head uncovered and in his shirt by soldiers on the orders of the incumbent chief of police Iwan Iwoltz Schukoff, and, after the aforesaid violent drubbing, was dragged in a bloodied state with a torn shirt through the whole town to the police station and was finally taken by the chief of police into his house and set free there by the same, 104, 105. On his return from the police station he went to the secretary of the Orenburg Expedition Andre Iwanoff, and showed him the evidence on his own body, bloodied and beaten as he was, and on this account gave him a *supplique* in German for the Orenburg Expedition Chancery, 105. The Woyword in Simbirsky throws him out of the free quarters that His Imperial Majesty had granted him four times over and for this reason he addresses an urgent complaint to Tatischoff but is consoled by the same and ordered to travel to Samara, 106. Arrives at Samara by water and is fortunate to be able to ingratiate himself with Councillor Tatischoff, 107, 108. Allows himself to be persuaded by this same Councillor to take service again with His Imperial Majesty and thereby receives his non-statutory wages and a new contract which finally ends in the year 1737 and at last receives after this year is long past his decommission, 108. Apologises for including this in his description of the Kyrgyz a few of the incidents that he has experienced, which was done not from any private motive but simply with a view to showing what the reward that State Councillor Iwan Kiriloff had promised so many times for what he had done at his own expense for the benefit of the Empire, and his very dangerous journey, and the merits that he thereby acquired, consisted of, whereby he begs that this should not be regarded as a complaint, page 108, 109.

Ayran is a drink made from sheep's milk.

Bachmetoff Peter Iwannewitz, a Russian Lieutenant-Colonel and father-in-law of State Councillor Iwan Kiriloff on the Orenburg Expedition, 98; is presented by the author with various reports in return for his wages and decommission, 98

Badachsan a town, the very one where lapis lazuli was found, 118

Barthaare [beard hairs] are plucked by the Kyrgyz, as from their entire bodies, leaving only a few hanging from their chins, 123

Baskiren, two loyal [Bashkir] men, through whom the author announced his arrival to State Councillor Iwan Kiriloff, 61

Baskirsches [Bashkir] Journal, which, along with the drawings pertaining to it, was stolen during the time when the author was attacked by the Sinbirsky military police and dragged to the police station, along with other things beside, 105, 106

Batur, among the Kyrgyz people this signifies a hero, 3

Begräbnis [burial], with the Kyrgyz, and how they go about it, 13

Bellusa, a fish, from which both isinglass and caviar or Ikra are made, 89

Beloselski, a Russian Knias, who is married to the daughter of General Tschernitscheff; accorded the author great honour, 94, 95

Bemühung [effort], by loyal subjects must be demonstrated in such a way that the latter always do more than is required of their official function, 2

Bey, is in Kyrgyz speech the same as nobleman, 143

Beybeck Augluck, a messenger of Abul Geier Khan to Orenburg, 6; comes to the author and conveyed the Khan's message, 16; summons the author to an audience with the Khan, 17; instructs the same in the ceremony on entering the Khan's presence, 18; returns in Orenburg with a further 3 persons from Jambeck Batur to ascertain whether the State Councillor had indeed arrived and whether the Eraly Sultan has been paid the funds he was, 73, 74; together with his people, was not given any provisions, whereupon they all came to the author, eager to put the blame on him, 74; presented, together with Mammet, the gifts that had been sent to the author by the Khan, 74, 75; arrived in the town of Jaick with the Kyrgyz men he had with him, 88

Beyhoscha, a man of the Tungau family is captured, 50

Beymarat Bey Batur, offers State Councillor Iwan Kiriloff 1000 sheep, 22, 67

BeyiSauby, foremost elder of Jambeck Batur, who promised that they would remain constant in their loyalty, 32

Bejoar Ziege [Bezoar goats] shot by the author, who has seen similar skeletons in various cabinets of art and natural objects and is sometimes found by the Kyrgyz to contain a stone, 46, 113; is caught with the pickurt bird, 21; during the winter they return to India and Persia, 113; Their size and characteristics page, 113, 114

Birla a river, of middling size which flows past the village of Resan, 95

Brandtewein [brandy], made by the Kyrgyz from mares' milk, which they call Arak, and which is distilled in 2 superimposed vessels, 134

Braut [bride], a Kyrgyz girl, whose brideprice is fixed according to their notion of beauty and whose parents will not convey her to the bridegroom until it has been paid in full, 125, 126

Bräutigam [bridegroom], a Kyrgyz man will pay as much as he has for his bride, once the transaction has been agreed, and will contribute the rest little by little from what he gains through raiding, 126 ; sends his new wife, once they have spent their first night together, 2 blouses, 1 pair trousers and a cloth to wrap around her head. What may happen next, 126

Brust [breast], which the Kyrgyz continually keep warm, even in the greatest heat, 123

Buberack Batur, the foremost elder of Iambeck Batur, spent 5 years as ambassador to the Kalmuks, 32

Buch [book] with strange characters, held by the mulla or priest when practising sorcery; 3 the present example must correspond with my journal, which is held in the Orenburg Chancery, 64

Bucharen [Bucharis] are subordinate to the Kyrgyz and pay them tribute, 121

Büchse or flintlock, was set off beneath the author when seated, 10

Butter, is placed by the Kyrgyz in their sheep's cheese beverage; they consider it the greatest delicacy and give it to the foremost persons, and smeared some on the author's mouth as is their custom.

Caffiar, see **Ikra**

started the rebellion punished, or if so desired to deliver them over to Russia, 29, 68; throws a great feast for all the elders present from 3 hordes 33, 68; complains about being forbidden by the Commandant in Orenburg from proceeding any further down the River Or, 36, 69; requests [permission] to build a house in Orenburg, and wishes to do this *item* to dedicate his 3 sons to Your Imperial Majesty and requires to keep no more people with him in Orenburg than he is permitted, 40, 69; asks the author to paint his wife and wishes to send him to Bucharia as his envoy, 41; presents the author with his best horse along with other things, 41, 42; is a lord of considerable stature, with a wise countenance and of such mighty strength, that no one in his entire nation can match him in spanning a bow, 141; his family was derived from Timerleck, which is supposed to be the same as Tamerlan, 142. Although he commands a force of 40000 men, his government is not at all sovereign, but depends on the approval of his elders, although [his government] is established through his orders which are approved by them, 142; has captured Conraicha, the leader of the Zungurish Kalmucks, with his own hand and has distinguished himself greatly against Bashkir Aidar, wherefore he was made Khan since which time he has been established beside the Aral Sea, 141. Would like to introduce one thing or another that could be of benefit to him, but may not undertake this without considerable assistance from his subjects, and other safeguards.

Characteurs, strange characters, were used in a book for Kyrgyz sorcery, page 13

Chiva [Khiva], a town that lies on the River Somuth, 120

Christin [Christian], a Russian woman who had been abducted from the town of Jaick, adressed the author in the Tartar tongue, and begged to be rescued. The author gave her an account of the return route, which she followed and arrived home, and was soon wed, 13, 14

Clima [climate] of the Kyrgyz land is warm, and the onset of winter is very mild, 110

Colika [colic], which most Kyrgyz suffer from, and in consequence must frequently chew grass, 138

Commando, at wartime the Kyrgyz are led by their elders but in such a manner that they are under the Khan's orders in all matters, 142

Commandant in Orenburg, did not wish to send any Russian envoys to the Kyrgyz, but gave the author permission to ride to the Khan at the request of Eraly Sultan, 3, 4; his opinion of the author's journey which he wrote to the State Councillor, 70; rejected the author's request for a convoy and instruments, with which to visit a mountain at no great distance from Orenburg on the River Tan-Atlack where the author had encountered traces of valuable lapis, 72, 73

Compliment [bow, greeting], made in the French style by the author at his audience, 18; and greeting, that the Kyrgyz people do on meeting each other, and how the women also do this to their men and closest relatives, 125.

Conjunction of the Bashkirs with the Kyrgyz against Russia that the author was able to observe rather than ascertain, 45

Contaischa [Kontaisha] a leader of the Zungurish Kalmucks, who Abas Geier Khan took prisoner with his own hand, 142

Convoy, of 24 Tartars was sent to the author and the Kyrgyz men he had with him to the newly-erected fort, 62

Cornu-Ammonis [ammonites] are frequently to be found on the Kyrgyz mountains, 117

Cosacke [Cossacks], one of whom ran off during the journey to Sackmara, 81; Jaick Cossacks have retained their Danube Cossack law, which consists of various prerogatives, 89

Cottoun [cotton], which the leading Kyrgyz people use for clothing

Cumis [kumiss], or mare's milk, is considered nectar by the Kyrgyz 11, 17; is frequently drunk by them, whereby they become extremely intoxicated, 134; and makes them fat, 136

136; to this pertains the leather vessels which are manufactured by Kalmuck and other girls.

Cur [treatment] for the Kyrgyz is practised by their priests and old women, who use it in a particular way, 1; the author treated some people on a few occasions, 138

Curtuck is a very wide lump of fat weighing between 20 and 30 pounds, which the Kyrgyz sheep have instead of tails, 117

Dankbarkeit [gratitude], supposed, is expressed by the Kyrgyz towards their benefactor during their repast by not killing the tame cattle that they have been seeking in their clothes all the while, but by throwing them on the ground alive, and leaving them for their host in his yurt, 132

Deen, River, takes its source in the Mahaschell Ayruck Tau or mountain [part of the Mugodzhar Hills] and flows into the River Jemm, 14

Delicatesse [delicacies], for which the Kyrgyz have their butter, which sits on top of the drink they make from sheep's milk, 47, 48

Derwisch [Dervish] is what the Kyrgyz call a religious or holy man

Desperater Mensch [desperate person], which the author was accused of being, quite undeservedly

Dieb [thief] Kyrgyz, had stolen 40 mares, was caught and punished for this.

Divertissement [enjoyment], for which reason the Kyrgyz men marry 3, 4 to 5 wives and as many as they can pay for, 125

Dollmetscher [interpreter], of whom the author had two, 6. During his audience with the Khan's sons, he was obliged to dismount from his horse and stand there, 15; were sent back to Orenburg by the author with a convoy of 3 men, bearing a letter to the Commandant in Orenburg with an account of the author's achievements, and bringing the author's horse and the gifts he had received, 47

Edelgesteine [gemstones], can be found frequently among the Kyrgyz, 118; which the author brought back from his Bashkir journey, and were subsequently taken from him by Iwan Kiriloff with no compensation, 96

Eigenshaften [characteristics] which are laudable in one

near Sackmara, 62; when in the camp, which lies 150 wersts from Ufa, receives from the author a journal written in pencil, 64, 65; to whom the author conveyed his reports on the hostile Bashkirs, 65, 70; is glad because the Kyrgyz envoys were presented to him by the author, thanks him in the name of Your Imperial Majesty and promises to send him to St Petersburg to be recompensed, page 70; informs the author of what the Commendant in Orenburg had written about his Kyrgyz journey, 70; orders the author to take a unit of 12 Cossacks and convey the Kyrgyz envoys and others of that nation who were there to the River Jaick, and afterwards to bring his choicest objects with him from Orenburg, 71. Although pleased with the samples of stones, ores and other curiosities that the author had found, and with the advantages that he had also secured from the Kyrgyz, 97, for this very reason does not keep his promise to the author and does not wish to send him to St Petersburg with his report or give him permission to travel to Moscow and instead prefers to pay him his wages little by little, 99; grows very angry with the author, for asking for his wages and permission to depart, and for sending his brother to the High Cabinet, 100; was continuously ill and died in Samara.

Europäer [Europeans], ruin their hearing by ensuring that their children, who are all brought into the world with sticking-out ears, have them trained back by placing a tight cap over them, thereby interfering with the course of nature, 122

Execution, which the Kyrgyz applied to a thief, 90; the process takes place by order of the Khan, 136

Feder [feather], from a particular type of goose that the Kyrgyz daughters fix, when leading their troupes alongside their caravans, to a silver clasp and set atop the tall pointed cap they wear on their heads, from which hangs a little bell, 128

Federwildprett [game birds], of which the Kyrgyz have but few since they lack woodland, though partridges inhabit the grasses beside the rivers, albeit such as there are the

Prayer 3 Matt Ch II

flesh is roasted on wild horse dung and promptly eaten,
6, 7

Gänse [geese], wild, among the Kyrgyz they inhabit the
lakes, whence they retire from cold lands in wintertime,
116

Gastfrey [hospitable], the Kyrgyz are obliged to be, and why
this has arisen, 130

Gastmahl [welcoming feast], such as the Khan provided
when the author arrived, to which the most important
elders in all 3 hordes were invited, 33, 68, 69; given by
the author for his Kyrgyz visitors in Orenburg, 75; how
the Kyrgyz provide such among themselves and what is
observed on these occasions, 131

Gebährden [grimaces], render the Kyrgyz mulla or priest
very dreadful when engaged in sorcery, 3

Geissel [hostage], in Orenburg was the Khan's son, the Eraly
Sultan, 3

Gegend [region], such as the Khan showed to have many
advantages for erecting a fortress, *item* where great riches
in gold and gemstones were to be found, 21, 60

Gehör [hearing], which the Kyrgyz are much better at than
Europeans 122

Gemüthsneigung [disposition] of the Kyrgyz is devious,
uncouth and suspicious, 123

Gerüste [structure], which the travellers assembled in order
to draw the equipage over the River Jaick, 52

Gesandten [envoys] from the Kyrgyz Khan Abul Geier,
why they arrived in Orenburg, 3; request a Russian envoy
and reveal their purpose at the same time, 4; Jambeck
Batur's envoys assert that he will remain true to the oath
of loyalty he made to Your Imperial Majesty in former
times, 32, 68; on account of which the Kyrgyz look to the
author, 8; on account of which the author is required by
the Khan to travel to Bucharia, 41, 65; the Kyrgyz men
accompany the author to the State Councillor, 65

Geschirr [vessels], wooden, in which the roasted meat from
a Bezoar goat is cooked with red-hot stones, 46; of which
the Kyrgyz have only wooden ones, 46

Gesundheit [health] of Your Imperial Majesty that the

Kyrgyz men have toasted, 7, 34, 68.

Gerickla, a little stream beside the town of Gericklinskoy, flows into River Ztchremschan, 95

Gold, silver and gemstones are not valued by the Kyrgyz, they do not understand these matters, 56, 118; gold-bearing sand, of which there is plenty in the Sir-Ami and River Tschiliztschu, 118, 120; booty, the Kyrgyz being wont to seize it from the Bucharis when the opportunity arises, 121

Gomouth, a river, beside which lies the town of Chiwa, 120.

Gott [God], whom the Kyrgyz people called on as witness to their undertaking to keep faith with Your Imperial Majesty, 33

Gowrin, a Captain from the Pensish Regiment, who commanded the newly-erected fortress near Sackmara and was a very good friend to the author, paying him every possible honour, 61

Grabmähler [monuments], of the ancient Mungal and Nogay Tartars, are very frequently to be found in the neighbourhood of Sackmara in the shape of a pyramid and are curiously formed, 57, 58

Gräber [graves] of the ancients, in which are to be found beside each dead body the latter's personal horse when alive with full trappings, along with everything that was conducive to his dignity when alive, 57, 58; how they are formed within, 57

Gränzen [borders] of the Kyrgyz and Khazak lands 110. The River Ami divides the Buchar from the Kyrgyz-Khazak lands, 120

Grass, in the Kyrgyz wilderness grows in bushels set half a foot apart, and is so sharp that it can also cut a man's shoe in half while he is walking, and serves no purpose other than providing the wild horses, goats and camels with their best nourishment, whereas the good grass is sought by the tame cattle along the streams and rivers, 111

Gresnuscha, or Rothigte, a little river which flows between the town of Jaick and the Oltschensirt mountains, where its source is found, and falls into the Sollona, 93.

Guder Bey, who was a very great man among the Kyrgyz, regarded the author as an envoy, assuring him that if he had not come, they would have attacked Russia within a couple of days, 8; whose eyes were treated with sugar by the author, 8

Haare [hair], which the Kyrgyz pluck from their entire body with a special hook, leaving only a little head hair on the chin, 123; from the beard, a Kyrgyz man will pluck it from another man as a courtesy and a loving service.

Haus [house], such as the Khan would dearly like to build for himself in Orenburg.

Hausblase [isinglass] is taken from the fishes, belluja, dewruja and assertina, which anyway resemble sturgeons, and the isinglass from the assertina is supposed to be far better than that from the other two fish, *item,* how it is made, 89

Haut [hide] from the upper part of a horse's leg, is made into flasks by the Kyrgyz and used as a drinking vessel when travelling, 48

Hechte [pike] are found in great quantities in the River Jaick, and are caught with a special instrument, this being an oval iron plate, and 4 of which can be purchased for a pipe of tobacco, 80, 81

Heinzelmann, previously assessor with the Orenburg Expedition and now Councillor, who on hearing the news that the author was dead, was authorised by his father to allow the author's estate to be extradited, 97, 98

Helleborum, or radix *hellebori*, which may be found in great quantities among the Kyrgyz

Hemde [shirt], a silk Persian one, removed from the author's own body and presented to the malcontent Kyrgyz men, to make them more willing to travel with him, 56. A cotton one was secured by the author as a gift from a Swiss man, Jacob Reiner, 64

Hengst [stallion], with the wild horses, *advenant* his years, has his share of 8 to 10 mares, is always the guardian of them and their foals, 114

Heuschober (haystack], which a Kyrgyz yurt resembles, given that it is round and curved at the top, 130

Hogg, an English merchant whom the author met in Samara, 94

Hügel [hills], in the Kyrgyz lands resemble nothing so much as the open sea, 111

Jaick [Yaik] **Stadt** [town] lies on a peninsula, and is described along with its inhabitants, the latter being surrounded by a crew of robbers consisting of Bashkirs, Kyrgyz and Kalmucks, and whose food is fish, isinglass and caviar, or ikra, 88, 89

Jaick [Yaik/Ural] **Strom** [river], where the fish are caught in such quantities as could scarcely be encountered anywhere in the world, 89. at three days' journey from Sackmara along this river is where rock salt is broken up, this being of extremely good quality and with this feature, that each time some is broken off, it increases by that much, 87; many chalk hills lie along it, close to the town, 88; along which are found many herbs, 88; flows into the Caspian Sea, 14; across which the author is obliged to swim, tied to a tail, 52; has its source two short days' journey away, in Siberia, close to Catharinenburg, 76

Jaickiscer Ottamann, from whom the author requested an 8-man convoy on two occasions, who refused him each time, and who reproached the author on this account, 60

Jambeck Batur, his envoy, 3, 31; his elders swear to remain loyal, 32, 68

Jaspis [jasper], traces of which the author encountered near River Tan-Atlack, and would gladly have visited this place, but that he was refused the necessary escort and the requisite instruments, 73. is also frequently found among the Kyrgyz, 118

Jemmstrom [River Emba], takes its source four and a half days' ride from Orenburg on a high mountain that is distinguished by two wings, and flows into the River Jaick near the town of Gurioff, 14

Jskra or caviar is made from the belluja, sewruja, indeed the very best, both fresh and pressed, comes from the assetrina, *item*, how it is prepared, 89, 90

Jirdisch [Irtysch], a river which has its source in the Ditschnsirt mountain and flows into the Volga, 94.

Junge, Mannschaft [youths and teams] of the Kyrgyz take the place of soldiers with them, and they surround

the caravan on all sides, keeping watch for the enemy
to prevent it from attacking the caravan, 129. The
Kyrgyz teams are a real quintessence of sheer good-for-
nothings gathered together from every nation, who live
from nothing but robbery, hunting and freeloading,
while wishing no good to anyone, and who are fed by
the Kyrgyz solely because they provide guard duty, and
butcher the sheep and horses that are presented for a
feast, which they do very promptly, 131; are commanded
by the Kyrgyz elders.

Jungens, Kyrgyz [boys], run around naked until their sixth
year, and their heads are shaved right from the start with
a knife, leaving only a tuft of hair on the crown

Jurden, Kyrgyz [yurts] and how they are made and formed,
129, 130

Iwan Kiriloff, see State Councillor, 70

Käse von Schafen [sheeps' cheese], upon which the Kyrgyz
people pour water, to turn it into a liquid that produces a
thirst-quenching drink.

Kalbeck, one of Abul Gaier Khan's gesauls or adjutants
with the Kyrgyz envoys, 6; is driven from the yurts with
whips. His stature and natural aspect, is a temporary
adjutant and a model for that penurious age (Bea – you
may wish to alter the main text?), 43, 44

Kamajur, a Schuwasisch village, beside a river of the same
name, 96

Karamsin, a Russian Lieutenant, who had been left behind
by his people, who drank away his mount and the author's
horse that he had shared with him, 83. Arrives all alone
on a barge dressed in a short linen smock, 92

Kargalet, a small lake, where many graves of the ancient
pagan people are to be found, and in the surrounding
region are to be found wild horses and goats, 46

Karaluk, a river, whose source lies in the Otschensirt
mountains and which flows into the Volga, 94

Kaufmannschaft [commerce] is very extensive among
the Kyrgyz on account of their wives, and once a deal is
concluded, that which they have is immediately handed

over, and the rest is acquired through robbery and gradually paid over, and the bride continues to work for her family until the last instalment has been paid, 126. With regard to bride and bridegroom it is considered proper for the husband to send his new wife, after he has spent the first night with her: 1 pair of trousers, 3 shirts, and a linen cloth to wind around her head, 126. For lacquer, cotton, sammet and silk objects, likewise for chagreen boots, iron and copper vessels, bits for horses, knives and other necessities, the Kyrgyz trade sheep, horses, and hides from the Buchars, 138. How such commodities are brought from Russia to India, is explained by the author, 76

Kilmeck, a Bashkir rebel who wished to form an alliance with the Kyrgyz against Russia, 4, 67. Who, following the author's arrival, lost all hope of securing the projected conjunction with the Kyrgyz

Kinder Kyrgyz [children], when the adults are travelling, are packed by dozens into baskets in a very curious manner, *item*, the children of Kyrgyz men that are born not of their wives but to girls they have taken captive, have the same rights as the children of a regular marriage, and are also as honourable, 127, 128

Kyrgyz people wished to be informed as to whether Orenburg was still occupied? and requested a Russian envoy, 3. took the author for a Russian envoy 8. took him for a skilful medicus, whose person and clothes appeared very strange to the Kyrgyz people, 8, 31. investigated the things on the author's person, and took him to be a sorcerer on account of his *perruque*, 10, 11. an elder boasts of having created cool air for the Khan, is inclined to practise his art, and will not teach it to the author, because he is not a Muslim, 15, 16; their common weapons, what they consist of, 20; are uncouth, 23, 123; swallow in the manner of the cassowary bird a handful of finely chopped horse flesh of 1-2 pounds in one go, 27; do not lightly commence any great undertaking unless the new moon is shining, 33; understand nothing of reading and writing, and have no skill at it, 33; are obliged to follow the course of the river on account of wood and fodder, 36; consider themselves far more fortunate than us, in that when eating they are not accustomed to forks as we Europeans are, but can eat with their fingers, 38, 12; young men with anxious faces come to the author, having been fiercely attacked without knowing by whom, 44; ensure they never drink bad water during their travels, to which end they take sheep's cheese with them, in order to make a drink from it, 47, 48; for which reason they take no provisions with them, relying as they do on game during their journey, 55; in the course of whose journey, think that Sackmara has disappeared and wish to turn back, 55; during our travels, are presented with the Persian silk shirt that the author was wearing on his body, which pleased them so much and which they divided among themselves, 56; no kind of money is valued by them, 56; come to the author with cheerful faces and report that they have made magic and thereby learnt that I will soon receive good news from the State Councillor, 62; are accused by Lieutenant Colonel Tschemaduroff for no reason of having attacked their Russian soldiers while travelling, for which reason he does not give them anything, 93; know nothing about laying-in hay, but early in the year they march with their herds along the rivers and watercourses towards Russia and in Autumn, they return with the wild geese to the Aral Sea, 111; give their horses, when they are engaged in raiding, little to eat, thereby ensuring that they run better, 117; take no interest in investigating the natural goodness of their own country, and do not know how to enquire into it, 118; their entire nation appears very mercurial to the author, 118; are of middling stature, well-proportioned, of similar colouring to us Europeans, and the men are uniformly black-haired, 121; have loyal hearts and are by no means as terrible as they are reported to be, if only a person would ingratiate himself among them, and know how to treat them honestly, 123; otherwise understand nothing of the sciences, unless it be those associated with the daytime sun and the moon and northern star at night-time, 4; including the 4 parts of the world, which enables their young captives to escape, and causes them great inconvenience, 123; cannot travel

Knochen des Lammes [lamb bones] are placed in a brass vessel to make magic, then burnt on the open ground and their ashes examined for portents, 13; the Kyrgyz people shift camp so cleanly that even the subtlest trail dog would be unable to find the slightest trace of meat or fat there

Koewa, a river of the Kyrgyz that flows into the Aral Sea, 130

Kopf des Lammes [lamb's head] used for Kyrgyz sorcery, whereby a light is placed in each eye socket, 12

Kranische [cranes] dwell in the Kyrgyz lands, on the lakes, where they retire to from cold lands in wintertime

Krieg [war], the manner in which the Kyrgyz conduct it, 143; and peace are all the same to the Kyrgyz, since they have no other object than that of despoiling their enemies of their women and children, and their cattle and baggage, 143

Kubeck, a Bashkir man, who was sent from Siberia by Colonel Teffkeleff, to the Contaisch of the Kalmucks, and after that to Abul Geier Khan, 91

Kusnitzoff, a Russian ensign, to whom the author presented a note of credit for 345 roubles 15 cop., but who paid no money.

Lamm [lamb] the bones of which are used by the Kyrgyz for sorcery, 12

Land der Kyrgyzen [Kyrgyz country], position and features, is infertile and consists only of wave-like hills ib. 28, 110, 111

Lapis-Lazuli, is frequently found near Badachsan, a Kyrgyz town, 118

Lexin, a Russian lieutenant, who was sent overland to the town of Jaick, with the horses and Cossacks, 83

Leppis, envoy of Jambeck Batur, bids farewell to the author on the pretext that he was likely to be retained too long by the State Councillor, 46

Leuchters [oil lamps] are made from the hooves of slaughtered lambs for Kyrgyz sorcery, 12

Lichter [lights], for Kyrgyz sorcery, are made from the fat of the lambs slaughtered for that purpose, 12

Liebesdienst [favours] among the Kyrgyz involve plucking hairs from each others' beards during their feasts, 132

Lieder [songs] of the Kyrgyz during their feasts recount the deeds of their deceased heroes, their chivalrous conduct during raids, their battles, and how they gave up their spirits in the process, but the melodies are frequently melancholy, 133

Luftus Dietrich, an apprentice, who the author employed as an interpreter on his Kyrgyz journey, 6; on the return journey, was sent to Orenburg by the author, along with the other interpreter, and who was entrusted with letters and the gifts that the author had received, 47

Mädgens, calmuckische [Kalmuck girls], are frequently captured by the Kyrgyz and taken to wife, 122; among the Nogay Tartar Nation the author saw some who were wearing a ring through one nostril, 124; for unmarried Kyrgyz girls, their costume, 124, 125; Kyrgyz children are left naked until their fifth year, 127; Kyrgyz make yarn from their horses' manes, 137

Männer, men, Kyrgyz, have the utmost *commando* in their homes, to the extent that the captured girls must serve them when they so command, 127; fashion their saddles and equipment during times of idleness, when they cannot sleep, and make particularly good gunpowder, which is in high demand, from the saltpetre that is found in the country, 137

Manier [manner] in which the Kyrgyz, when they are guests, are accustomed to treat their benefactor, 125, 130; in which the Kyrgyz conduct war, 143

Manufacturen [manufactured goods] about which the Kyrgyz understand nothing, apart from a few sorts of felt and felt caps that their wives and daughters make, and the wild animal skins for various kinds of pelt that the men bring back from the chase, 137

Marschieren [marching] the Kyrgyz are not good foot walkers, 124

Marmor, figurierter, [figured marble], which is far better than the Florentine, quantities of which are to found among the Kyrgyz, 118

Medicus, the author was considered to be a skilful one, 8

Medizin [medicine] for this, arak or brandy made from mares' milk is used for the principal men, 135

Menage [household] is formed by Kyrgyz men when they marry captured Kalmuck girls on account of not having to pay so many mares for them, 122

Miseer, the son of the Bashkir rebel Ultar, who leads 200 Bashkirs, 66

Monsur, a Buchar Ugun or priest, 3

Motscha, a river which has its source in the the Oltschensirt mountains and flows into the Volga, 94

Münze [coins], are nothing at all to the Kyrgyz and even the Khan knows nothing about them, page 144

Mulla, or a Kyrgyz priest, performs the sorcery ceremony by crooning in the Arabic tongue, and threatens the Devil with a whip, conjuring him to keep away from all righteous Muslims, 12, 13; have learnt nothing about reading and writing 136; treat ill people, 258

Muselmann [Muslim] is what the Kyrgyz people call a true believer, 16

Murmeltier [marmot], of which there are many in the Kyrgyz lands, 112

Mursa [murse] means the same as prince in the Kyrgyz tongue, 267

Nachfolge [The results] of a bold enterprise are frequently completed and made an example of by others, 3

Negoce [commerce] could, in the author's opinion, be conveniently conducted through the town Orenburg to India, and he shows the way there, 77

Nemkoff, Irwan Iwannewitz, Woyvode in Sinbirsty gives the author no satisfaction with regard to his petition or *supplique* [that was] presented within 44 days against the incumbent Chief of Police, and instead has him thrown out of the free quarters provided in accordance with Your Imperial Majesty's contract, on 4 separate occasions and with the greatest *solemnité*, 106

Nutzen [uses] of Orenburg could perhaps be most fully employed through trade with India, 77

Nijas Sultan is a brother of Abul Geier Khan, page 23

Pray. 3 Mat. Chap II

Obeleck, a little river so weak it almost eludes notice, which flows into the River Jaick

Ohren [ears], with the Kyrgyz they do not lie flat against the head as they do with us Europeans, but are larger and stick out, 125

Oltschensirt, a mountain which lies between the town Jaick and the town Samara, 93, 94

Orenburg, on the River Or, where the author settled to develop this town, 2. he arrived there in the yr 1735 on the 12 Aug. 75, 76; his description of it, 75, 76; should be forced by hunger, 77; could serve extraordinarily well for commerce with the Buchars, Taskents, and all Asiatic peoples.

Osernov, a newly-founded township by the River Jaick, set half-way between Orenburg and Sackmara, and beside a hill with a wooden guardhouse with the Imperial flag, where Cossacks keep guard, 81, 82

Osorka, a fortress, which was established 120 wersts on this side of Orenburg, 71

Ottaman, a Jaick man, who the author twice asked for a 8-man convoy, who refused him twice and reprimanded the author, 58, 59

Ottomanische Pforte [The Ottoman Porte] incites 4000 Kyrgyz to form an alliance against Russia with the Bashkir rebel Kilmeck, 6, 4

Palstoff, a Russian lieutenant, who has a very disagreeable encounter with Captain Elton, page 94.

Patienten [patients] of the Kyrgyz are borne along on camels while undergoing their treatment because they have no waggons, 259. As soon as one of them grows so ill he can no longer sit on a horse, he really does see death standing before him, in that he is immediately abandoned, and laid quite apart in a small yurt, and his meals are put out some distance away until he dies, 259

Peitsche [whip], the mulla or priest threatens the Devil with this, 13

Persiko or bitter almond tree, with the Kyrgyz it grows 2-3 hands in height, and is burnt almost every year with the grass, 112

Pfeile [arrows], the end-parts are set end to end, and sorcery is practised in order to find the right way, 52

Pfeilnath, see *satura sagittalis* [sagittal suture]

Pferd [horse], when one is to be slaughtered, it is first of all be led out and shown alive, to the person who shall approve it, 130

Pferde [horses], are of a Persian race, their characteristics and description, 117; wild, how they are captured and cannot be tamed, 114, 115; fat is one of the Kyrgyz' greatest delicacies, it is a mighty cause of sweating and maintains the body in an open condition, 37; milk is the nectar of the Kyrgyz, 11, 27; horse droppings, wild, are used by the Kyrgyz to roast meat, 7, 86; the tail, to which the author was bound and in such a manner transported over the water, page 53, 54

Pickurt, a bird, which the Kyrgyz use when hunting for goats and horses, 21

Pimpenelle [pimpernel] grows in great quantities with the Kyrgyz, 21

Pischpermack, a Kyrgyz meal, which is made of horseflesh chopped small, 118

Porphyr [porphyry] is frequently encountered among the Kyrgyz people

Prärogatio [prerogative] is not enjoyed at all by the Khan, other than that his commands are dependent on the approval of his elders, 265; and that the elders who command during wars are under his orders in all matters, also that he may dine at any time wherever he wishes, 263

Presente [gifts], which the author presented to the consort of the Khan, 25

Priester [priests], which are called mulla by the Kyrgyz people, are few in number, and furthermore are learned in nothing, apart from a little reading and writing, 254

Process [trials] are not extensively held among the Kyrgyz, but are conducted swiftly and they also have a martial law, 255

Pulver [powder] for shooting of a particularly good quality is made by the Kyrgyz from the saltpetre that is found on their land.

171

Purgatorium [Purgatory] is believed in by the Kyrgyz, 260

Quint-Essenz [a quintessence] of braggart good-for-nothings gathered together from all nations constitutes the Kyrgyz fellowship of young men

Ragusin, Captain of a regiment of dragoons who the author consults for advice, but who questions him about his rank, and likewise the reply that the Ottaman Weroskin gives, 59, 60

Rhapontica, grows in great quantities with the Kyrgyz, III.

Räubers [robbers] who start a rebellion near Orenburg, are to be punished or handed over to Russia if so required, 29, 68

Rauch [smoke], that should not rise from any Kyrgyz home, lest one or more hungry men should spy it and fall on this home and demand hospitality, 130

Regale [regalia], of which the Khan has none, unless that he may dine whenever he please wherever he wishes, 268

Regierung [government], the Khan's is not at all sovereign, and joined to the approval of his elders, 265

Reiner, Jacob, a mason and Swiss man from St Gall, gives the author another shirt to wear, 64

Reinlichkeit [cleanliness], of the Kyrgyz consists in wiping their hands after eating, first on their boots, then they complete the task properly on their heads and beards, 248

Reise [journey], from Orenburg to the Kyrgyz people took a southerly direction, 6

Reißzeug, a complete [set of drawing materials], was presented to the author by a young Kyrgyz man, who thought that the compasses inside it were used for eating instead of forks, 38

Reiten [horse races], whereby a little boy won the prize allotted by Abul Geier Khan, 34; on which occasion sheeps' cheese is made into a drink by pouring water onto it and turning it liquid, 48.

Relation [account] of his activities is reported by the author to State Councillor Iwan Kiriloff, page 65

Religion of the Kyrgyz, what it consists of, 283

Revenüen [revenues], are raised by the Khan from his

Kyrgyz people in meagre quantities, just sufficient to enable him to live, 266

Revieres [rivers] of the Kyrgyz generally rise sharply due to the snow in winter and the rain in spring-time, and overflow, wherefore the precious grass grows in these places, III

Rüben [beetroot], red, were brought to the author, these being unusually large, albeit yellow and firm within, 87

Roskolschicken, many of whom are to be found on the right side of Sackmara, 82; are runaway Russian servants, who live in the wilderness, are considered to be settlers and nourish themselves by catching fish, 84; many of whom also live in the neighbourhood of Jaick, 84

Russland [Russia], is able to inspire a special sense of awe in its people, 2; its peril drives the author to travel to the Kyrgyz people, 4, 5

Sackmara, the old town, which was destroyed by the Bashkirs 30 years ago, lies at a distance of 30 wersts from the new town Sackmara, 83; the new town derives its name from the river Sackmara; its description: its environs resemble the Elysian Fields, 57; hereto 5 Cossacks were sent by Lieutenant-Colonel Tchermaduroff, with orders to seek out the 3 officers who had been ordered to ride overland with the horses from Orenburg to the town of Jaick, 83

Sackmarastrom [River Sackmara], at whose mouth the author had shown the Lieutenant-Colonel a place where a peninsula shape has been formed with the assistance of the River Jaick, which is exceptionally suitable for a fortress, 83, 84

Sakamsky-Linie [line], is 400 wersts long against the Bashkirs, with a fortress every 15 wersts, 95

Salpeter [saltpetre] the finest, with which the entire land of the Kyrgyz is filled, 117

Salz [salt], which the inhabitants of the town of Jaick procure for their caviar or ikra from a lake that lies at 12 days' distance, where the salt is found floating on top like ice, 91

Samara-Strom [River Samara] flows past the town of the same name into the Volga, 94

Satisfaction, which the author cannot obtain in the slightest degree against the Simbisky Chief of Police, neither from the presiding Woywode, nor from Expedition Chancery in Orenburg, 104

Schafe [sheep], which were slaughtered when the author arrived in the first Kyrgyz yurts, and Your Imperial Majesty's health was drunk during the subsequent feasting, 8; when about to be slaughtered by the Kyrgyz, are first of all led out to be viewed and God is called on to shower a thousand-fold blessings on the giver, 106

Schaafe, Kyrgyz [sheep], a description, and their flesh is far more delicate than English [sheep], 117; join the train of a Kyrgyz caravan, a herd to each family, with the drivers on foot, each fitted out with a long horizontal pole on his back, and this is how they are herded, 129

Schafe-Milch, [ewes' milk] dried, of which the author was presented with a bagful by a young Kyrgyz man, 37, 38

Schager-Bey, the Khan's envoy, 16

Schemacki, the Khan of the middle Kyrgyz-Kazakh horde, who is powerful and, along with his district, owns the town of Turkestan, 262.

Scheremka, a river which is very broad and fast, 95

Schild-Kröten [tortoises], of which there are terrible quantities among the Kyrgyz, 116

Schockoloff, a Russian ensign, who was shot by Kyrgyz robbers when travelling with his unit, 83

Scholbars, is the Khan of the first and pre-eminent Kyrgyz-Khazak horde, who, along with the rest of his district, also owns the town of Taskent, 262

Schriften [writing], the Kyrgyz use reeds dipped in Indian ink and write from right to left, 254

Schukoff, Iwan Lwowitz, Chief of Police in Sinsbirsky, told a Sergeant and 16 men to throw the author out of his house and drag him with many blows to the police station, and then let him go free again, 104, 105

Schweine, wilde [boar], are plentiful with the Kyrgyz but are not relished by the inhabitants, 116

Schwestern [sisters] of Eraly Sultan honour the author with a visit, bringing a gift of soured ewes' milk, 35

See [lake] of which one is filled with sky-blue water which tastes aluminous, 7; is filled with green and very stinking water, in which the author nearly drowned, 54; of which there are very many, on which pure salt floats, 119

Seele [soul], of a living person, may take true pleasure in the district of Sackmara, 57

Serpillum [wild thyme], grows frequently in the land of the Kyrgyz, 112

Sewruj a fish from which both isinglass and caviar are taken, 89

Sir [Sïr Darya], a river whose source rises in the mountains above the town of Tashkent and which flows into the Aral Sea and contains much gold-bearing sand, 120

Situation, where an advantageous fortification could be erected, item where great treasure and gemstones are to be found, is shown to the author by the Khan, 21, 67

Sock, a little river near to Krasnoyiahr, of middling size, with a bridge over it, 95

Soldaten, sick Russian [soldiers] were transported on 3 chaloupes to the town of Jaick, and attacked by Kirgis robbers on the way to Sackmara, whereby 2 Russians were killed and 3 wounded, 85, 86. From the police force in Sinbirsky who, together with a Sergeant, attacked the author within his quarters and conveyed him to the police station, 104.

Solennität [ceremony] among the Kirgis, when a person supplies the food for a feast, 130, 131

Sollona, a river that flows between the town of Jaick and the Oitschenfirt mountains, whence it springs, and flows into the Tchagan, 93.

Speisegeschirr [vessels for food] are simply made of wood among the Kirgis, 245.

Staatsdiscourss [discourse on matters of state] among the Kirgiz the most eminent such consist of the tales of fighting and robbery that they recount during their feasts, 245

Steinsalz, rock salt, is mined along the River Jaick at a distance of 3 days' journey from Sackmara, which increases constantly, 87

Steine, edle [gemstones] which the author brought back from his Kirgis journey and which Iwan Kiriloff gradually

Tiegerkatzen [tiger cats] are numerous in Kyrgyz country, 112

Timerleck or **Tamerlan**, from whose family Abul Geier Khan is descended, 265

Toback [tobacco] is used by the Kyrgyz during their feasts when they smoke a curious sort of pipe, 252

Tochter [daughter], the most beautiful of which in a Kyrgyz family will ride in the caravan's train on their finest horse, and lead her family's herd, dressed in her finest costume, 128

Tractamenten [feasts] such as the Kyrgyz put on and observations on the same, 245

Trank [drink], of sheeps' cheese, such as the Kyrgyz are used to make when travelling, the same being thirst-quenching, 48

Trappen [bustards], to be found on the lakes in Kyrgyz country, where they retire to from the cold lands during the winter, 116

Trat, silberner, [silver thread], hung around the neck of a corpse, and crushes it, 47

Trifolium [clover] grows in great quantities among the Kyrgyz, 206

Trommetarii [trumpeters] are frequently to be found among the Kyrgyz, 112

Trunk [drink], which the Kyrgyz avoid when they are heated, 123; made of sheeps' cheese as used by the Kyrgyz when travelling, 48; and they call it ayran, 252

Tschagan, a river, into which the Stresnuscha and Lollona flow, whose source lies between the town of Jaick and the Oltschensirt mountain, and which flows into the River Jaick, 92

Tschemaduroff, Jac. Feodrowitz, Lieutenant-Colonel and Commandant in Orenburg, 3; did not wish to send any Russian envoys to the Kyrgyz, but, following a request by Eraly Sultan gave the author permission to ride there, 4, 5; issued a ban against the Kyrgyz, which they complained about, 36, 70; denied the author the convoy and instruments he requested in order to visit a mountain where he had found traces of precious lapis, 73; reproached the author quite unwarrantedly for being

Vergnügen [satisfaction] that the author should have derived from his very perilous yet fortunate undertakings among the Kyrgyz, which has now been thwarted, 109

Vitriol, is frequently found in Kyrgyz country, 119

Vogel Pickurt [pickurt bird], is used for hunting wild goats, 12

Wachteln [quails], frequently dwell among the grasses by the rivers among the Kyrgyz, 116

Wachtler, a German surgeon, accompanied the author, 95

Wasser [water], bad, is not drunk by the Kyrgyz when travelling, but they take sheep's cheese along with them, which they pour water onto and it turns liquid while they are riding, 47

Wappen, the principal Kyrgyz [weapons] and what they consist of, 20

Weg [route] to India, a very convenient means for Russian trade, shown by the author, 77

Weiber, [wives] of which Kyrgyz men sometimes have, 3, 4, 5 and as many as they can pay for, 125; among themselves the one who bears the first son is distinguished by her Kurdish title, which she retains forever, 127; also, when a family is on the move, pregnant women often ride along with the household effects, often with 2 to 3 children, some still at the breast, and some who can neither walk nor stand, packed beside her on her horse, 129; may not eat openly with their men and must perform all the work, saddling the horses, feeding them and lifting the men off when they return, 127

Wilder Kirschbaum [wild cherries], grow to about 2 to 3 hands among the Kyrgyz, and most years are burnt with the grass, 112; garlic, often grows in Kyrgyz country, 111; horses, how they are caught, item, their natures and characteristics, 114

Wildprette [game], on which the Kyrgyz people rely and on account of which they take no provisions with them on their travels, 55, 11; of which there are many sorts, 112

Wilde Schweine [wild boar], are plentiful among the Kyrgyz, but are not eaten by the inhabitants, 116

Wissenschaften [sciences], the Kyrgyz have none at all,

and consequently are as foolish as their cattle.

ABBREVIATIONS

AVPRI	Archiv vneschnei politiki Rossiskoi imperii
E.I.	*Encyclopaedia Islamica*, New Edn., Leiden:Brill.
GAO (O)	Gosudarstvennyi arkhiv Orenburgskoi oblast
IKRI	*Istoriia Kazakhstana b Russkikh istochnikah*, 6 Vols., Almaty: Daik Press.
LMA	London Metropolitan Archives
MERSH	*The Modern Encyclopaedia of Russia, Soviet and Eurasian History*, Vols.1-55, Florida: Academic International Press
PSZ	*Polnoe sobranie zakonov Rossisskoi imperii*, 1645-1825,Vols. 1-45, (M.M.Sperankii); 1825-1881 Vols. 1-55; 1881-1913, Vols. 1-55, St. Petersburg.
RGADA	Rossiskii gosudarstnennyi arkhiv drevnikh aktov
RGIA	Rossiskii gosudarstvennyi istoricheskii arkhiv
Rychkov, *Istoriia*	*Istoriia Orenburgskaia* (1730-1750), St. Petersburg, ed. 1896
Rychkov, *Topografiia*	*Topografiia Orenburgskaia*, St. Petersburg 1762
Tevkelev, *Diary*	"Zhurnal bytnosti v Kirgiz-Kazatskoi orde perevodchika Mametia Tevkeleva 1731-1733 gg.", *IKRI* 3, 2005, pp.65-142
TsGARKaz	Tsentralnyi gosudarstvennyi arkhiv Respubliki Kazakhstan

BIBLIOGRAPHY

Aitov, Lieutenant [1846] "Materiali po kazakhskomu obychnomu pravu, sobrannye chinovnikami Orenburgskoi pogranichnoi komissi v 1846 godu," *Qazaqtyng ata zandary* (also known as *Drevnii mir prava kazakov*), Vol. 6, 2005, Almaty: Zheti Zhargy, pp.176-82.

Akiner, S. 1996 "Islam, the State and Ethnicity in Central Asia in Historical Perspective", *Religion, State and Society*, Vol. 24 nos.2/3, pp.91-132.

Aksan, V.H. 2012 "Ottoman Military Power in the Eighteenth Century", in ed. B. Davies, *Warfare in Eastern Europe 1500-1800*, Leiden: Brill, pp.315-47.

Asfendiarov, S.D. and Kunte, M.A. eds. 1997 *Proschloe Kazakhstana v istochniakkh i materaliakh, Sbornik 1*, Almaty.

Balkarek, P. 2012 "Two Byzantine Slabs of Near-Eastern Origin", *Byzantoslavica*, 1-2, pp.131-39.

Barrett, T. 1999 *At the Edge of Empire: the Terek Cossacks and the North Caucasus Frontier 1700-1800*, Boulder.Co.: Westview Press.

Barbarunova, Z.A. 1995 "Early Sarmatian Culture", *Nomads of the Eurasian Steppes in the Early Iron Age*, Berkeley, Ca.: Zinat Press, pp.121-36.

Bardanes, Ch. c.1770 "Kirgizskaia, ili Kazatskai chorografia", *IKRI 4*, 2007, Almaty: Daik Press, pp.93-194.

Barthold, W. and Hazai, G. 1986 "Kirgiz", E.I. 5, pp.134-36.

Bell, J. 1763 *Travels from St Petersburg in Russia to Various Parts of Asia*, Glasgow.

Belov, Provincial Secretary [1846] "Sobranie svedenii o priniatikh poriadkakh suda, raspravi, semeinykh, obychaiakh i obriadakh ordyintsev, kochuiuschkih, v raione Uralskogo ukrepleniia," *Qazaqtyng ata zandary* (also known as *Drevnii mir prava kazakov*), Vol. 6, 2005, Almaty: Zheti Zhargy, pp.183-85.

Black, J.L. 1986 G.-F. *Müller and the Imperial Russian Academy*, Kingston and Montreal: McGill-Queen's University Press.

Bodger, A. 1980 "Abulkhayir, Khan of the Kazakh Little Horde, and his oath of allegiance to Russia of October 1731", *The Slavonic and East European Review*, Vol.58/1, pp.40-57.

Borschberg, P. 2010 "The Euro-Asian Trade in Bezoar Stones (approx.1500-1700)", *Artistic and Cultural Exchanges between Europe and Asia, 1400-1900*, ed. M. North, Surrey: Ashgate, pp.29-43.

Bregel, Y. 2003 *An Historical Atlas of Central Asia*, Leiden, Boston: Brill.

Bronevskii, S.B. [1831], "O zakonakh Kirgizov", *Qazaqtyng ata zandary* (also known as *Drevnii mir prava kazakov*), Vol. 6, 2005, Almaty: Zheti Zhargy, pp.144-50.

Burnes, A. ed. 1973 *Travels into Bokhara and a Voyage on the Indus*, 3 vols., London, New York, Karachi: Oxford University Press. (First ed. 1843, John Murray).

Castagné, I.A. ed. 2007 *Drevnosti Kirgizskoi stepi i Orenburgskogo kraia*, Almaty: Daik Press.

Chibiliev, A.A. 2010 ed. Rychkov, *Topografiia Orenburgskaia*, Orenburg: Dimur.

Chistiakova, M.B. 2007 "Stone Cutting in the Urals. Articles of Masters from Ekaterinburg in the Fersman Mineralogical Museum", *New Data on Minerals* 42, pp.97-113.

Cook, J. 1770 *Voyages and Travels through the Russian Empire, Tartary and Part of the Kingdom of Persia*, 2 vols. Ed. A.L. Fullerton 1997, Newtonville MA.: Oriental Research Partners.

Cross, A. ed. 2007 *By the Banks of the Neva, Chapters from the Lives and Careers of the British in Eighteenth Century Russia*, Cambridge: Cambridge University Press.

D'André [1847] "Materiali po kazakhskomu obychnomu pravu, sobrannie chinovnikom osobykh poruchenii d'Andre v 1846 godu," *Qazaqtyng ata zandary* (also known as *Drevnii mir prava kazakov*), Vol. 6, 2005, Almaty: Zheti Zhargy,pp.151 ff.

Dale, S. 2002, *Indian Merchants and European Trade 1600-1750*, Cambridge: Cambridge University Press.

Davies, B. 2011 *Empire and Military Revolution in Eastern Europe, Russia's Turkish Wars in the Eighteenth Century*, London: Continuum.

De Weese, D. 1994 *Islamization and Native Religion in the Golden Horde*,

University Park: Pennsylvania State University Press.

De Weese, D. 2009 "Islamization in the Mongol Empire", *The Cambridge History of Inner Asia, the Chinggisid Age*, eds. N. di Cosma, A.J. Frank and P.B. Golden, Cambridge: Cambridge University Press, pp.120-34.

De Weese, D. 2012 *Studies on Sufism in Central Asia*, London: Routledge.

Demidova, N.F. 2001 *Orenburgskaia ekspeditsiia i bashkirskie vosstannia 30 kh. godov XVIII v., Materialy po istoriia Bashkortostana*, Vol. 6, Ufa: Kitap.

Dobromyslov, A.I. 1900 *Materialy po istorii Rossii. Sbornik ukazov i drugikh dokumentov, kasaiuschchikhsia upravleniia i ustroistva Orenburgskogo kraia*, Vol. 2, Orenburg.

Donnelly, A.S. 1968 *The Russian Conquest of Bashkiria 1552-1740*, New Haven and London: Yale University Press.

Dvornichenko, V.V. "Sauromatians and Sarmatians of the Eurasian Steppe: the Transitional Period from the Bronze Age" and "Sauromatian Culture", *Nomads of the Eurasian Steppe in the Early Iron Age*, Berkeley, CA.: Zinat Press, pp.101-104; 105-120.

Dury, A. and Sayer, R. 1761 Russia in Asia, in *New General and Universal Atlas*, London.

Ebulgazi Bahadir Han, Khan of Khorezm 1729-30 *A general history of the Turks, Moguls, Tatars, vulgarly called Tartars*, 2 vols. London.

Egorov, V.L. 1985 *Istoricheskaia geografia zolotoi ordi b XIII-XIV vv.*, Moscow: Nauka.

Epimakhov, V. 2007 see under Koryakova.

Epimakhov, V. 2009 "Settlements and Cemeteries of the Bronze Age in the Urals: the Potential for Reconstructing Early Social Dynamics", *Social Complexity in Prehistoric Russia*, eds. B.K. Hanks, K.M. Linduff, Cambridge, New York: Cambridge University Press, pp. 74-90.

Erofeeva, I.V. 2001 *Simboli Kazakhskoi gosudarstvennocti*, Almaty: Arkaim.

Erofeeva, I.V. 2005 "Sluzhebnie i issledovatelskie materiali rossiskogo diplomata A.I Tevkeleva po istorii i etnografii kazakhskoi stepi (1731-1759gg.)", *IKRI* Vol.3, Almaty: Daik Press.

Erofeeva, I.V. 2007 *Khan Abulkhayir: polkovodets, pravitel, politik*, Almaty: Daik Press (first edition 1999, Almaty: Sanat).

Erofeeva, I.V. 2011 ed. (with L.E. Masanova and B.T. Zhanaev), *Istoriko-Kulturni Atlas Kazaskhgogo naroda*, Almaty: Print-S.

Falk, J.P. 1785-86 *Topographische Kenntnisse der Russichen Reiches*, St. Petersburg.

Frank, A.J. 1998 *Islamic Historiography and 'Bulghar' Identtity among the Tatars and Bashkirs of Russia*, Leiden and Boston: Brill.

Frank, A.J. 2009 'The Qazaks and Russia', *The Cambridge History of Inner Asia, the Chinggisid Age*, eds. N. di Cosma, A.J. Frank and P.B. Golden, Cambridge: Cambridge University Press, pp.363-79.

Frank, A.J. 2012 *Bukhara and the Muslims of Russia*, Leiden, Boston: Brill.

Fuchs, C.L. 1981 *Obychnoe pravo kazakov v XVIII- pervoi polovine XIX veka*, Alma-Ata: Nauka.

Fyodorov-Davydov, G.A. 1984 *The Culture of the Golden Horde Cities*, Oxford, British Archaeological Series, International Series no.198.

Hanway, J. 1753 *An Historical Account of the British Trade over the Caspian Sea: with a Journal of Travels from London through Russia into Persia*, 4 vols. London.

Hennin de, G.W. 1992 ed. *Description of Ural and Siberian Factories in 1735*, ed. E.A. Battison, Washington D.C.: Smithsonian Institution Libraries and the National Science Foundation.

Hughes, L. 2002 *Peter the Great, a Biography*, New Haven and London: Yale University Press.

Georgi, J.G. 1780-83 *Russia: Or a Compleat Historical Account of All the Nations which Compose that Empire*, 4 vols., London.

Gmelin, J.G. 1751-52 *Reise durch Sibirien von dem Jahr von dem Jahr 1733 bis 1743*, 4 vols. Göttingen.

Jackson, P. and Morgan, D. 1990 *The Mission of Friar William of Rubruck: his journey to the court of Great Khan Möngke, 1253-1255*, London: Hakluyt Society.

Hellie, H. 1984 "Tatischev, Vasili Nikitich", *MERSH* 38, pp.190-96.

Kahan, A. 1985 *The Plow, the Hammer and the Knout*, Chicago: Chicago

University Press.

Kappeler, A. 2001 *The Russian Empire*, Harlow: Longman, Pearson Education Ltd.

Khodarkovsky, M. 1992 *Where Two Worlds Met, the Russian State and the Kalmyk Nomads, 1600-1771*, Ithaca and London: Cornell University Press.

Khodarkovsky, M. 2004 *Russia's Steppe Frontier, the Making of a Colonial Empire 1500-1800*, Bloomington and Indianapolis: Indiana University Press.

Kirilov, I.K. 1727 *Tsvetuschee sostioaine Vserossiiskogo gosudasrsva*, St. Petersburg.

Kirilov, I.K. 1734 *Atlas Vserossiiskoi imperii*, St. Petersburg.

Koryakova, L.N. and Epimakhov, A.V. 2007 *The Urals and Western Siberia in the Bronze and Iron Ages*, Cambridge: Cambridge University Press.

Laurie, R. and Whittle, J. 1806 "The Russian Empire in Asia", in *Laurie and Whittle's New and Elegant Atlas*, London.

Levshin, A.I. [1820] "Obraz upravleniia i zakoni [kirgizov]", *Qazaqtyng ata zandary* (also known as *Drevnii mir prava kazakov*), Vol. 6, 2005, Almaty: Zheti Zhargy, pp.123-26.

Levshin, A.I. 1840 *Descriptions des hordes et des steppes des Kirghiz-Kaii'zzacks...traduite du Russe par Ferry de Pigny, revue et publié par E. Charrière*, Paris: Imprimerie Royale.

Levshin, A.I. 1996 *Opisanie Kirgiz-Kaizach'ikh ili Kirgiz-Kaisatskikh, ord i stepei*, Almaty: Sanat.

MacGregor, A. 2007 *Curiosity and Enlightenment, Collectors and Collections from the Sixteenth to the Nineteenth Century*, New Haven and London: Yale University Press.

Major, R.H. ed. 1857 'The Travels of Athanasius Nikitin' (translated by Count Wielhorsky), *India in the Fifteenth Century, being a collection of narratives of voyages to India, in the century preceding the Portuguese discovery of the Cape of Good Hope; from Latin, Persian, Russian and Italian Sources, now first translated into English*, London: Hakluyt Society, pp.201-33.

Malikov, Y. 2011 *Tsars, Cossacks, and Nomads*, Berlin: Klaus Swarz Verlag.

Marincola, J. 1996 ed. *Herodotus, the Histories*, London: Penguin Books.

Martin, V. 2001 *Law and Custom in the Steppe*, Richmond: Curzon Press.

Masanov, N.E. 2011 *Kochevaia tsivilizatsiia kazakov*, Almaty: Fond Nurbulata Masanov.

Matvieskii, P.E. 1958 "Dnevnik Diona Kestlia kak istochnik po istorii i etnografii kazakhov", *Istoria SSSR* (1958), no.4, pp.133-45.

Moll, H. 1732 *Atlas Minor*, London: Thomas and John Bowles.

Monardes, N. 1569 *Dos Libros, el uno que trata de todas las cosas que traen de nuestras Indias Occidentales, que siruen al uso de la medicina, y el otro que trata de la pietra bezzar, y de la yerua escuerçonera*, Sevilla: Hernando Diaz.

Morgunova, N.L. and Khokhlova, O.S. 2006 "Kurgans and nomads: new investigations of mound burials in the southern Urals", *Antiquity* 80, pp.303-17.

Moshkova, M.G. 1995 "Middle Sarmatian Culture", "Late Sarmatian Culture", *Nomads of the Eurasian Steppes in the Early Iron Age*, eds. J. Davis-Kimball, V.A. Bashilov, L.T. Yablonsky, Berkeley, CA: Zinat Press, pp.137-48,149-64.

Muraviev, N.N. 1871 *Muraviev's Journey through the Turcoman Country, 1819-20. Translated from the Russian 1824 by P. Strahl...and from the German by...W.S.A. Lockhart*, London: British Library, Historical Print Editions.

Olcott, M.B. 1987 *The Kazakhs*, Stanford, California: Hoover Institution Press.

Ovchinnikov, R.V. 1983 "Rychkov, Petr Ivanovich (1712-1777)", *MERSH* 32, pp.238-39.

Pallas, P.S. 1788-93 *Voyages de P.S. Pallas en differentes provinces de l'empire de Russie, et dans l'Asie septentrionale, traduit de l'Allemand par Le C. Gautier de la Payronie*, 5 vols., Paris.

Penati, B. 2012 Review of Malikov, Tsars, Cossacks and Nomads, *Central Asian Survey*, pp.375-77.

Perdue, P.C. 2005 *China Marches West, the Qing Conquest of Central*

Eurasia, Cambridge, Mass., London: Belknap, Harvard University Press.

Portier, L. 1984 *Le Pélican: histoire d'un symbole*, Paris: Éditions du Cerf.

Poujol, C. 2000 "Turkistan", E.I. 10, pp.680-81.

Privatsky, B.G. 2001 *Muslim Turkestan, Kazak Religion and Collective Memory*, Richmond: Curzon Press.

Raeff, M. 1969 *Michael Speransky: Statesman of Imperial Russia, 1722-1839*, The Hague: Nijhoff.

Rowell, M. 1980 "Linnaeus and Botanists in Eighteenth-Century Russia", *Taxon* 29/1, pp.15-26.

Rychkov, P.I. [1750] "Kratkoe izvestie o tatarakh...", *IKRI* 4, 2007, pp.60-79.

Rychkov, P.I. 1896 *Istoriia Orenburgskaia 1730-1750*, Orenburg (first published 1759).

Rychkov, P.I. 1999 *Topografiia Orenburgskoi gubernii*, 2 vols., Ed. A.A. Chilibieva, Ufa: Kitap.

Rychkov, P.I. 2010 *Topografiia Orenburgskaia*, 2 vols. (reprint of St. Petersburg 1762 publication, with maps), Ed. A.A Chilibieva, Orenburg: Dom Dimir.

Samokvasov D. Ia. [1824] "Obychai Kirgizov" (of the Middle Horde), *Qazaqtyng ata zandary* (also known as *Drevnii mir prava kazakov*), Vol. 6, 2005, Almaty: Zheti Zhargy, pp.127-43.

Searight, S. 2004 "Elton, John (d. 1751)" revision of E.I. Carlyle, online DNB.

Semionov, V.G and V.P. 1999 *Gubernatory Orenburgskogo Kraia*, Orenburg: Orenburgskogo Kraia.

Shangin, I.P. [1816] "Dnevnie zapiski putescheshtviia v stepi kirgiz-kaisakov srednei ordi", *Qazaqtyng ata zandary* (also known as *Drevnii mir prava kazakov*), Vol. 6, 2005, Almaty: Zheti Zhargy, pp. 119-23.

Shaw, D.J.B. 2010 "Utility in Natural History: some Eighteenth-Century Russian Perceptions of the Living Environment", *Studies in the History of Biology*, Vol.2/4, pp.1-16.

Singaevskii V. 2006 *Russkii Muzei Imperatora Alexsandra III*, St.

Petersburg: ACT.

Slare, F. [1646] *Experiments and Observations upon Oriental and other Bezoar Stones, which prove them to be of no use in physick...*, London, 1715.

Slezkine, Y. 2001 "Nationalists versus Nations: Eighteenth-Century Russian Scholars Confront Ethnic Diversity", in D.R. Brower and E.J. Lazzerini eds. *Russia's Orient: Imperial Borderlands and People*, Bloomington, IN: Indiana University Press, pp.27-57.

Smith, E.F. and Christian, D. 1984 *Bread and Salt: a Social and Economic History of Food and Drink in Russia*, Cambridge: Cambridge University Press.

Sokol, E.D. 1987 "Yaik Cossacks", *MERSH* 44, pp.144-51.

Spilman, J. 1742 *A Journey through Russia into Persia: By Two English Gentlemen*, London.

Subrahmanyam, S. 1995 Review of S.F. Dale, Indian Merchants and Eurasian Trade, 1600-1750, in *Bulletin of the School of Oriental and African Studies*, Vol.58/2, 1995, pp.390-91.

Teissier, B. 2011 *Russian Frontiers*, Oxford: Signal Books.

Teissier, B. 2012 'Russia', *The Edinburgh History of the Book in Scotland, Vol.2, Enlightenment and Expansion 1707-1800*, eds. S.W. Brown and W. McDougall, pp.254-57.

Tevkelev, A.I /M. [1731-32] "Donoschenie perevodschika kollegii inostrannykh del A.I. Tevkeleva v kollegiiu inostrannykh del o priniatii rossiikogo poddanstva kazakhami mladshevo i srednogo zhuzov ot ianvaria 1732 g.", *IKRI* 3, 2005, pp.50-64.

Tevkelev, A.I /M. [1731-33] "Zhurnal bytnosti v Kirgiz-Kazatskoi orde perevodchika Mametia Tevkeleva 1731-1733 gg.", *IKRI* 3, 2005, pp.65-142

Tevkelev, A.I /M. [1748] "Donoschenie brigadira A.I. Tevkeleva Kollegii inostrannikh del o sostavlenii im rodoslovnikh kazakhskikh khanov i sultanov i opisaniia rodoplennogo sostava Mladshego, Srednogo i Starshego zhuzov ot 24 sentabria 1748", *IKRI* 3, 2005, pp.298-304.

Thadeu, E.C. 1984 "Tatischev, Vasilii Nikitich, *MERSH* vol.38, pp.196-200.

Toropitsyn, I.V. 2006 "The Beginnings of the Mining Industry in Russia", *CIM Magazine*, Vol.1/5, pp.1-3.

Uyama, T. 2004 "Kazakhstan", E.I. Vol.12 (supplement).

Valikhanov, Ch. 2009 *Izbrannye proizvedeniia*, Almaty: Aris.

Volstenburg, E.O. 1995 *Khudozhniki narodov CCCR*, Akademia Khudozhestva SSSR: Iskusstvo.

Yablonsky, L.T. 2010 "New Excavations of the early Nomadic Burial Ground at Filippovka (Southern Ural Region, Russia), *American Journal of Archaeology*, Vol.114, pp.129-43.

Zimanov, S.Z. 2004 "Was There a Golden Century of Justice in the Ancient Land of the Kazakhs?", *Qazaqtyng ata zandary* (also known as *Drevnii mir prava kazakov*), Vol. 3, Almaty: Zheti Zhargy, pp.26-32.

Zimanov, S.Z. 2008 "Ten Samples of biy judgement", *Qazaqtyng ata zandary* (also known as *Drevnii mir prava kazakov*), Vol. 9, Almaty: Zheti Zhargy, pp.97-110.

Zimanov, S.Z. 2010 "The Kazakh biy courts were kept and remained in the memory of generations as independent, professional and wise justice", *Science of Central Asia*, no.4, pp.18-24.

Zimanov, S.Z. 2011 "Three legislators and legends of the century", *Science of Central Asia*, nos.1-2.

Zimanov, S.Z. 2012 "The Kazakh biy court is the common cultural value", *Science of Central Asia* no. 1, pp.20-29.

Zonn, I. Glantz, M. and Kostianoy, A. 2009 *The Aral Sea Encyclopaedia*, Heidelberg: Springer Verlag.

INDEX